CAMBRIDGE IBERIAN AND LATIN AMERICAN STUDIES

Gabriel García Márquez
New Readings

Gabriel García Márquez

New Readings

EDITED BY
BERNARD McGUIRK
AND
RICHARD CARDWELL

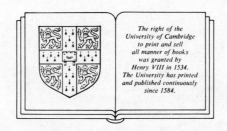

The right of the
University of Cambridge
to print and sell
all manner of books
was granted by
Henry VIII in 1534.
The University has printed
and published continuously
since 1584.

CAMBRIDGE UNIVERSITY PRESS

CAMBRIDGE
NEW YORK   NEW ROCHELLE
MELBOURNE   SYDNEY

Published by the Press Syndicate of the University of Cambridge
The Pitt Building, Trumpington Street, Cambridge CB2 1RP
32 East 57th Street, New York, NY 10022, USA
10 Stamford Road, Oakleigh, Melbourne 3166, Australia

First published 1987

Printed in Great Britain at
the University Press, Cambridge

British Library cataloguing in publication data
Gabriel García Márquez: new readings. –
(Cambridge Iberian and Latin American
studies)
1. García Márquez, Gabriel – Criticism
and interpretation
I. McGuirk, Bernard II. Cardwell, Richard A.
863   PQ8180.17.A73Z

Library of Congress cataloguing in publication data
Gabriel García Márquez: new readings.
(Cambridge Iberian and Latin American studies)
Bibliography.
Includes index.
1. García Márquez, Gabriel, 1928– – Criticism
and interpretation. I. McGuirk, Bernard. II. Cardwell,
Richard Andrew. III. Series.
PQ8180.17.A73Z674   1987   863   86-24424

ISBN 0 521 32836 5

Contents

Note on the translations

In each case, the contributors to this volume have opted to provide their own version of extracts from García Márquez's original text. A list of available published translations of his major works may be found in the select bibliography.

Contributors

Dr Carlos J. Alonso is Assistant Professor of Romance Languages and Literatures in the Wesleyan University, Middletown, Connecticut, USA. Among his interests is the *novela de la tierra* on which he has published a monograph study. He has also written articles on Carpentier, Cortázar, Donoso, Sarmiento and other Latin American writers.

Dr Richard A. Cardwell is Professor of Modern Spanish Literature in the University of Nottingham, England. His major interests are in Romanticism and the European *fin de siècle*. He has written books on Espronceda, Blasco Ibáñez and Juan Ramón Jiménez, numerous articles on Spanish literature and has published editions of Gil, Reina and Icaza. He is currently writing a study of *modernismo* and Symbolism in Spain.

Dr Robin W. Fiddian is Lecturer in Spanish and Latin American Studies in the University of Newcastle upon Tyne, England. His research interests embrace the Spanish novel in the twentieth century and contemporary fiction in Latin America. He is also interested in aspects of comparative literature and the Spanish cinema since the Civil War. He has published studies of the Spanish Generation of 1898 and of the novels of the contemporary period in Spain and Latin America.

Dr Aníbal González is Assistant Professor of Spanish American Literature in the University of Texas at Austin, USA. His academic interests are *modernismo*, nineteenth-century Latin American fiction, Hispanic Caribbean literature and literary theory. He has published a book on the *crónica modernista*, articles on Rafael Sánchez and others; he has a forthcoming study of the *novela modernista hispanoamericana* and is working on the influence of journalism on the development of the Latin American narrative.

Dr Eduardo González is Associate Professor in the Department of Hispanic and Italian Studies in the Johns Hopkins University, USA. His major field of interest is Latin American fiction. He has published numerous articles in this field, a book on Carpentier, a book on psychoanalytical criticism and a forthcoming study of Cortázar. He is at present working on Roa Bastos.

Dr Clive Griffin is Fellow and Tutor in Spanish in Trinity College, Oxford, England, and University Lecturer in Latin American Literature. His interests embrace the history of printing in sixteenth-century Spain and Latin America, on which he has recently published a book, and Latin American prose fiction. He is currently writing a study of Azuela's *Los de abajo*.

Jo Labanyi is Senior Lecturer in Spanish in Birkbeck College, University of London, England. Her major interest is in the fiction of the modern period in Spain and Latin America on which she has written a series of articles, including a book on Luis Martín Santos. She has also translated contemporary Spanish and Latin American poetry and fiction.

Dr Gerald Martin is Professor of Hispanic and Latin American Studies in Portsmouth Polytechnic, England. His interests lie in the social and historical aspects of literary creativity. His publications include an edition of Miguel Ángel Asturias and articles on Latin American literature and culture.

Dr Bernard McGuirk is Lecturer in Hispanic Studies in the University of Nottingham, England, where he is also responsible for postgraduate studies in critical theory. He has written on the application of contemporary literary theory to works in French, Spanish and Portuguese. He is currently writing a book on post-structuralist approaches to Latin American literature.

Dr Mark Millington is Lecturer in Latin American Studies in the University of Nottingham, England. His academic interests include the application of recent narratological theory to Latin American fiction, critical theory and the cinema. He has published a book on Onetti and articles on Borges and García Márquez.

Dr René Prieto is Assistant Professor of Spanish in the Southern Methodist University of Dallas, Texas, USA. He specializes in the application of critical theory to contemporary Latin American fiction. He has published numerous articles in this field including studies of Arguedas, Borges, Onetti, Sarduy, Vargas Llosa, and is presently completing a book on the *indigenista* fiction of Miguel Ángel Asturias.

John Wainwright is Assistant Librarian at the Taylor Institution Library, University of Oxford, England, where he is in charge of Hispanic collections.

Dr Edwin Williamson is Lecturer in Spanish and Latin American Studies in Birkbeck College, University of London, England. His principal interest is in the fiction of sixteenth- and seventeenth-century Spain and he is author of a major study of Cervantes. He is also working on Latin American fiction and its historical background.

Introduction

BERNARD McGUIRK

The present volume of essays on Gabriel García Márquez was originally conceived in 1983, shortly after he was awarded the Nobel Prize for Literature. Apart from extending critical appreciation of his work to an English-reading public, its principal objective was to reflect the breadth and variety of current critical approaches to literature applied to a single corpus of writing. By no means all of the writer's prolific output is dealt with here, though his major novels and a selection of his short fiction are covered. Equally, the range of critical method, while not exhaustive, seeks to encompass practical criticism, thematic, formalist-structuralist, anthropological, psychoanalytical, Marxist, philosophy of language and deconstructionist readings.

The first three contributions deal with the early phase of short fiction which García Márquez himself saw as the key to his first universally acclaimed masterpiece *One Hundred Years of Solitude*. Richard Cardwell's analysis of the techniques of characterization in *Big Mama's Funeral*, specifically in 'One of these Days' and 'Tuesday Siesta', reflects the pluralistic critical approach of liberal humanism, elaborating on the writer's avowed commitment to 'write well' by demonstrating one of the principal resources of García Márquez the 'teller of tales'. In contrast, Eduardo González approaches a single story from the same collection from an angle of anthropology. His study, involving a critique of the structural method, views 'Baltazar's Prodigious Afternoon' in the light of the celebrated Marcel Mauss essay on 'gift-exchange'. By juxtaposing story and essay, he rejects an 'empty' formalism, demonstrating and situating various narrative parallels within a socio-ethnic function of fable. Whereas the previous study isolates one action in one story, René Prieto follows a single theme in *No One Writes to the Colonel* – that of hunger. He treats the

I

concomitant preoccupation with the 'lower' bodily functions in a quasi-Bakhtinian manner, uniting the politically subversive and psychoanalytical within a Freudian application of oral and anal phases to the protagonist-colonel's ideological and personal liberation.

Two juxtaposed readings of *One Hundred Years of Solitude* follow, the one thematic, the other theoretical. Edwin Williamson traces the narrative pattern, rather than the theory, of incest with a view to exposing the 'inefficiency' of a taboo-regime. In the process, a so-called 'magical realism' – defined here as 'the fascination with the past, the escape from history into memory, the longing to recover a pristine innocence, and the surrender to mindless erotic desire' – is rejected as a misreading of history. Complementary to Williamson's essay, Aníbal González's analysis of the theory of translation, drawing principally on Walter Benjamin, proposes, however, a very different treatment of Melquíades's notorious 'deciphered' manuscript. A broadly geneticist analogy of family and language provokes the conclusion that not only incest but also the act of translation itself is an improper act'. Aníbal González's passing suggestion of a parallel function in Cervantes's Cide Hamete Benengeli and García Márquez's Melquíades is taken up by Clive Griffin, albeit from a wholly different critical perspective. His study of the humour of the novel avoids, for instance, the Bakhtinian approach and, firmly in the empirical tradition of Anglo-American 'common-sense' criticism, takes up García Márquez's own warning that *One Hundred Years of Solitude* is 'completely devoid of seriousness'. Cataloguing a variety of comic devices, his essay provides a counterblast to the many analyses which have naturalized or neutralized the most famous of García Márquez's writings by association with one or another 'world-view'. In direct contrast, Gerald Martin argues for an ideological approach both to this novel and to the problems of the over-used restrictive label of 'magical realism'. Martin's is an unapologetically dissenting voice raised against the inevitable 'otherness' of any European and North American reading of Latin American literature. He attempts to confront, polemically and from a socialist viewpoint, a 'racist', even if unconscious, conspiracy on the part of much Anglo-Saxon criticism to ignore the ontological, epistemological and historical implications of García Márquez's work in favour of the metaphoric spiral of decline which, he argues, is myth-reading. And misreading.

The most systematically theoretical essay in the volume is Mark Millington's narratological treatment of the stories of *Innocent Eréndira*. Following Genette, he isolates such narrative structures as episodic deferral, reversal, causality versus non-causality, and interlocking repetitions, and passes from the formalism of narrative patterns to engage with the thematics of emptiness, reticence and expansion, broaching, too, with overt reference to Bakhtinian 'carnivalization', the social and ideological implications of narrative open-endedness.

The last three essays have in common a preoccupation with the philosophy of language. Jo Labanyi's study of *The Autumn of the Patriarch* is a meditation on writing in which she reactivates the spoken/written distinction by juxtaposing García Márquez's practice, in this novel, with Derrida's views on *écriture*. Arguing that writing refers back to an absent source, she questions the traditional view that to control language is to wield power. The questioning of the authority of the written word is taken up by Carlos Alonso in his analysis of language and ritual in *Chronicle of a Death Foretold*. Drawing on Austin/Searle speech-act theory, he suggests that the function of narration in this novel is performative rather than referential, a re-enactment of a 'crime' which, far from seeking to understand, traditionally and hermeneutically, attempts mastery over the sacrificial act only by restaging it. He argues that the text amounts to a further act of violence, that the novel is a perfect analogue of writing itself. Carlos Alonso also strikes a Derridan note, when he points to the text's 'drive to abolish the differences that constitute it'. In the final study, Bernard McGuirk echoes Derrida's notion of language and *difference*, applying the latter's practice from 'Speculations – on Freud' in a series of overlapping speculations on *Chronicle*. Taking up the generally ignored ludic element, he is nonetheless at pains to stress the ideological potential of post-structuralist criticism by showing how the text deconstructs the founding myths of Latin American consciousness.

In January 1986, García Márquez published a new novel, *Love in the Times of Cholera*. The editors wish to thank Robin Fiddian, of the University of Newcastle upon Tyne, for the judicious post-script in which he anticipates possible humanist, feminist and Americanist critical responses to this most recent novel.

It is envisaged that the collection, given the dual objectives outlined at the outset, will extend knowledge of the work of García Márquez and introduce to both the general reader and to students of literature a plurality of current critical approaches.

The volume closes with Richard Cardwell's rendering into English of the author's Stockholm Nobel acceptance address and an index, and John Wainwright's select bibliography, including criticism available in English.

I

Characterization in the early fiction of Gabriel García Márquez

RICHARD CARDWELL

The early fiction has been viewed as the necessary literary preparation for the mature work and especially of *One Hundred Years of Solitude*. Yet to suggest that the short stories are apprentice pieces is to detract from their real artistry, their subtlety and their narrative techniques. Given their remarkable literary qualities, it is strange that they should have received such scant critical attention. In this essay, I should like to consider one technique, that of characterization, as a starting point for a fuller appraisal of the early stories and, perhaps, of the major works. After all, García Márquez once said in conversation to Miguel Fernández-Braso, 'in reality one only writes a single book' (*Gabriel García Márquez (una conversación infinita)*, Madrid, 1969, p. 44). He went on to reveal his consuming interest in his early characters which culminated in *One Hundred Years of Solitude* 'which is the basis of the jigsaw which I have been assembling in my early books. The key, therefore, is to be found in my first works.' In what follows the analysis is necessarily selective, a starting point for a complete study.

Much of the appeal of the stories in *Big Mama's Funeral*, as much as in the major novels, lies in the subtlety and allusiveness – even elusiveness – of characterization. Many of his characters are taken from the classical repertoire of the eternally comic, including characters who through their disharmony or absurdity in behaviour or dress, or who by involvement in disguises, tricks, beatings, petty criminality, or indecent behaviour, create humorous situations which can affect all readers at all times. Some of these shock elements appear in *Big Mama's Funeral*. There remains, however, one further type who appears in a number of guises in the early fiction: the heroic colonel, the courageous dentist, the resolute mother, or the stubborn cage-maker. These have a number of qualities in common. To varying

5

degrees they become involved in a confrontation with the authorities: the regime, the mayor, the church, moneyed influence. But García Márquez's combined feelings of humour and affection towards his characters allow him to delineate them in a very special way. He avoids the 'exemplary' figure who might be used to catechize. García Márquez's ideological and political affiliations are well known; yet his use of irony and ambiguity, the allusive and elusive nature of his material, points to a perspective and a breadth of vision in character-ization and in his narrative. It is quite unlike the sermonizing one might find among fellow Latin American committed writers. García Márquez has said that his commitment is 'to write well'. He is, then, primarily a literary creator, a teller of tales, a creator of character, and it is these features which may absorb the reader independently of the many interpretations that have been laid on the work. The focus, then, might properly be on literary techniques, those of narration, use of imagery, characterization.

In *Big Mama's Funeral*, as in *No One Writes to the Colonel*, García Márquez seems to be attracted to humble, unassuming people who, while often poor or crushed by life's adversities, can, nevertheless, demonstrate enormous resourcefulness, can still find the courage of spiritual heroism to resist oppression and defeat, can still dissent, defend a deeply held principle or, almost unconsciously, confront and overcome the forces ranged against them. The colonel himself is an obvious member of this gallery of characters. He must be included with the mother in 'Tuesday Siesta', the dentist or Baltazar. They all, in their different ways, oppose the pattern of behaviour which is expected of or laid down for them, oppose authority, whatever its guise, in a surprising but unspectacular way. The mother is not welcome in the town; the dentist is expected to pull the tooth and be servile, silent and obliging; Baltazar to take home without protest his masterpiece. But the resistance of these characters forces their oppressors off guard to reveal that, at certain moments, an individual can enjoy glimpses of freedom by refusing to accept the status quo.

To pursue such a line might produce an interpretative view of character rather than a technical analysis of how the text discloses such dissenting spirits. Leaving aside the reasons for García Márquez's choice of this particular character type let us consider the means whereby they are presented.

But we must return to the theme of confrontation. To be persuasive the author must delineate the nature of and reasons for the confrontation. The character is placed in such a situation as to produce a crisis in his personality. His acceptance of the dictates of authority or the servile compliance with the prejudiced, uncritical and unreflective patterns of behaviour of the majority are placed under strain in such a way that a minor transformation takes place in the character himself, a change which could not be effected without the presence of the figure who stands in a position of power or influence over the character. In *No One Writes to the Colonel* the confrontation is presented in a diffuse way, for the figures of authority – the mayor, Don Sabas, the guard, the clergy, etc. – appear and reappear. But we cannot doubt that the personality of the colonel undergoes a change. One might have expected a crisis point in the confrontation in the casino between the guard, the murderer of Agustín, and the colonel. Yet García Márquez understates the moral superiority of his colonel at this point to reassert it in a spectacular way in the colonel's final words and when the reader least expects it. Thus the ground or the nature of the confrontation is often allusive rather than explicit; surprising rather than predictable. In the cases of Don Aurelio, or the mother of Carlos Centeno or of Baltazar, the encounter and the direction it takes are unexpected. The dentist's surgery, the priest's waiting room and Montiel's patio become, of a sudden, arenas of opposition or resistance to the patterns of behaviour expected in such a situation. This, then, is the first aspect of such characterization: a specifically selected type who might pass unnoticed in a crowd but who, in a given moment, stands prominent in the affirmation of his personal integrity. Secondly, the necessary presence of a figure of authority; thirdly, the occasion of the conflict itself when the forces of expected compliance collide with the irresistible or indomitable will of the unassuming individual; fourthly, and perhaps the most novel aspect of many of the short stories, is the unpromising location chosen as a backdrop for the confrontation which is to emerge. This last aspect, together with the unassuming central character, contributes to the constant and consistent element of surprise which is a central feature of all García Márquez's fiction. Finally, we might include another technique which, like the last, is both a narrative as well as a characterizing one. In each of the cases we have been examining, and commonly in other short stories, character conflict and change are also stimulated by an arrival (often of the protagonist himself or sometimes by an object like Baltazar's cage). As Mark Millington points out in his essay in this collection, 'The effect of the arrival is to disrupt – it introduces instability into a pre-existent situation, and that instability produces interest and also movement.' In this context it also produces movement of character, movement in the sense of development along a new and unexpected path. The character is destabilized, forced in a new direction, to undertake an action which signifies change and a return to a new equilibrium. By the same token, of course, departure is used to terminate the process which the arrival inaugurated and so close the development. The mayor leaves, the mother steps out into the street, Baltazar leaves the patio for the casino to begin a new cycle of arrival/departure, etc. García Márquez uses the departure motif narratively to close his stories and as a closure for characterization. It is the perfect technical fusion.

One common means of conveying character in narrative fiction is through dialogue; another is description, another symbolic language. All these techniques are used to consummate effect in *No One Writes to the Colonel*: in the conversations; in the description of the colonel and those who stand against him; in the symbolism of the climatic conditions, the letter and the cock. A further technique, used with both economy and skill in the short stories, is that of signposting stages in the development or chronology of the story. Finally, we should not overlook the ironic or ambiguous general statements nor the allusive details of milieu or setting. All of these are used in 'One of these Days' and 'Tuesday Siesta', the two stories chosen for analysis. The story of Baltazar, the colonel or others might also serve as evidence for the present study.

Let us consider the elementary presentation of the dentist. Aurelio Escovar is granted from the outset of the story the courtesy title of Don. It is given by the narrator alone, for no one else in the story addresses Aurelio in this fashion. No specific interpretation can be applied to this fact, however, for the man's son is unlikely to use it. The fact that the mayor, the only other figure in the story, does not use it may suggest that the mayor views Aurelio as an inferior, unworthy of the title. Perhaps the narrator is conveying not only his own esteem but that of Aurelio's fellow townsmen. Perhaps it is used ironically, for the positive effect of the 'Don' is immediately deflated by the following description of 'unqualified dentist', only for the ironic – or positive? – thrust to reassert itself in the phrase 'an early riser' and, as we learn, a hard and diligent worker. The reader is perplexed. We are not told why Don Aurelio never qualified or why he rises early. The surgery itself suggests penury and the struggle to make a modest living. The early rising suggests hard work and continuous effort to the same end. The spareness of the opening delineation also suggests that the town senses that it is fortunate, indeed, as the 'Don' implies, to have a man who can practise with skill and care. The descriptive technique, then, is economic yet richly suggestive. The rest of the description tells us of the inner man rather than of his social position. By far the greater part of the ensuing description evokes a single impression. We are given the following details of physical make-up and aspect:

He was stiff, spare, with a gaze which rarely matched the moment, like the look of the deaf . . . He seemed not to reflect on what he was doing, but he worked stubbornly, pedalling on the drill even when he was not using it . . . He went on working . . . The voice of his son . . . aroused him from his abstraction.

After a short interlude of dialogue we learn further that:

He held [the tooth] at arm's length and examined it through half-closed eyes . . . He went on examining the tooth . . . His expression still did not change . . . Without haste, with an extremely quiet movement, he stopped pedalling the drill, withdrew it from the chair and opened the bottom drawer of the table.

The characterization, we note, becomes increasingly verbal with description indicated by minimal adverbialization: 'smoothly', 'with a careful pressure of the fingers', 'still without haste', etc. It is a transition from nominal and adjectival description of the man to description of his actions. The dentist becomes animate; it is he who dominates the scene, monopolizes the movement and the conversation in the arena of implied conflict. The physical characteristics of the absorbed or abstracted demeanour are prepared for by his earliest actions, the preparations in the surgery: 'he placed on the table a handful of instruments which he laid out in order from the largest to the smallest, as in an exhibition'. Despite his lack of qualifications and evident poverty, the author implies a richness of personality. The outer man, somewhat ridiculous in his braces over a striped shirt with a gold stud but no collar, belies the inner composure. The physical description is, in reality, the bearer of an implied spiritual description. The qualities evoked are resilience, orderliness, determination, concentration, tenacity, joy in work well done, that is, inner harmony.

But the shift in emphasis in this description (from adjectival to verbal), from the man beginning a weekly routine to a man exacting payment for sins committed, is signposted by three further devices: dialogue, surprise and symbolism.

The introduction of dialogue is used, of course, for narrative effect. It bears the burden of tracing the mayor's discomfiture and the payment for past sins. But it also signposts the development of character. The first is the dentist's ' "Tell him I am not here." ' The effect is to carry narrative and character development in an unexpected direction. The reader has been prepared for inner composure but not outright antagonism and rudeness. The next stage in the building process is the laconic ' "Better" ', whose effect is underpinned by the readiness to allow a rupture with the expected norm – of social grace as well as of vocational duty to treat the suffering – implied in the speech itself and in the contrastive refusal to allow the present task – that of polishing the tooth – to be interrupted. The next stage of the process again coincides with the dentist's further reply in the elaborate charade of offence by proxy. Again this laconic utterance is embedded in a series of actions: 'stopped pedalling', 'withdrew it from the chair', 'opened', 'swung the chair'. The building up of tension in the series of precise actions whose narrative burden points to confrontation implies a corresponding tensing of will in the person of the dentist himself. The threat of the mayor's revolver is met by that of the dentist. But the implied violence of the mayor's threat is matched by coolness and control on the part of Don Aurelio. García Márquez does not overtly describe this quality; rather it is implied in the sentence beginning 'Without haste, with an extremely quiet movement' and the concluding line of the sequence leading to the appearance of the suffering mayor: 'He closed the drawer with his finger tips and said softly, "Sit down." ' We are presented, then, with a slightly ridiculous and unassuming figure. Yet by the moment of the invitation to be seated the dentist has grown in inner strength and in authority. What the dentist sees in the eyes of the mayor is a further device of characterization, for it explains the veiled contempt of the closing of the drawer and the lowered voice. The control of action and of voice emphasizes, by contrast with the violent threat and the effects of prolonged suffering in the mayor's face together with the submission of the mayor to the ministrations of his antagonist, an upsurge of moral superiority. Physical well-being implies spiritual well-being. García Márquez charts this last phase of the change the dentist undergoes by a contrast of relative calm, suggested by the description of the room and of the mayor seated in the chair, and the return to dialogue and movement. Again surprise is used to add to the effect in the revelation that anaesthesia cannot be used. It is an ironic comment for both men understand what is happening. The refused smile indicates the increasing gravity of the dentist and points to the next stage of Don Aurelio's role. But García Márquez does not allow his dentist to torment the mayor further for he is now to assume another, more symbolic role, that of retributive justice. The confrontation moves, at this point, from an implied social, perhaps political one, to a metaphysical one. Where the dentist could have caused pain 'he only moved his wrist'. The change in characterization is signalled first, then, by verbal action, second by the adverbial 'without rancour . . . with a bitter tenderness', last by dialogue, with which the theme of retribution is made explicit: ' "Here, lieutenant, you are making us payment for twenty killings".'

The rest of the story neatly combines both realistic and symbolic readings. The surprising command to wipe away tears where to wipe the mouth would have been more appropriate points to the theme of social interaction and humiliation of an antagonist. But the final question concerning the destination of the bill, while combining both, emphasizes the theme of retribution, for in the final words of the mayor (and of the story), he is forced by the dentist to admit that public office has become private patrimony.

Contrasts of dress (neatness against untidiness), of bearing, of speech, etc. further interact to characterize. But there remains one last level of implied delineation: symbolism. As with other techniques, so here García Márquez employs a diffuse, implicit, allusive mode of presentation. The apparently incidental details of the buzzards on the roof, the gold tooth and the cobweb in the window serve to focus the topos of confrontation. The buzzards evoke an atmosphere of predation and death which, subsequently, the mayor comes to incarnate. The infected tooth also suggests decay. But the gold tooth becomes the dentist's symbolic sword in the moment he resists the mayor. Ironically the mayor is resisted by gold, a metal only he and his supporters might be supposed to afford. He is resisted by the image of his own class. But the gold theme becomes more complex and subtle when we recognize that it is used not only thematically (in the confrontation) but as a means of characterization. The dentist is associated with incorruptible metal (perhaps to become at the point of retribution the 'shining sword of the avenging angel'); the mayor's tooth is abscessed, corrupt. Similarly, the contrast of 'the clear sky' and the 'dusty cobwebs filled with spiders' eggs and dead insects' reinforces the characterization of both protagonists and underscores the nature of the symbolic conflict. The 'clear sky' seems to suggest idealism, aspiration, hope; the cobwebs a structure which inhibits, even prohibits, the surging flight of such idealistic aspiration. The 'spiders' eggs' appear to make less possible that hopeful bound of the human heart in that more spiders will appear to spin more webs. The corpses of the insects, the victims of the spiders, suggest defeated ideals, aspirations and hopes and, as the telling statement concerning the payment for murders committed by the mayor, the death of idealistic men. Against such forces the indomitable spirit of the dentist seems doubly powerful.

The mother of Carlos Centeno Ayala who appears in 'Tuesday Siesta' is, arguably, very similar to the hero of *No One Writes to the Colonel*. The poverty which, in a strange way, confers a heroic grandeur and nobility on the colonel is also borne by this woman. We never learn her name but she is carefully and subtly described. Unlike the tale of Don Aurelio, this story eschews the motif of confrontation and of surprise at its outset. The introduction to the story is allusive in its narrative quality and generous in description. Dialogue, too, is eschewed in favour of monologue, for only the mother speaks during the train journey. All of her utterances evoke the same qualities of personality: solicitude for her child and an awareness of social proprieties, of appearances. Her statements are authoritarian yet combined with gentleness as witnessed in the 'gentle expression' with which she returns the look of the child. The primary burden of characterization at the outset is, however, by description. The pair are travelling third-class, their belongings are of cheap materials, the flowers wrapped in newspaper, they are dressed in 'rigorous and poor mourning clothes'. The reasons for the mourning are not yet disclosed. The journey, the flowers and the solicitude of appearances all suggest, as the story confirms, a visit to the grave of a near relative. The description goes on to reveal the mother as prematurely old, a shapeless, ill-dressed figure. Life, clearly, has been unkind and, as the setting suggests, is still unkind. The smoke, the heat and the smells are used as incidental background description but they also suggest the forces ranged against her. The brooding silence and the crushing heat of the siesta subsequently perform the same function and prepare the way for the corporate hostility to the couple as the story closes. But the description and, thus, the characterization takes on a new direction with the insertion of two key sentences. The first notes how she travelled 'with her spine pressed firmly against the back of the seat'.

Her physical posture is the bearer of her spiritual strength. Physical rectitude is moral rectitude. This is confirmed by one of García Márquez's most revealing portrayals of character, one which we might associate with the person of the colonel, the author's most enduring hero: 'She had the scrupulous serenity of those people accustomed to poverty.' The combination of words denoting the outward manifestation of pride in oneself, a dignity devoid of arrogance or the parade of poverty together with a sense of propriety ('scrupulous') is twinned with the implication of inner resolve, self-possession, calm, inner harmony ('serenity'). The juxtaposition of words, as with other similar instances in 'One of these Days' and other stories, typifies the skill of the narrator to evoke the abstract and elusive nature of spiritual strength and power. We find, too, in this story a singular transparency of characterization, a simplicity not only of detail or of significant feature but a revelation, in the simplest and most economic of language, of the inner core of personality. Nothing is obscured, nothing ambivalent. The mother shows no naivety or ingenuousness, she is the victim of no humour or irony. In her we perceive the indestructible core of the essential self which Vargas Llosa has noted in the writings of García Márquez. This simplicity of characterization is, arguably, one of the most prominent aspects of his technique.

With the arrival in the town, the inimical forces reappear, suggested by the silent anonymity of the sleeping town and the tiny eyes behind thick lenses of the priest's sister. The mode of characterization changes at this point from physical description and telling juxtaposition of word to verbal and adverbial delineation: gesture, tone and inflection of voice, regard, demeanour. The inner serenity and integrity of a woman undertaking a sad and uncomfortable journey grows stronger at this point in the story. It coincides, as we have already seen in 'One of these Days', with a moment of confrontation. She refuses to be deflected from her purpose. ' "I need . . ." ',' "It's pressing" ', 'insisted', suggesting resolve, all culminate in another typical word pairing: 'reposed tenacity'. Strength of will with serenity, resolve with relaxed control. She refuses to wait for an hour and miss her train. Now dialogue bears the burden of characterization and the refusal spoken in a tone of voice 'still gentle, with a variety of nuances' conveys the same combination of qualities as 'reposed tenacity'. The impression is evoked by physical demeanour and inflection of voice of a force of personality to be reckoned with. The mother might be poor, haggard, a victim of life's uneven hand. But her will, her integrity and dignity, her serenity of inner control all emerge in the conversation with the priest. The burden of their dialogue is shaped to highlight these qualities.

The unpromising story takes on a promising direction (and explains the mourning clothes and the hostile silence) with the emergence of the soporific priest and the request for the cemetery key. When he finally understands who she is, he reacts in a very special way. He 'scrutinizes her'. García Márquez adds nothing else. But the text discloses, in the reaction of the mother, further details. We return to the theme of confrontation. The priest accuses with his stare; the mother returns his look 'with a quiet authority'. Such is the intensity of her gaze that the priest blushes. The accuser yields the psychological advantage to the accused. If, in the first confrontation, the issue was one of convenience now the arena of conflict has shifted to a moral ground. It is an example of the signposting alluded to earlier. In this shift the mother undergoes another significant change and, in so doing, grows in moral stature. But the priest, though humbled, cannot resist the question, ' "Did you never try to direct him on the proper path?" ' This marks a further crisis point or signpost in the ordering of the story coming, as it does, after the flashback of the son's tragic death. The inner serenity and control hold firm and she replies only after she has signed the ledger. She offers no justification, only an affirmation of her son's goodness. This statement, too, is revealing. Clarity of conscience needs no justification. The adjective *inalterable* is used here to singular effect. This is what the priest comes to recognize and here, as in 'One of these Days', the interaction of character is used to establish character. The priest's reaction tells us more about the mother than the priest himself. Indeed, the whole section which follows, giving the bare essentials of a morality divorced from the morality of a property-owning society, leads the priest to the point of capitulation. His utterance of a pious cliché and García Márquez's revelation that 'he said it without much conviction, partly because experience had made him a little sceptical, partly because of the heat', marks a high point in the spiritual ascendancy of the mother. But it is not the highest point, for once more the story takes an unexpected direction and we return to the implicit theme of hostility. And yet this frail creature, whose physical condition belies that inner core of growing strength, like the colonel, when faced by the challenge to her morality and her value system, accepts and takes on the challenge.

There is a remarkable similarity of spiritual strength, resolve and integrity of selfhood in the final lines of the two stories, in spite of the difference of tone and register. The mother will not be deflected from her duty; she will not accept the easy compromises or excuses offered by the priest and his sister; she faces the hostility of the prejudiced townsfolk resolutely and squarely. All this is implied in the words of the priest and sister. In the two final verbs of the story the mother transcends the compromise of life and towers in magnificent moral ascendancy over her fellows: 'She took the child by the hand and went out into the street.' We cannot doubt that she outfaced the entire town.

Thus we can see that characterization is achieved in an original way. García Márquez relegates the role of omniscient narrator in favour of a more indirect and allusive approach to the delineation of his favoured type of character. His stories begin in an unassuming, even unpromising way. His protagonists are similarly unassuming. Yet, with the introduction of another figure, representing vested interest or authority (spiritual or temporal), the chosen character begins to develop. The chosen milieu, too, may seem unpromising yet the background details serve a further but importantly symbolic role. The combination of the given arena of conflict and the chosen antagonist produces a point of crisis in the development of the humble character. From the simple and economic sketching in of outward physical attributes which, as we have seen, are often the bearers of an implied inner being and condition, the delineation is taken over principally by action (verb and adverb) as the 'character' emerges and by speech (the dialogue revealing the emergent spiritual qualities). Nor should we overlook the careful marking, in the narrative, of key points in the development of character. In the end, we perceive that, while García Márquez is able to present a realistic portrait of these characters, his interest is primarily in alluding to their 'spiritual' or 'moral' character. 'The moral of a story is like the iceberg', revealed García Márquez in conversation with Plinio Apuleyo Mendoza, 'it must be held afloat on the part that is not seen: in study, reflection, the material included but not directly employed in the story' (Gabriel García Márquez: *El olor de la guayaba*, Barcelona, 1982, p. 43). The same is true of the building of 'moral' character. And the reader must perceive that process in a study of and reflection on the literary text itself. We return to the point made at the outset of the essay and García Márquez's commitment 'to write well'. He is, above all, a literary artist. Yet he is also a political writer and commentator whose ideology and views are well known. His art, however, never becomes the handmaid of pamphleteering. In any reading of his fiction we need to consider the less conspicuous features of his story-telling for much of García Márquez's 'artfulness' and his skill as a narrative innovator lie in what critics have called his 'magical realism'. In fact there is little that is 'magical' in these early stories (save in the sense of imaginative excitement) for we are dealing rather with an extreme subtlety of technique, the transformation of the raw stuff of reality, even the very ordinary and insignificant, into a social reality and a commentary on it. But the very tenor of his article in 'Tabla Redonda' (*Imagen*, 40, Caracas, 1969, p. 8) suggests a preference for artistic honesty and integrity created out of real, lived experience over 'arm-chair' political theorizing. The message must not control the artistic creation, rather the meaning is conveyed by suggestion. There can never be a question of sermonizing.

In the face of García Márquez's own conviction that much of Latin America suffers from a form of political bankruptcy, he offers, in these stories and the mature fiction, a vision of humble but potent idealism. His evocation of spiritual values in his writings, of which his unassuming characters are the bearers, is part and parcel of that conviction he expressed memorably in his speech of acceptance of the Nobel Prize in 1982, that there is a need for change in society and in its outlook. In the practice and commitment to 'write well' and in the evocation through that writing of an alternative vision of human conduct and of human and spiritual values he emphasizes and exemplifies his own part in that need for change. It is hoped that the foregoing commentary has helped to provide some understanding of the practical and technical aspects of García Márquez's commitment.

2

Beware of gift-bearing tales: reading 'Baltazar's Prodigious Afternoon' according to Marcel Mauss[1]

EDUARDO GONZÁLEZ

Jésus se fût obstinément refusé à faire des prodiges que la foule en eût créé pour lui; le plus grand miracle eût été qu'il n'en fît pas; jamais les lois de l'histoire et de la psychologie populaire n'eussent subi une plus forte dérogation. Les miracles de Jésus furent une violence que lui fit son siècle, une concession que lui arracha la nécessité passagère. Aussi l'exorciste et le thaumaturge sont tombés; mais le réformateur religieux vivra éternellement.
(Ernest Renan, *Vie de Jésus*)

Speaking of the main task of his *Essai sur le don* (1925), Marcel Mauss says that he intends 'to catch the fleeting moment when a society and its members take emotional stock of themselves and their situation as regards others'.[2] In the wake of recent structuralist complexities Mauss's words appear forthright and endowed with a kind of naive authority. Of particular interest is his emphasis on emotions and feelings as pre-eminent objects of analysis. In *The Gift*, Mauss rebuilt an instance of social being which was significant in that it seemed to be total and, in spite of its aberrant display of excess and waste, practical. He saw the act of gift-exchange, or total presentation, as that juncture in time and space where structure and event intercept each other. As an object of story-telling, the group *becomes*, it begins at such a moment: social reality originates as *kairos*, as an occasion overruled by its own disclosures.

Behind Mauss's faith in rational analysis, there was a sober awareness of having to be timely in its exercise; for the surest attribute of social phenomena is not found in their constancy, but in how quickly the full force of their meanings might perish. The deftness of his dissertation creates the illusion that the practices it dissects and illustrates are being held hostage to inquiry within a fleeting measure of time which will not again be accessible. In this fashion, the accent and style of Mauss's explorations bring him closer to the story-teller than to the semiotician or other recent practitioners of the structuralist science.

The lasting exemplariness of Mauss's practice might be demonstrated by a reading of Gabriel García Márquez's short tale, 'Baltazar's Prodigious Afternoon', as if it were an occasion akin to the one that Mauss saw in gift-exchange.[3] I shall outline a way of construing the story as a fable concerning the origin of the *social* as an alienating domain.[4] With this exercise I hope to demonstrate how, without embedding stories in a particular ethno-social context, our structural knowledge of them is bound to remain an empty formality. However, by context I shall understand not so much the story's realistic setting (in this case the Colombian countryside) as the implicit links existing between a story and those instances of ethno-social learning which give genealogical antecedents to a given tale. At issue will be what we might call the canonical significance of stories (or of narrative cycles) aimed at disclosing the meaning of persons as social beings.

Readers of García Márquez's *One Hundred Years of Solitude* will be familiar with the elder José Arcadio Buendía's fondness early in that novel for wild experimentation and relentless tinkering, as he is driven by the spell cast on him by Melquíades, the Gypsy Magus. In Macondo's morning, objects and instruments of all kinds rise from their slumber when reached by the zeal of the elder José Arcadio become demiurge. The plot of 'The Prodigious Afternoon' hinges on a similar act of creative frenzy. As the story opens, its protagonist, the humble and naive carpenter, Baltazar, has just spent much toil and disturbed sleep building a birdcage. His talents as craftsman have exceeded carpentry; on this occasion he has managed to fashion a prodigious object, worthy of the skills seen only among master artisans of former times.

Baltazar lives, unmarried and childless, with the level-headed Ursula. Upon its completion, the birdcage soon becomes the centre of increasing polemics. From the start, Ursula is exclusively interested in the product's cash value, while on his part Baltazar seems to agree with her strong sense of profit; but, in the end, a motive other than obtaining cash will rule over his actions. The town's children are the first to gather as celebrants of the cage's beauty, but soon a more keenly disposed observer appears. Doctor Octavio Giraldo wants to offer the cage to his invalid wife, a bird lover. Giraldo's prodigality is spent in rhetoric. His speech is at once terse and hyperbolic. He addresses the cage, and through it Baltazar, as if instead of buying it he were engaged in selling it to its maker. Giraldo's rhetorical elegance transforms the cage into a synoptic illusion. Metaphor acts here as a kind of homeotropic gesture which foreshadows the cage's imminent tonality: Doctor Giraldo is the first executor of this tropism when he puts into play his gift for metonymic sympathy. There is no need, he says, to put birds in the cage, 'It would be enough to hang it in the trees so it could sing by itself' (p. 127). Baltazar's contact with the cage's resonance is of a different sort, perhaps one nearer the object's tacit occupancy of space, a form of public dwelling which is meant to resist metamorphic seizures: he indexes the cage's intricacies and then sounds it with one definitive flourish of his wrist: ' "The measurements are carefully calculated" – he said – pointing to the different compartments with his forefinger. Then he struck the dome with his knuckles, and the cage filled with resonant cords' (p. 167). The cage becomes a tuning fork which registers the resonances of each individual's perception of it.

In the end, the good doctor's efforts are thwarted. According to Baltazar, the cage has already been promised to Chepe Montiel's son (Montiel enjoys the accursed reputation of being Macondo's rich man). Giraldo quibbles to no avail: can Baltazar prove that the cage is meant for troupials and not for other birds?; did the child give him a blueprint to follow? During the bargaining Ursula supports Baltazar, moved by her desire to sell the cage to the richer Montiel.

It is to be noted also that it is Ursula, and not Baltazar, who first mentions Montiel as the buyer when she estimates the best price which the cage is likely to command. The reader might surmise at least two things: that Baltazar has told her (in the implicit past of before the story) about the child's request; or that, led by her common sense and good business practice, she takes for granted that if Baltazar has ended up building such an extravagant cage, it had better be for the only person in town with the means to buy it. The point is a crucial one since, as we are about to see, the story offers a minute account of the role played by inference in social affairs.[5] For instance, in strictly discursive terms, the cage rises before the reader's imagination in full detail as if in seeming complicity with the doctor's arrival on the scene. His presence brings before our eyes the achieved object in all its complexity. Until then, the cage has existed as sheer inference, as rumour devoid of form; subsequently, it becomes a visual reality as well as an individual mental perception.

The doctor's visit establishes several things: first, it forces both

Ursula and Baltazar to declare that the sale to Montiel has in fact already taken place (which of course is not the case); second, it underscores the fact that selling a product involves more than the ability to exact the best possible price: social prestige and power (being a Montiel and not a Giraldo) might be stronger factors in creating commercial ties than just the amount of money exchanged; and last but not least, Giraldo's visit heightens the conflict between maker and user concerning the thing made, its value and contingent meanings. The first paradoxical outcome of the story's plot is to be found in Giraldo's odd victory over Baltazar, for the doctor's failure to obtain the sale through rhetorical ploys cannot match the lasting contagion produced by his diagnosis. As a failed owner, he still manages to prescribe the spreading force of word over deed, of unstable metaphor over the presumptive accuracy of action or labour (perhaps Giraldo is destined to own only a wealth of words in which the never-to-be-owned object lies buried in the shadows of rhetoric's illusion).

In a curious way which testifies to the depth of practical wisdom conveyed to the tale – in the manner of a medieval *exemplum* – Giraldo's devious attempt to buy the cage anticipates Montiel's subsequent refusal even to consider buying it. Both men would seem to regard the transaction as something of far greater importance than a simple commercial deal. Giraldo's quaint elegance and cunning give way to Montiel's beastly alertness. No matter how much his son raves there will be no deal. It is at this point that readers of Mauss's *The Gift* might see in Montiel's refusal to honour his son's request, as well as in his suspicions of Baltazar's motives, something more than just the fear of parting with money at the whims of a child.

With respect to exchange, and surrounding the meanness of Montiel, there lies an area of intertextual prodigality which, in this particular case, happens to deal with the unrestrained giving and taking of objects. As is well known, Marcel Mauss understood communal gatherings (such as the potlatch) as affairs in which primitive groups engaged in prolonged bouts of gift-giving and taking, under the common and necessary belief that a pervasive force – a sort of 'mystic cement' in the words of Marshall Sahlins – existed binding donor and recipient; a force conveyed in and by the thing given, a force whose flow could not be arrested: receiving meant giving in turn to a third party and so, relentlessly and sometimes for weeks, men bound themselves through reciprocity.

In refusing Baltazar, Montiel manifests a tacit and inadvertent sense of the logic mapped out in *The Gift*. His character becomes attuned, pretextually, to the knowledge of the central moral put forth by Mauss. Montiel seems aware of something in the sale which exceeds the mere notion of a transaction, something in the order of a reciprocal bond, more deeply rooted in human soil than the overt exchange of cash for object. In other words, and in line with Mauss's lexicon, it is fear of *connubium*, of a lasting dwelling in the other, and of the other in oneself, through the force held in what is given. It is such apprehension which haunts Montiel into breaking this act of attempted *commercium*. On the social plane he fears the rupture of hierarchy in the feeling of being beholden.

Baltazar's excessive and, until now, unfocused zeal meets in Montiel's denial a fitting and complementary force. The clash of wills brings about a shift from market affairs to the older stricture of gift-exchange: Baltazar's zeal and frenzy (which remain mystifying and naive at a narrowly realistic level) point beyond selling, while Montiel's refusal grasps, negatively, the gift element dwelling in the object, its poisonous talents, its gravity. Here I am of course alluding to Mauss's use of etymology to create his own sense of analytic contagiousness: in several languages, including German, *gift* and *poison* stand in neighbouring complicity (cf. Wagner's *Tristan*). In our story, Montiel's refusal to buy is followed by Baltazar's gift of the cage to the child, an act far more offensive and threatening to Montiel than the attempted sale itself. This again points to social rupture.

In terms of the need to reciprocate shown by Mauss, Montiel gets away without buying because nothing like the gift relationship exists in Macondo (and this in itself is revealing). One must see the archaic norm of symbolic exchange as hypothetical, being the opposite of function, yet working in not working. Had it been actual, it would have answered Montiel's refusal with strife. But Baltazar's gift is as unreciprocal as Montiel's non-buying: it shows as the poison foreshadowed in the refusal. As Montiel knew well, something archaic and potentially threatening lurked beneath the blank mirror of the carpenter's face.

I have tried to show that our understanding of the meeting between Montiel and Baltazar is heightened when merged with the textual contingencies activated by *The Gift*. I would also argue that when Mauss interprets the act or institution of gift-exchange he is dealing with the phenomenon of heightening itself. In other words, he is dealing with the problem of whether or not an occasion can ever arise where social phenomena might be grasped at a heightened pitch, an occasion at once so singular and general as to amount to a total social deed. Without such heightening of communal purpose, the structuralist project could not meet its proper object of study, an object both discrete and universal. 'Nothing in our opinion', writes Mauss, 'is more urgent or promising than research into "total" social phenomena'; adding that

the advantage is twofold. Firstly there is an advantage in generality, for facts of widespread occurrence are more likely to be universal than local institutions or themes, which are invariably tinged with local colour. But particularly the advantage is in realism. We see social facts in the round, as they really are. In society there are not merely ideas and rules, but also men and groups and their behaviours. We see them in motion as an engineer sees masses and systems, or as we observe octopuses and anemones in the sea. We see groups of men, and active forces, submerged in their environment and sentiments.   (Mauss, p. 78)

These words should explain how the institution of gift-exchange became the inaugural structuralist construct. Lévi-Strauss sees *The Gift* as such a beginning when, in his introduction to the main writings of Mauss, he recalls experiencing 'the entire gamut of emotions' upon reading the essay for the first time, comparing his experience with Malebranche's evocation of his first reading of Descartes: 'a thumping heart', 'the head boiling', in other words, a total seizure.[6] From this we may gather that poets and story-tellers are not the only creators ruled by the jubilant but also anxious discovery of their powerful predecessors.

Mauss's emphasis on the possibility of transcribing feelings and of moving beyond ideas and rules, casts him in a heroic role, given the reductive and arid character of much of what nowadays is offered as a semiotic account of social action. At any rate, he aims at a total gathering of social means, feelings and imaginings held in normative concert. Such a total construct achieves both its integrity and logic by opposing, replacing or holding at bay other, equally encompassing and frequently lethal, domains. In the case of *The Gift*, the adversary turns out to be war itself. Just as gift-exchange must become total in order to prevent strife, Mauss's reconstruction of it must also achieve analytical integrity and wholeness if it is to stem chaos and randomness in the realm of anthropological analysis. As the American anthropologist, Marshall Sahlins, has so elegantly demonstrated, *The Gift* shows the savage state of constant 'war' against 'warre', amounting to 'a new version of the dialogue between chaos and covenant'.[7]

Just as the anthropologist reduces randomness in the very act of surmising how the savage stems war through the battle of the gifts, Baltazar defeats Giraldo, but only after the doctor erects before his very eyes an already odd and prodigious cage wrapped in a veil of words. Thus the plot of the story unfolds as a series of polemics, it makes itself – or thus is our illusion as readers – out of a primal ground of reciprocal contingencies. I am reminded of Paul Ricoeur's rhetorical exclamation when confronting the ingenuity of the structuralist who, like the Argonauts, builds his vessel as he sails on it. 'Now', says Ricoeur, 'this is quite a strange brand of imitation which comprises and constructs the very thing it imitates!'[8]

Even critics not concerned with Marcel Mauss have read 'Baltazar's Prodigious Afternoon' in terms of latent warfare. The Peruvian novelist, Mario Vargas Llosa, speaks of 'the war which creates divisions in fictional reality' and of the primordial struggle which, active at the heart of the story, transcends a narrowly defined socio-economic understanding of its incidents.[9] Following this notion of struggle, one could see how Baltazar prevails in his meeting with Doctor Giraldo only at the level of reality (he manages to preserve the cage for Montiel's child), while being bested at the level of metamorphic or figural value: the doctor prescribes norms of understanding which transcend the immediate, the practical and urgently useful, just as Baltazar did when creating the cage in all its sumptuousness, before he came to the business of having to sell it. In his meeting with Montiel, however, Baltazar deviates into transcendent significance. He recognizes and seizes upon the prodigy of the cage that is the gift; he defeats meanness in Montiel and, as a result, he engages ruin. His surrender of the cage seems to be at once ridiculous and magnificent. The reader is left with a heightened sense of the conflicting meaning held in abeyance by the notion of prodigality embedded in the title. Is to be prodigal to be reckless, wasteful and even idiotic, or is it perhaps to exercise the noblest of human talents? Answering this question involves addressing the complex issue of the christological aspect of Baltazar's figure broached in my epigraph, placing emphasis on the theological and existential hiatus that separates *Jesus* from *Christ*.

Baltazar will remain oblivious to certain metaphoric gains. Instead of proclaiming his triumph by basing it on the prestige of giving gifts to the children of the rich (thus acknowledging his failure to sell and to profit), he will accept his now numerous followers, hosting them while being acclaimed for defeating Montiel's meanness through a sale. Thaumaturgic generosity, and its embarrassment of symbolic riches, is thus defeated by a different sort of metamorphic excess. As such, Baltazar's flight into the realms of metaphor is inflationary. It is so at least in a triple sense: he pays for the celebration of his own heroics with money from a sale that never takes place; not having such money, he leaves his watch at the saloon as token of future payment to be made with wages not as yet earned; and, once drunk, he dreams of building thousands of cages until becoming a millionaire. One might ask if such inflation could not be something meant to imply the inherent fictionality of both monetary and personal values, something that betrays the ill-begotten powers put into these tokens in order to abstract from flesh, toil and thing their specific talents, their concrete modes of being. We have here an allegory of alienation: could it be that ours is like the fate of things which become commodities and, further, tokens of exchange? Baltazar's fate tells us about feelings, about times lived and felt, time known in the deed; but it tells us about all of it becoming, in the long run, not a form of being, but one of having been, of having to lag behind ourselves, lengthening the hiatus of our own life told as a tale of dispossession. The allegorical drift of the individual towards abstraction and alienation just sketched amounts to a move on the part of both plot and character into the latent realm of political economy and away from any other modes of exchange and symbolic value.

Jean-Pierre Vernant has described the status of artisans in ancient Greece in pertinent terms.[10] Working under a system of values which raised the use of products over their making, artisans made objects whose worth depended on the designs of their intended users. The models provided by the latter were the ones which ruled over the product's significance and social place. Men acted only when they used and not when they made things; they stood free, on account of this reigning ideal, only when they acted as users and not as makers. In fact, according to Vernant making was denied the philosophical status of being an action. But such had not always been the case. In archaic times, before the flowering of the *polis*, there were *thaumaturgoi* or wandering makers shrouded in demonic prestige. These men engaged in making marvellous *thaumata* or *agalmata*, objects as sumptuous in their intricacies as they were useless, which these magicians displayed before their audiences. Building such captivating devices rested on the faculty (demiurgic as well as, in a radical sense, poetic) to seize the right occasion, the *kairos* or pregnant moment when the maker's labours stood the best chance of achieving the rhythms linking them with the force and values latent in matter. It should be clear that the same principle of sumptuous excess and prodigality discerned by Mauss is at work here, in the art of the thaumaturgus.

Baltazar, too, inscribes his actions as maker within a similar domain of values, although in his case the spellbinding uselessness of the cage proves ephemeral. His increasing failure to resist the encroachment of the contending forms of use value which others would impose upon the cage equals his own drift (as constant as his heartbeat) towards the politics of economics and the economics of politics. It seems that there is in the order of things a cunning sort of reciprocity which pays the tribute of awe before the thing made, only to exchange it immediately for the appropriation of use value. Nothing of value can exist free from two temporal modes: first, the one in which value is found and, second, the one which marks the object's fate as exchangeable value as it becomes currency.

This temporal drift characterizes the strictures of political economy. In his *Le miroir de la production* (Paris, 1973), Jean Baudrillard argues in favour of regarding political economy as a category set within the Western, European and, by extension, capitalist understanding of production.[11] He goes on to theorize that the Marxian critique of economic modes reinforces the basic concepts of production which it attempts to demystify, being an extension of the very system of political economy that it sets out to subvert. In his view, the systems of symbolic exchange that characterize archaic or savage societies of the sort treated by Mauss are not economic. In viewing them as such, Marxist and other theories of production perform an act of cognitive imperialism. Regardless of the validity of Baudrillard's thesis in the realm of pure economics, I would like to underline its relevance to practical criticism: to subject literary fictions to semiotic transcription might result in a similar act of imperial appropriation. Without necessarily having to return to a subjectivist or emotionalist approach to literary values (or, for that matter, without turning literature into the eternal savage within our midst), one might search for modes of understanding more in sympathy with that aspect of literary fictions which remains a wayward act, a gesture not exhausted by being reflected in the atomistic mirror of semiotic jargons.

I now turn to 'Baltazar's Prodigious Afternoon' to suggest that the story resists economic closure. For example, there are the women: Ursula is a Penelope who awaits and keeps time slicing onions and who, like her namesake Ursula Iguarán from *One Hundred Years of Solitude*, joins each single day with the next to form an endurable measure of life. There is Giraldo's wife, the enigmatic invalid from the short novel, 'In Evil Hour', always silent, bird-like in her gilded isolation. Finally there is Montiel's wife, who is better known to us as the widow of 'Montiel's Widow', and whose only moment of graceful acquaintance with life seems to have been her welcoming of Baltazar into the house and her delight at the cage. Her son, who is dismissed by most critics as a spoilt brat, exceeds such a minor role, being perhaps twice an orphan: orphan to Montiel's callousness and to Baltazar's childless prodigality. Between child and cage there is a transparent affinity – 'the child jumped up, embraced the cage which was almost as big as he was, and stood looking at Baltazar through the wirework without knowing what to say' (p. 175). Both child and cage are contested objects, two marks of disownment, the cage in its joyous emptiness as the vanishing point of the tale's allegories, the child as the inheritor of the blessings through which his dual orphanhood twice denies him the chance of becoming prodigal.[12]

Besides these instances of characterization, it is instructive to focus on the two meetings between Baltazar, Giraldo and Montiel, to fix the plot upon a given site, an imaginary point in time and space large enough to encompass the main deployment of the action and yet small enough to allow for coherence in procuring a central fable, that of passing from feeling and desire into symbol and, ultimately, into abstraction. Giraldo is seen as diagnostician of Baltazar's predicament, offering neither a prescription nor a cure for his increasing isolation. Matching Giraldo's eloquence with some borrowed jargon, I would call Baltazar a *hysteresiac*. In other words, he might be said to suffer from belatedness; he lags behind the effects of his own wilfulness and craft, vibrating to the tune that someone else plays with his creation. By hysteresis I do not mean a psychological malady, but rather a rupture of temporal and semantic immediacy taking effect between person and surroundings, an acute state of ontological displacement with respect to life, habits and common values.[13] Baltazar's 'Prodigious Afternoon' is emblematic of his falling into literature, of the layered disclosure which heightens his being as an affliction open to reading. Only as such could these few hours be at once catastrophic *and* blissful. The plot that befalls Baltazar removes him from his social cradle, from the contrived space and time which his craft carves out.

If there is a token of literature in the tale, or a critical point where this peculiarly modern affliction is best registered, it might be found in the protagonist's resistance to structure. For all that we know, when at the end Baltazar lies by the wayside in death-like sleep ('The women who passed on their way to five-o'clock Mass didn't dare look at him, thinking he was dead'), he might be enjoying that exorbitant condition of abjectness which Georges Bataille places as the unassailable realm of meaning known as the *heterogeneous*.[14] With Baltazar we obtain either the residual oddity left behind by a hero of everyday toil, or just a patient awaiting some disciplinary judgement of his ills.

In juxtaposing García Márquez's story and Marcel Mauss's essay, I have tried to outline what should be regarded as a basic structuralist ploy, of which *The Gift* is a seminal example. It consists of arresting the flux of social phenomena at a virtual point in time, or at a moment of potential crisis when systems of belief as well as practices can be grasped in dualistic confrontation. When the ethics of structuralism are imagined, it becomes apparent how (perhaps from Hegel) the method has invariably tried to break such dual confrontations by means of generating a third realm of synthetic resolutions. This moral fable is a persistent one in the history of structuralist discourse: beginning with the insoluble and crisis-laden bond of signifier/signified (or Symbolic/Imaginary, as in Lacan), continuing with the master split Nature/Culture (plus its endless derivations) and gathering an ever-growing lexicon of polarities, the method remains poised on the line which *must* separate seemingly alien and yet reciprocal spheres in need of meditation.

I have tried to suggest that both essay and tale heighten for us the perils of passing from randomness to culture, doing so through a sort of transactional cadence. The giving and taking of gifts liberated culture from what Mauss saw, in line with other French moralists, as a brutish and stagnant condition. But in so doing he altered the views of classical contract theories by demonstrating that chaos had not preceded commonwealth, that before civilization coercion had not been the price of order (such is the case made by Marshall Sahlins). Similarly, the tale helped us establish a minimum coefficient of sociability in Macondo's life. In both essay and tale, culture swings precariously between confrontation, its risks, and the dispersal of energies. Culture is fragile, menaced by corruption and distrust, but in *The Gift* it still remains free from the force of the body politic. García Márquez tells the story of Macondo as a struggle to remain reciprocal, or to believe in the alien graces of the other, to welcome the gift of his arrival, thus sustaining what Melville calls in *Moby-Dick* 'the Siamese connexion with a plurality of other mortals'. Sooner or later, however, social affairs will break away from the gift's enclosure. Macondo will evolve from Eden-like hamlet to boom town to ghostly ruin. The gypsy Melquíades's early offerings (those marvellous toys which José Arcadio changed to the point of madness) become in the end the Book itself, the one gifted occurrence which some characters will have to unravel, making of their own lives a fitting tune for its mute script.

If, as Gérard Genette has said, structuralism views language as a process of inexorable degradation of the symbol into the sign, the transfer of gifts offers us one of the earliest instances of such a drift. For archaic symbolic exchange encompasses a struggle, a *pugna* where symbol and thing meet, as the former is being institutionally born. But before the motivated character of the symbol with respect to that which it embodies gives way to the unmotivated and arbitrary sign, a prior severance will have occurred: the thing would have been designated or named, all perceptive immediacy between persons and world having thus been broken (a passage which structuralism can adopt or simply assume, but could not describe without going beyond its own epistemological strictures). The tale brings us closer to this primal scenario than does the essay, since for Mauss gift-exchange must amount to at least a rudimentary institution, while in García Márquez's text the birdcage would exceed all stable linguistic designations, being either an unnamable aspect of thinghood, or a generator of the most extravagant efforts to describe it.

The theoretical preoccupations of Jacques Lacan tell us how close gift-giving was to the earliest vestiges of symbolic practice known to humans. *Symbol*, or what might correspond to our notion of it, designates in several languages 'bond', 'intercourse', 'twisting together', 'knotting' and, in archaic Greek, 'a contribution to a common meal or feast'.[15] In parallel terms, Vladimir Propp sees the origins of folktales as a narrative detachment from ritual, in which a story is cast off from a ceremony where an object or amulet played the central role of being transferred into story; the object was eventually lost or simply replaced by a nucleus-plot dealing with the search for it and its recovery (a fitting if historically dubious genesis for stories such as 'Baltazar's Prodigious Afternoon').[16]

However, what seems at stake here is not history as such, but rather casting our knowledge of fable-making in terms of tale-telling itself, a project which leads to the nostalgic sense of having lost contact with objects whose making and ritual possession the stories uphold in memory. Walter Benjamin also left us a fable of the story-teller's craft and of its imagined historical origins.[17] The narrative elements of his well-known essay heighten the loss and eventual recovery of an object which remains at the heart of the tale's origin. Thus at one point in his essay Benjamin speaks of how 'traces of the storyteller cling to the story the way the handprints of the potter cling to the clay vessel'. For him the teller of tales ventures 'into the depths of inanimate nature' (p. 207), a thematic thread which gains in prominence as the essay nears the end, finding perhaps emblematic resolution in his retelling of Johann Peter Hebel's story where a would-be bride recovers the crystallized body of her deceased betrothed after years of burial at the bottom of a mining shaft, an outcome that lends to the human form, recovered in jewel-like perfection, the status of an object at once pristine and definitive, like those which the art of the story-teller is said to seek.

The ethnographic records favoured by Lacan bear affinities with the views of Propp and Benjamin. In them, thought, action and discourse become available to the archaic mentality as extraneous additions and support of gifts circulated in ritual. What discourse replaces and supplements into eventual obliteration is a touchstone-like object which, in an even more primordial sense becomes a site-of-sites, a clinging-to-place, a holding-fast-place, a dwelling place in need of being rent or cast asunder from itself.[18] Though structuralism must leave such primal grounds in haste, searching for other, more structurable terms, readers of literature may refuse such flight into abstraction, holding fast to the enigmatic gift-object.

To conclude, the merging of gift-bearing tale and essay suggests that, in what is likely to prove the most enduring aspect of structuralism, there is at work a grand fable which narrates the untuning of savage harmonies and tells us how there used to be an active embedding of the individual in his communal and natural environments. These harmonies the fortunate enthnographer might arrest and transcribe before they fade out for ever. What literature might have to offer in answer to such a stern nostalgia for a bygone integrity of thought, action and setting is its own problematic sense of structure. Problematic because, in spite of some recent critical efforts, object/texts such as 'Baltazar's Prodigious Afternoon' have a structural character which might be at best dubious and at worst trivial. Critics bent on structuring (and even some trying to emulate deconstructions) do not seem to have learned the lesson conveyed in recent fiction by writers as different as Carlos Fuentes, Manuel Puig, Thomas Pynchon, Michael Tournier and, of course, García Márquez. For them, semioticians of literary fictions would seem to be engaged in a rather ponderous removal of the Emperor's new clothes. Last but not least, these novelists themselves remain as much connoisseurs of randomness as they are counterfeiters dealing in structures.

It is in grasping the structural contingency and excess of literary fictions as well as of hermeneutical strategies, and not in redeploying them structurally, that the beginning of the critical task lies. In this sense, to read a tale by means of an essay may be understood as a fictive and allegorical retelling aimed at disclosing the grounds of the interpreter's choices and ploys. Here the reader is caught in the need to answer an always unfulfilled call for reciprocity embedded in the fable itself.

Notes

1 This is a revised version of an article which appeared in *Modern Language Notes*, 97 (1982), 347–64.
2 Marcel Mauss, *The Gift. Forms and Functions of Exchange in Archaic Societies*, translated by Ian Cunnison (New York, 1967), pp. 77–8. All quotations come from this edition.
3 'La prodigiosa tarde de Baltazar', Penguin Parallel Texts: Spanish Short Stories II (Harmondsworth, 1972), pp. 162–77.
4 In the preface to the English version of his *La police des familles*, Jacques Donzelot gives a new twist to the *social*, viewing it as the 'strange aquarium that has become, in a brief period of time, the reality principle of our societies'. I shall follow Donzelot in regarding the *social* as the implied and taken for granted mode of cohesiveness which grounds the discursive knowledge of the *social* itself, making of it an insulating and alienating domain. What is thus abstracted is not the individual as much as his or her concrete needs and conflictive moral and political aims.
5 The nuances of signification are not readily perceived in the most sustained analysis of 'La prodigiosa tarde' that I have come across, David William Foster's 'García Márquez and the *écriture* of Complicity: "La prodigiosa tarde de Baltazar" ', *Studies in the Contemporary Spanish-American Short Story* (Columbia & London, 1979), pp. 39–42.

6 Claude Lévi-Strauss, 'Introduction à l'oeuvre de Marcel Mauss', in Marcel Mauss, *Sociologie et anthropologie* (Paris, 1950), p. xxxiii. The full passage reads: 'Peu de personnes ont pu lire l'*Essai sur le don* sans ressentir toute la gamme des émotions si bien décrites par Malebranche évoquant sa première lecture de Descartes: le coeur battant, la tête bouillonnante, et l'esprit envahi d'une certitude encore indéfinissable, mais impérieuse, d'assister à un événement décisif de l'évolution scientifique'.

7 See 'The Spirit of the Gift', in *Stone Age Economics* (Chicago, 1972), pp. 149–83.

8 Quoted by Clifford Geertz in his *Negara. The Theatre State in Nineteenth-Century Bali* (Princeton, NJ, 1980), p. 121, an undertaking whose importance as a study of symbolic systems in their historical settings the literary critic should not ignore.

9 Mario Vargas Llosa, *Gabriel García Márquez: historia de un deicidio* (Caracas, 1971), pp. 372–9, i.e. 'la guerra que divide a la realidad ficticia'.

10 Jean-Pierre Vernant, 'Aspects psychologiques du travail dans la Grèce ancienne', in *Mythe et pensée chez les Grecs II* (Paris, 1971), pp. 37–67.

11 Translated and introduced by Mark Poster as *The Mirror of Production* (St Louis, 1975).

12 Besides implying the meanings of *prodigalidad* already discussed, the plot extends the echoes of *prodigiosa* at least along two more lines: 1. as *prodigio* (*prodigy*), the cage appears aberrant, excessive, and also (*prodigy: pro-agium*, 'a thing said', OED) as the object from which omens and prognostic utterances issue; and 2. as *pródigo* (*prodigal*), what surfaces is Baltazar's eventual return to Ursula and to everyday time, but beyond this, there remains a sympathetic affinity between the cage and Montiel's son, which creates a triangular relationship (focus of a possible reading according to Lacan's notion of the *nom de père*) whose two other points would be marked by Montiel's barren withdrawal of paternal blessings and Baltazar's fertile artisan gifts, which seem to stand in place of his own lack of children and, in particular, a son. At this level, the tale would allude to the contractual uncertainties of male descent and their attendant cultural prestige, this being the same deep-seated theme which binds all male inheritors and makers of the *Book* (of the sovereign cultural object) in *One Hundred Years of Solitude*.

13 I borrow the term as it is abundantly applied by Pierre Bourdieu throughout his *Outline of a Theory of Practice* (Cambridge University Press, 1977), pp. 63–4, 81–8; see also index entry under *habitus*, p. 234.

Michael T. Taussig has provided a spirited account of grassroots resistance on the part of some Colombian agrarian workers against the habits and values enforced upon them by market economics. See the first part of *The Devil and Commodity Fetishism in South America* (Chapel Hill, NC, 1980), pp. 3–139. Although Taussig's interpretations attempt to incorporate into Marxist theory the practices of these peasant workers, his deeper understanding of them tends to confirm Baudrillard's critique of the assimilation of archaic or magical conceptions of exchange into the patterns of political economy. Taussig's is also a good example of how to penetrate beyond the alienating category of the *social* as described by Donzelot.

14 The full intensity of Bataille's views on *hétérogénéité* can be grasped in the dossier of his polemic with André Breton. In place of a complete summary of the concept which cannot be attempted here, it might be enough to say that the *heterogeneous* frames degrees of being which society must keep at bay in order to function, having recourse to them in deflected or mediated fashion. Although it involves what Eliade would call the *Sacred*, the *heterogeneous* remains in many of its manifestations a realm of earthly immanence harbouring forces which range from those manifested in sadism to the ones which characterize religious ecstasy. The

heterogeneous occupies the edges of community, or those regions viewed by Victor Turner as liminal, although Bataille places a heavy emphasis on the degree of pollution present in these forces. Contact with such realities is usually obtained through orgiastic excess, of which the potlatch itself is a prominent instance. Also the dynamics of scape-goating are very much in evidence at the heart of this realm, with the presence in it of masses of miserable beings and their repellent objects, all victims of conquering abuse. One might also see in these manifestations of the abject a status of extreme forlornness not unlike Durkheim's *anomie*, which in the upper reaches of literary discourse would show forth as melancholy's terminal prestige. I have had access to this phase of Bataille's work through the anthology in Spanish selected by Mario Vargas Llosa: *Georges Bataille. Obras escogidas* (Barcelona, 1974), pp. 243–308, and also through *La part maudite* (Paris, 1967).

15 See the notes contributed by Anthony Wilden to Lacan's *The Language of the Self. The Function of Language in Psychoanalysis* (Baltimore, Md, 1968), pp. 118–21.

16 Vladimir Propp, *Las raíces históricas del cuento* (Madrid, 1974), pp. 523–35. A strong critique of Propp's theories regarding the origins of folktales can be found in David E. Bynum's *The Deamon in the Wood* (Cambridge, Mass., 1979). See in particular its fourth chapter, 'The Ritual Phallacy', pp. 149–254. One should add, however, that in refuting Propp's account, Bynum reinforces the notion of there being a primal link between story-telling and a given object, in this case through the contact between the hewer of wood and the two trees which this character confronts; see 'Inter Duos Arbores', pp. 85–146.

17 Walter Benjamin, 'The Storyteller. Reflexions on the Works of Nikolai Leskov', *Illuminations* (New York, 1968), pp. 83–109.

18 Compare the account of this primal site in Wilden (ed.), *Lacan's 'The Language of Self'*, pp. 120–1 which belongs to a descriptive genealogy whose most illustrious ancestor is Maurice Leenhardt's superb *Do Kamo. La personne et le mythe dans le monde mélanésien* (Paris, 1947), particularly the ninth chapter, 'La parole', pp. 164–86.

3

The body as political instrument: communication in *No One Writes to the Colonel*

RENÉ PRIETO

Has a work of fiction ever been as spuriously transparent as *No One Writes to the Colonel*?[1] Crisp and direct to the point of being laconic, this tale of a retired colonel who waits away his life, dying of hunger for a pension which never comes, could well be just what it seems and nothing more: a brilliantly terse indictment of social injustice in Latin America. Certainly in 1961, when it was first published, the story was seen in this light, which is to say, that it was read on its most unmistakable level. More recently, critics such as Peter Earle and Graciela Maturo have duly noted the complex network of symbols which sustain the main theme of García Márquez's novella, recognizing, once and for all, how this author always delivers more than mere appearances.[2] Earle, for one, notes at least three features instrumental to our understanding of *No One Writes to the Colonel*: 1) the novella has a musical structure programmed on the basis of two voices, 'discouragement' and 'illusion'; 2) there is a dialectic between desire and death housed within the persona of the protagonist; and 3) the rooster, prize possession of the colonel's slaughtered son, must be seen as 'an allegory of vigilance and resurrection'.[3] Maturo's concerns are of a more religious nature: she views the chronological development in the light of the Christian liturgical calendar. The action, starting around the time of the October equinox, concludes at Christmas and suggests to this critic 'the spiritual regeneration of man'.[4]

What these readings both share and bring to our understanding of García Márquez's novella is, first, the importance of the theme of renewal, secondly, the fact that the story is a rite of passage during which the colonel frees himself from the oppression and sense of discouragement which typify him at the onset and, thirdly, the notion that, in Earle's own words, we must speak in terms of an 'apparent

33

simplicity' when we refer to García Márquez's most celebrated short work.[5] Apparent because, even when the sentences are clipped and the syntax plain, *No One Writes to the Colonel* has the 'simple' complexity of a gothic cathedral: the structure is disciplined, almost severe, but the result is labyrinthine if we speak in terms of the complex layering which spells out the message. Fortunately, all labyrinths have a centre and *No One Writes to the Colonel* is no exception. Not surprisingly, a direct path to it is suggested by Mario Vargas Llosa in his monograph on García Márquez, *Historia de un deicidio*.[6]

In this study Vargas Llosa underscores the importance of the 'demons' or obsessions 'which appear and reappear converted in themes' in all works of fiction.[7] Something about this remark, forthright though it is, catches the attention. Critics approaching *No One Writes to the Colonel* have concerned themselves with the net result of Vargas Llosa's equation – the themes – instead of directly tapping the wellspring. It is unquestionable that the fighting cock, and the rain, and certain numbers are fundamental to the development of this novella. They are pieces of the narrative puzzle but not, as far as I can see, a central obsession from which the entire thematic development emerges. And yet, such an obsession is present. Redundance and obviousness do much to camouflage it, it is true, but should in no way detract from the fact that a concern with eating functions is the matrix of *No One Writes to the Colonel*. To demonstrate the centrality of this theme, I propose to start from the beginning, with an overview of the narrative development. I will then focus on the role of food and study its ramifications in the fiction before discussing the semantic content and the three-tier technique of García Márquez's ostensibly simple architecture.

The action of *No One Writes to the Colonel* begins on a morning in October and ends on a Sunday in December, late at night. The protagonists are a 75-year-old man and his wife. He is a dreamer, an inveterate optimist; she, a woman of a 'naturally hard character, hardened even more by forty years of bitterness' (p. 101). They are unable to make ends meet, having waited for over fifteen years for a war pension which the man, a retired colonel, should have received in recognition of his service. They have no money left, no provisions and no guarantees for the future. Their son, Agustín, was shot nine months previous to the beginning of the action for distributing clandestine political literature at the cockfights. His legacy to his parents is his fighting cock, a sure winner at the fights scheduled for January. The problem is that, having no resources, the couple will have to choose between feeding it or feeding themselves.

The day and the action begin simultaneously when the colonel takes the lid off the coffee can and realizes 'that there was only one teaspoonful left' (p. 7). He throws half of the boiling water down the drain and scrapes the inside of the can with a knife, to get at 'the last coffee grounds mixed together with rust from the can' (p. 7). This initial occupation, not to say preoccupation, with food and drink, is only the first of many in the story and, some might argue, could well be a reflection of the fact that García Márquez wrote *No One Writes to the Colonel* while living in Paris on a shoestring budget.[8] Real hunger will undoubtedly force the hand of an author, but mention of eating in this instance is no mere coincidence. Food, consuming it and discharging it, buying it, preparing it or refusing it, is in fact Theseus's thread to unravelling the protagonist's knotted evolution and grasping the otherwise problematical outcome of García Márquez's novella.

If we concern ourselves exclusively with the three members of the main household – the colonel, his wife and the fighting cock – we can count twenty-four instances of eating and drinking in the 106-pages-long Biblioteca Era edition of *No One Writes to the Colonel*.[9] In and of itself, from a critical perspective, such insistence could add up to no more than a mere fixation. What makes the references to eating and drinking so revealing is that, until the last of seven sections, and with only one exception, all mention of food and drink brings forth, immediately following, a reference to death. Clearly, it is not possible within the framework of this article to quote all of these instances. Nevertheless, a few examples will suffice to convince the reader that the systematic association between consumption and death in the first six sections of the novella is far from gratuitous.

To begin with, in the first scene, when the colonel is waiting for the coffee to brew, he 'experienced the sensation that poisonous mushrooms and lilies were growing in his bowels' (p. 7). Soon after, when his wife, prostrated in bed after an asthma attack, drinks the last sip of coffee left in the house, the omniscient narrator declares: 'at that moment the bells began to toll. The colonel had forgotten the burial . . .' (p. 8). Even as his wife finishes drinking, 'she was still thinking about the dead man' (p. 8). Later in the action, she recovers her proverbial pluck and fixes a stew by boiling together 'all the edible things that tropical lands are capable of producing' (p. 27). As they are about to finish their meal, their doctor pushes the door open and cries out: ' "are all the sick dead?" ' (p. 28). The colonel answers him along the same morbid lines, ' "So it seems doctor . . . I've always said that your watch keeps time with the buzzards" ' (p. 28). And his wife, never one to stay silent, develops her husband's theme: ' "One of these days I'll die and I'll take you to hell, doctor" ' (p. 29). In the meantime, however, she offers him a cup of coffee which he turns down with revealing irony, ' "No, thank you very much . . . I absolutely deny you the opportunity of poisoning me" ' (p. 29). During yet another meal, prepared by borrowing some corn from the rooster's provisions, the colonel mournfully reflects, ' "I am thinking about the employee responsible for my pension . . . Fifty years from now we will be resting in peace underground while that poor man will be in agony every Friday as he waits for his own pension" ' (p. 66). The following day, as they finish up the rest of the corn stew, it is the wife's turn to feel despondent: ' "I am thinking" ', she says out of the blue, ' "that the man is dead going on two months and I haven't given my regrets yet" ' (p. 68). The dead man turns out to be the same one for whom the bell tolls at the beginning of the story, his body conveniently dragged out as the topic of food turns up once again. This topic is tainted with death, moreover, whether provisions are available or not, and it is alluded to, both metaphorically, ' "we are dying of hunger" ' (p. 81), or, as in the previously quoted examples, 'factually', within the fiction.

Relentless, obsessive and systematic, the association between consumption and death reaches a climax at the end of part six in a scene which functions as the turning point of the novella. The colonel goes to the pool hall on Sunday evening. A friend of his son's slips him a sheet of clandestine political propaganda. The colonel pockets it and, almost immediately after, the music stops. It is a police raid and he realizes that, like his son Agustín, he is caught red-handed. To boot, the man conducting the raid, the very one who shot his son, is now facing him, 'his rifle pointing right into his stomach' (p. 89). The man stares at him unblinkingly while the colonel feels 'swallowed by those eyes, mashed, digested and immediately expelled' (p. 89). Significantly, however, the murderer lets him walk out of the tight spot with the words: ' "Go ahead, colonel" ' (p. 88). More significantly still, the next and final section of the novella, immediately following the scene in which the hero is metaphorically 'swallowed and expelled', opens with a complete reversal of all previous premises. Six of the seven sections take place during the humid Colombian 'winter' or rainy season. The seventh unfolds at the beginning of the spring-like dry season: 'He didn't have to open the window to identify December' (p. 90). To say that the overall tone of the novella changes dramatically after this point would be an understatement. Earlier in the action man and nature were hopelessly sick, unremittingly dreary, whereas the brave new world of section seven glistens with newness. All of a sudden, the backyard is a 'patio maravilloso' (p. 90) inviting the colonel to set out for the quay, as usual on Fridays, to wait for the mail boat. Instead of stepping out into the rain as on previous occasions, however, his walk becomes 'a prodigious moment, made of a clarity not yet tried out' (p. 92) and the colonel, taking his cue from new-fledged surroundings, feels crisp and clean 'as if made out of glass' (p. 92).

The pain of waiting is over, even if waiting itself is not. The letter may still not come but hope is in the air. In keeping with the festive mood, the circus arrives, 'the first to come in ten years' (p. 93) and ushers in – with a typically carnivalesque sense of inversion – the transposition of all previous conventions. The sun begins to shine, the sick man heals. The relationship of the central couple evolves in unison. He, heretofore uncertain, starts December full of mettle, just like the fighting cock which his wife is so adamant about selling. During an argument on the subject he 'discovers, with no astonishment, that she awakens neither compassion nor remorse in him' (p. 97) and, 'with unfathomable kindness', proceeds to inform her that ' "The fighting cock is not for sale" ' (p. 98). Their relationship evolves not only in what they say to each other but, more importantly, in the manner in which they say it. Up until the spring section, the wife typically resorts to the imperative voice when addressing her husband and tends to treat him like a child: ' "Those shoes are ready to be thrown out" ', she tells him in section two, ' "go on wearing the patent leather boots" ' (p. 20). Later, wrangling over their most typical bone of contention, she orders him thus: ' "You get rid of that rooster immediately" ' (p. 52) and, on a different subject, ' "You take him the clock right away, you put it on the table and you tell him: Alvaro, I am bringing you this here clock" ' (p. 54). Adamantly demanding money, she finally informs her husband, ' "Don't you come back here without the forty dollars" ' (p. 55). The colonel's flaw is not merely (in the words of his wife) that he 'lacks character' (p. 79) but that, in keeping with the inversions which typify relationships in *No One Writes to the Colonel*, he is often reduced to the status of a child while she, the voice of authority, behaves like his parent. The colonel's infantile behaviour is strongly suggested during four different scenes. The first takes place at the post office when the hero turns toward his friend, the doctor, 'with an entirely childish look' (p. 23); soon after, in a discussion about politics, the physician reminds him, ' "Don't be naive, colonel . . . we are already too old to be waiting for the Messiah" ' (p. 24). Finally, much later in the action, when the disgruntled colonel tells his friend, ' "If I were twenty years younger things would be different" ' he is reminded, somewhat cryptically, that he ' "will always be twenty years younger" ' (pp. 83–4). Being fussed over parentally by his own wife further reinforces the theme of the old man's childishness. Not only does she direct and scold him throughout, she enhances his protracted boyishness whenever possible as, for example, by 'taking twenty years off [his] back' (p. 35) when cutting his hair and persuading him to keep on wearing what to him, frankly ' "look like orphan's shoes" ' (p. 20). When he demurs she is quick to refresh his memory with the fact that they are indeed ' "orphans of their son" ' (p. 21).

The role of child is superseded in the last section, however, where, in addition, the wife's use of the imperative to address her husband is substituted in the Spanish text for a series of non-assertive interrogatives which fully qualify her new station in the novella and function as foils introducing the colonel's thrustful new tone:

1 ' "And if he doesn't come?", asked the woman.
   "He will come." ' (p. 98)
2 She:' "And if they don't understand?"
   He: "Then they don't." ' (p. 99)
3 She:' "And if it doesn't arrive?"
   He: "It will arrive." ' (p. 100)[10]

But the series of carnivalesque inversions in part seven does not end here. The references to food in this section, for one, are associated with death in the case of the wife's discourse exclusively, never that of the husband. During lunch, deprived of her authority, she informs him, ' "You should realize that I am dying, that what I suffer from is not a disease but an agony" ' (p. 102). And later that evening, after mumbling prayers in bed – the original version has, revealingly, 'chewing' her prayers: 'masticó oraciones' (p. 102) – she complains, ' "I don't want to die in the dark" ' (p. 103). There is one other significant change in this last section: the colonel is finally rid of his digestive troubles. 'He feels good', we are told, 'December had wilted the flora from his viscera' (p. 92). So not only does he prepare and consume food that is untainted from affiliation with death, but, just as importantly, he is rid of the excremental curse which hounds him throughout the six earlier sections.

The fact that the actual fully-fledged 'demon', the obsession, in this novella should comprise not one single ingredient but rather a kinship of contraries – food and excrement – should come as no surprise for we are dealing with a narrative scheme in which the supporting elements function in pairs (husband/wife; winter/summer; assertive/submissive). The scatological fixation should surprise us even less. The anal weapon is brandished through García Márquez's fiction, from *In Evil Hour* to *One Hundred Years of Solitude*. After all, carnival (and the carnival literature which these works epitomize so precisely) is also, according to Bakhtin, a celebration of the forces of the lower body, a 'mighty thrust downward'.[11]

This thrust penetrates the novella from the first page, where the protagonist is assailed by the invading sensation already alluded to, the 'poisonous mushrooms and lilies growing in his bowels' (p. 7). This same curse reappears, as a leitmotif, thirteen times throughout the tale, as has been noted by critics such as George McMurray in his excellent study on García Márquez.[12] However, McMurray's sense of propriety gets the better of his analysis when it comes to investigating the colonel's ailment, which he identifies as 'gastritis'. A close study of the matter is enough to ascertain that the colonel's curse is, however, quite different from McMurray's diagnosis. After 'agonizing many hours in the privy, sweating ice, feeling that the flora of his viscera was rotting and falling in pieces' (p. 52), the hero painfully learns that all was really 'a false alarm' (p. 26). Squatting on the platform of rough-hewn boards, he anxiously experiences 'the uneasiness of an urge frustrated' (p. 26). His trouble, in other words, is not an inflammation of the lining of the stomach as McMurray would have us believe but rather, to put it bluntly, constipation – an inability to relieve himself. It is an inability which is resolved at the very beginning of section seven, as we have seen, after the colonel feels swallowed and rejected by his son's murderer. The physiological resolution in turn drains a thematic bottleneck and warrants the utterance of previously censured scatological material.[13] To his wife's last injunction, '"Tell me, what do we eat"', the colonel rebelliously answers, ' "Shit" ' (p. 106), bringing together in this manner the two poles of the symbolic matrix in an echo of Freud's succinct formula, 'excrement becomes aliment'.[14] The obvious question at this juncture is, how does this confluence fit within the scheme of the action? It is at this point that we can grasp the complexity of García Márquez's conception.

In *No One Writes to the Colonel* meaning is apprehended on three autonomous but also interwoven levels. On the first and most obvious we read the injustice of the political system which afflicts the hero. The second level records the evolution in the relationship between a man and his wife and, read in the light of the first, raises a pivotal question, namely, why is the colonel's battle fought, which is to say, depicted, on the home front? Since the context is the family (i.e. what is common to all) and not the battlefield, I would suggest that García Márquez's aim in this novella is to portray the urgency of evolving beyond the submissiveness which lies at the base of all social injustice, abetted by the men who wait rather than act. After all, the well-worn phrase applied to the last Aureliano in *One Hundred Years of Solitude*, 'the habit of obedience had dried up the seeds of rebellion in his heart',[15] could just as easily apply to the retired colonel at the beginning of this tale. But unlike Aureliano, the colonel clearly evolves toward a self-realization which culminates at the conclusion of the novella when he feels 'pure, explicit, invincible' (p. 106). What is less manifest is the fact that this evolution is depicted through the figuration of bodily functions, a physiological frame which operates as the third level of the narration and one which García Márquez plainly conceives on the basis of psychoanalytic theory.

From this theory, for example, we know that the oral phase is a period of dependence, a phase during which the human infant is incapable of accepting separation from the mother. Cast in the same mould, the hero's dependent phase in García Márquez's scheme is haunted by a fixation with food.

Twenty instances of eating and drinking take place during the time the colonel submits to his wife and is treated like a child (addressed in the imperative voice and directed in his actions). Psychoanalysis further teaches us that the incapacity to accept separation from the mother turns out to be, in Norman O. Brown's classic formula, 'the core of the human neurosis'.[16] Neurosis because separation confers individual life to all organisms while, at the same time, it leads to death. Man's inability to deal with this prospect makes him repress the death instinct but, in so doing, he ironically denies life which can only come through individuation. In other words, during the oral dependent stages, a fixation with the body of the mother brings together the nourishment which provides life and the subjection which denies it, a fact which distinctly illuminates the nexus between food and death in *No One Writes to the Colonel* and one that also explains the denial of elimination (the colonel's 'urge frustrated') in the first six sections of the novella. Antithetically, the oral phase foregrounds incorporation while the anal is typified by separation. Freud sees in this separation a path through which the organism's innate destructive instinct (the death instinct) is channelled. 'The organism converts the destructive energy into an aggression directed unto others', he argues, 'which preserves it from harm and makes its own existence possible.'[17] But we must not see in this aggression forces which are ultimately destructive of the organism itself. On the contrary, rejection is, in fact, the very mechanism of reinstatement driving the organism forward in a dynamic confrontation and involvement with life. It is, as Julia Kristeva points out, 'le mécanisme même de la relance, de la tension, de la vie'.[18] In the light of Kristeva's remark, we can better grasp the full tenor of the colonel's evolution and recognize how the climactic ending of the novella betokens in every way the beginning of a new life for its hero. We can also see how the conclusive invective at the end signals a release; it is not 'ironic' as McMurray would have us believe, or even a 'new way of expressing violence' as Angel Rama suggests, but rather the most fundamental step on the path to self-realization.[19] The hero has evolved away from submissiveness and become capable of asserting his independence. It is not surprising that he should feel 'pure, explicit, invincible' (p. 106) as he prepares to oppose the will of his wife and assert his own for the first time in the action. It is even less surprising that the word used to affirm this newly acquired self-sufficiency should be the emblem of the rejection he is about to carry out. And by rejection I do not mean that he breaks away from his wife but, simply, that their relationship evolves until the climactic conclusion which takes the hero one step beyond the threshold of a fresh involvement with life.

No One Writes to the Colonel is, therefore, a eulogy to independence (pictured as an organic evolution) and a portrayal of the struggle required to achieve it (dramatized in the continuing dialogue between husband and wife, authority and subordination, 'parent' and 'child'). It is also an indictment of political injustice and, implicitly, an injunction to the men who, through their passivity, make it possible. Fully in keeping with his political aims and his firm belief in social evolution, the novella is conceived in complete accordance with García Márquez's wholly original artistic creed. And by this I do not refer to his artful technique but, rather, to the less conspicuous undercurrents of his fiction, since so much of his innovation lies in what is not so readily apparent, as, for instance, in his transformation of reality and, more specifically, of political reality. He has always repudiated the misjudgement inherent in the bending of artistic inspiration to serve political aims. In a very revealing article published in 'Tabla Redonda' in 1960, he intimated what was to become the basis for all his fiction: 'It is perhaps more rewarding to write honestly about what one is capable of telling for having lived it', he declares, 'than to write, with the same degree of earnestness, about that which our political position suggests must be told, even if it means inventing it'.[20] Forcing the pen to fit the message, in other words, leads unremittingly to failure. With equal conviction, he indicates that the best means of eliciting reader response is through suggestion and challenge not through pontification. All this by way of saying that, in keeping with both his political and artistic beliefs, the message of *No One Writes to the Colonel* does not meet the reader at every turn. The *violencia* which tore through Colombia starting in 1948 is suggested, implied, alluded to throughout, but García Márquez does not write a tale of war.[21] He portrays a much more penetrating message: namely, a struggle between two people cannily conceived on two levels. As the body is the mirror of the soul, he allows the vital processes of his protagonists to dictate the dynamic evolution of their relationship. Food and the colonel's 'frustrated urge' are as important in understanding *No One Writes to the Colonel* as the dialogues between the characters, perhaps even more so. For, through the universal language of the body, García Márquez voices both a tale of struggle and a panegyric to action which applies equally to all men. In this sense, it is perhaps the most political and far reaching of his novels.

Notes

1 Gabriel García Márquez, *El coronel no tiene quien le escriba* (Mexico: Biblioteca Era, 1984). All page references are to this edition; all translations in the text are my own.
2 Peter G. Earle, 'El futuro como espejismo', in *Gabriel García Márquez* (Madrid, 1981). Graciela Maturo, *Claves simbólicas de García Márquez* (Buenos Aires, 1977).
3 In his article, 'El futuro como espejismo', Peter Earle refers to J. E. Cirlot's *A Dictionary of Symbols* (New York: Philosophical Library, 1962), p. 49, in order to interpret the role of the rooster in *No One Writes to the Colonel*.
4 Graciela Maturo, *Claves simbólicas*, p. 105.

Communication in *No One Writes to the Colonel*

5 Peter G. Earle, 'El futuro como espejismo', p. 82.
6 Mario Vargas Llosa, *García Márquez: historia de un deicidio* (Barcelona, 1971).
7 *Ibid.*, p. 136.
8 In 1955, García Márquez was sent as foreign correspondent to Europe by the Colombian newspaper, *El Espectador*. He travelled first to Rome and then to Paris, only to discover, a few months after his arrival, that the paper had been shut down by order of the Colombian dictator, Rojas Pinilla. Instead of returning home, García Márquez decided to sell his ticket and stay in Paris to write. He lived in the Latin Quarter, at the Hôtel de Flandre, eking out an existence mostly from the sale of empty bottles and used newspapers, but he managed to finish the manuscript of *El coronel no tiene quien le escriba* in less than a year. Interested readers can find an illuminating personal account of the writer's first stay in Paris in an interview conducted by Jean-Michel Fossey, 'Entrevista con Gabriel García Márquez', published in *Imagen*, 40 (Caracas, 1969), 8.
9 Pp. 7, 8, 10, 20, 27, 28, 29, 32, 33, 38, 51, 53, 66, 68, 71, 72, 78, 86, 89, 90, 99, 101, 102, 104.
10 1   '–Y si no viene–preguntó la mujer.
          –Vendrá'.
   2 She: '–Y si no entienden
      He: –Pues entonces que no entiendan'.
   3 She: '–Y si no llega.
      He: –Llegará'.
11 Mikhail Bakhtin, *Rabelais and his World*, trans. Hélène Iswolski (Cambridge, Mass., 1965), p. 370.
12 George R. McMurray, *Gabriel García Márquez* (New York, 1977).
13 García Márquez underscores the fact that his hero strongly dislikes profanity early in the action. When he goes to see Alvaro to sell him the clock, one of the young man's friends is amazed at the sight of the colonel's very old-fashioned shoes and exclaims, ' "Shit, colonel" ' (p. 56). The colonel is very taken aback by this remark and requests that there be no swearing; Alfonso protests by saying that the colonel's shoes are quite a sight and the older man answers him in a firm tone, ' "But you can say that without swearing ... These monsters [the shoes, that is] are forty years old and it is the first time they have heard a swear word" ' (p. 57). It is no coincidence, of course, that this swear word should be the very one the colonel utters at the conclusion of the novel. I do not think I am forcing the point by suggesting that García Márquez wished to emphasize the fact that the colonel's last injunction is much more than simple profanity. It is for this reason that he makes clear the hero's dislike (actually, more than dislike, condemnation and even rejection) of swearing. The conclusion must be read, therefore, at face value, with the full force of its connotation. It is a purposefully chosen word vehemently signalling the act of emancipation with which the action concludes.
14 Sigmund Freud, *Collected Papers*, vol. 2, ed. J. Rivière and J. Strachey (New York and London, 1924–50), p. 48.
15 Gabriel García Márquez, *Cien años de soledad* (Buenos Aires: Editorial Sudamericana, 1969), p. 308.
16 Norman O. Brown, *Life against Death* (Middletown, Connecticut, 1970), p. 284.
17 Sigmund Freud, *Beyond the Pleasure Principle*, trans. by C. J. M. Hubback, 2nd ed. (London, 1922), p. 69.
18 Julia Kristeva, *La révolution du langage poétique* (Paris, 1974), pp. 136–7. Throughout her earlier writings, *Recherches pour une Sémanalyse* (Paris, 1969), *La révolution du langage poétique* and *Polylogue* (Paris, 1977), Kristeva makes much of the

sublimation of the anal impulse in the work of writers such as Artaud, Bataille and Joyce (we could easily include García Márquez in this list) whose narrative discourse unhinges the epic integrity of what she refers to as the 'sujet unaire' (the subject subordinated to the law – whether such law is emblematized by God, the father, logos or reason).

19 McMurray, *Gabriel García Márquez*, p. 22; Angel Rama, 'Un novelista de la violencia americana', in *Nueve asedios a García Márquez* (Santiago de Chile, 1972), p. 119. In a slightly different version, the first part of this article (entitled 'García Márquez: la violencia americana') appeared in the Montevidean weekly, *Marcha*, 201:1 (17 April 1964), 22–3.

20 Fossey, 'Entrevista con Gabriel García Márquez', p. 8.

21 In *Historia de un deicidio* (pp. 34–5, 44–5) Vargas Llosa gives a succinct account of the political holocaust which left behind between two and three hundred thousand victims and almost completely destroyed the province of Tolima (Colombia) between 1949 and 1962. Readers wishing to consult a more detailed account of *la violencia* should refer to Germán Guzmán, Orlando Fals Borda and Eduardo Umaña Luna, *La violencia en Colombia*, vols. 1 and 2 (Bogotá, 1963 and 1964).

4

Magical realism and the theme of incest in
One Hundred Years of Solitude

EDWIN WILLIAMSON

For all the attention it has received since its publication, *One Hundred Years of Solitude* remains an elusive and enigmatic novel. Although accepted as one of the major examples of Latin America's contribution to modernist writing, the problem of understanding how its highly acclaimed technique of magical realism actually works is still unresolved. At the level of simple definition there can be little disagreement: magical realism is a narrative style which consistently blurs the traditional realist distinction between fantasy and reality. Beyond this, critical opinion is divided as to whether magical realism is entirely self-referring or whether it establishes a new kind of relationship between fiction and reality.[1]

According to the former view, *One Hundred Years of Solitude* is analogous to the *ficciones* of Borges; its fictional world is autarchic, creating through the act of narration special conditions of development and meaning which enable the fictive imagination to achieve a free-floating state of pure self-reference akin to the exhilarated innocence of children at play.[2] The difficulty with such a view is that it cannot explain the political and historical allusions in the novel. To be consistent, it must absorb these also into the realm of ludic autonomy, and it therefore leaves García Márquez open to the charge of having 'aestheticized' the history of Latin America.

The other account would have magical realism expand the categories of the real so as to encompass myth, magic and other extraordinary phenomena in Nature or experience which European realism has tended to exclude.[3] This explanation derives from Alejo Carpentier's early ideas about 'lo real-maravilloso', and it is especially satisfying because it endows García Márquez's particular brand of modernism with a unique Latin American character.[4] What is more,

García Márquez himself has often talked about magical realism in just this way.[5] Nevertheless, this explanation, in so far as it re-introduces a denotative link to an external reality – albeit more inclusive than European realism – produces a very negative, pessimistic reading of the text. The novel ends with the realization of a curse and the fulfilment of a prophecy, and so it apparently vindicates the mystical power of a malign fate. As such, it would appear to condemn Latin America to a hopeless condition of historical failure, allowing no scope for change or free human action.[6]

In either account, difficulties arise in reconciling magical realism as a narrative style with the actual movement of the action in the novel. Both accounts regard magical realism as an entirely positive, liberating feature and, in consequence, they are equally hard put to explain the nature of the Buendías' degeneration and the reason for Macondo's destruction.[7] But if one examines how magical realism actually functions in the narrative, it will become clear that there is an intimate connection between it and the degenerative process described in the novel; indeed, magical realism can be shown to be a manifestation of the malaise that causes the decline of the Buendía family.

Magical realism creates its aesthetic impact by fusing terms that are in principle opposed to each other. The effect upon the reader of such a fusion of fact and fantasy or innocence and knowledge is, however, not one of absolute identification with the characters but rather a mixed reaction of sympathy and comic detachment. Let us take as an example José Arcadio Buendía's encounter with ice. In the first instance, the narrator describes the ice in a de-familiarizing way which allows the reader to share in the character's wonderment at the mysterious phenomenon:

When the giant opened it, the chest let out a chilly breath of air. Inside it there was just an enormous transparent block with countless internal needles which broke up the light of the setting sun into stars of many colours. (p. 22)[8]

And yet, when it comes to *explaining* the mystery, the difference between José Arcadio Buendía's innocent awe and the reader's knowledge is sharply drawn within the text itself, producing an effect of comic irony:

Taken aback, yet knowing that his sons expected an immediate explanation, José Arcadio Buendía dared to murmur, 'It's the biggest diamond in the world.'

'No,' the gypsy corrected him, 'it's ice'.   (p. 23)

José Arcadio Buendía's awe at the discovery of ice remains unimpaired – he pronounces it 'the greatest invention of our time' – but the reader can no longer share in that response since it is evident that García Márquez intends the gypsy's correction as a signal that the character is touchingly misinterpreting phenomena which the reader is presumed to take for granted in his own experience of the world. The sense of the marvellous afforded us by magical realism is therefore transient, for soon enough García Márquez tips the wink at his reader, as it were, creating a complicity behind the backs of the characters who remain circumscribed by an elemental innocence which charms but is not, of course, meant to convince. Such humorous complicity exists in the more fantastical instances of magical realism, as in, say, Remedios the Beautiful's assumption into heaven in a flurry of white sheets (p. 205). Even though the inhabitants of Macondo might accept this as a true event, as far as the reader is concerned, the fact of its being narrated in the text does not strengthen its claim to literal, historical truth. Rather the opposite, it de-mystifies the phenomenon because of the underlying assumption (as in the ice scene above) that the reader's world-view is at odds with that of the characters.

In spite of its ostensible fusion of fantasy and fact, magical realism is conceived as a wilfully specious discourse that inevitably betrays its hallucinatory character in the very act of its being read by the kind of reader García Márquez is addressing. Were the reader to participate wholly in the perspective of José Arcadio Buendía, there would be no humour in *One Hundred Years of Solitude*; its discourse would be all too solemnly denotative. But García Márquez sets up an ironic interplay between the *identity* of opposites promoted by the magical-real discourse and the inescapable sense of *difference* retained by the reader. The novel is, then, predicated upon a dialectic that opposes the experiences of the world *inside* the fiction to that which lies *outside* it.

The dialectic between identity and difference does nevertheless operate symbolically within the fictional world of Macondo. It is conveyed through the motivating theme of incest. Like magical realism, incest tends towards the fusion of differential categories, and as such constitutes a threat to social organization, since it weakens the vital distinction that underpins cultural order: the difference between self and other. In this sense, incest can be taken as a symbolic equivalent of the solipsism that underlies magical realism. For, when kinship differences are not properly marked, communication or constructive social intercourse are rendered ineffective. The family becomes a focus of centripetal energy, attracting the separate individuals that compose it back into an undifferentiated generic identity.

The fundamental impetus of *One Hundred Years of Solitude* springs from the wish to *avoid* incest. Initially, the Buendías react to the threat of incest in two ways: Ursula seeks to uphold an ancestral taboo against it, whereas her husband José Arcadio Buendía, having defied this taboo by killing Prudencio Aguilar and forcing intercourse with his wife, looks to establishing a new order. He leaves Riohacha to make contact with 'civilization' beyond. The nature of this 'civilization' remains vague, but there are indications that it corresponds to that which exists outside the fictional world. In any case, its distinguishing characteristic is scientific knowledge. José Arcadio Buendía in the early stages of the novel is a man in search of science. He undertakes innumerable projects and experiments 'with the self-denial of a scientist and even at the risk of his own life' (p. 10); his imagination, we are told, 'reached beyond the spirit of nature and even beyond miracle and magic' (p. 9). When his sons see a gypsy and some children fly past the window of his laboratory on a magic carpet, José Arcadio Buendía declares, 'Leave them to their dreams. We shall fly better than them with superior scientific resources than that wretched bedspread' (p. 34). Although the humour that characterizes the narrative style of magical realism is not forsaken in the account of José Arcadio Buendía's endearingly perverse quest for useful, scientific knowledge, his efforts are directed, as is indicated above by the last quotation, precisely towards undoing the mentality of magical realism within which he is himself imprisoned. He hopes to move out of the world of the novel, so to speak, and into the world of the reader, where 'dreams' such as flying carpets can be successfully distinguished from aeroplanes.

Science, then, would be José Arcadio Buendía's defence against the threat of incest, since its basic concern to discover objective facts about the material world excludes by definition the introverted, solipsistic mental attitudes represented by incest. Ursula's form of control – through superstitious acquiescence in a taboo – restricts but cannot of itself overcome the problem of introversion and subjectivism; it is essentially a holding operation against incest, reinforced by a suspicion of self-assertion and by irrational fears of malign forces beyond the will of man.

José Arcadio Buendía's search for scientific understanding is soon frustrated, not just because his mentor Melquíades is an alchemist whose knowledge is rooted in occultism and medieval learning, but chiefly and decisively because he chooses to abandon it and give way to Ursula's priorities. Even though an exhaustive exploration of the region convinces him that Macondo is not well placed to make contact with 'civilization', he refrains, under pressure from his wife, from moving to a more propitious location. He is, none the less, aware of the consequences: 'We shall never get anywhere . . . We'll rot our lives away here without the benefits of science' (p. 19).

José Arcadio Buendía's act of resignation provides the key to the significance of Macondo's decline. It shows that the process of degeneration is set in train by a free human choice, a loss of nerve in fact, and not by some irresistible force of destiny which mysteriously impels the Buendías towards a predetermined end. The unbreakable circle of fate that will appear to enclose the history of the Buendías is, as we shall see, an illusion created by the characters. The founding father's decision not to move on in his quest for 'civilization' puts into reverse the rebellious drive against the incest-taboo which had motivated his departure from Riohacha.

There are two main consequences of this reversal. In the first place, it condemns the Buendías to a life without science, to a state of mind, that is, which cannot make firm distinctions between objective fact and the subjective projections of desire. Subsequent generations will find themselves prey to urgent promptings of dream, imagination and memory; their perceptions of the external world will be coloured to such a degree that their hold on reality remains dangerously fragile, leaving them open to delusion or, worse still, deception and exploitation.

Second, the decision deeply affects José Arcadio Buendía's conception of time. Just before his 'deep sigh of resignation' we are told that 'something occurred inside him; something mysterious and definitive which uprooted him from his actual time and carried him adrift through unexplored regions of memory' (p. 20). Now the ghost of Prudencio Aguilar returns to haunt him, rekindling the fear and guilt associated with his original defiance of the taboo. He begins to neglect his experiments and takes to conversing with ghosts until his communion with the past intensifies to a point at which he smashes up his laboratory and, believing it to be forever a Monday in March, imagines that he has abolished time altogether (pp. 73–4). By abandoning himself to his memories, he shuts out the uncertainties of the future and attempts to bend time back upon itself as if to recover a state of pristine innocence that would spirit away by magic those acts committed in the actual course of his life. This magical escape from history into a kind of cycle of nostalgia will become yet another powerful legacy in the Buendía family.

After José Arcadio Buendía renounces his search for science, the undifferentiated chaos threatened by incest can only be kept at bay by Ursula's reinstatement of the taboo-mentality. Ursula's regime provides the basis for a social order of sorts, but it is an order which requires constant vigilance. Ursula, the lynchpin or axis of this order, is always frantically busy – cleaning the ancestral home, keeping her wayward family in check, defining the legal ties of kinship, overseeing the upbringing of the young, and generally providing a line of continuity from one generation to the next for as long as her energies allow. But for all that, the moral economy of the taboo-regime is repressive, artificial and inefficient. Just as the original observance of the taboo had kept Ursula and her husband from making love until José Arcadio violently defied it, so too does its re-establishment foster a climate of sterility and frustration in the family. Ursula's order cannot eradicate the urge to incest, for it is based on fear rather than understanding and, as such, precludes the possibility of discriminating between different types of desire. For instance, of her son José Arcadio's prodigious sexual endowment she feels that 'it was something as unnatural as the pig's tail her cousin was born with' (p. 29). But equally, her other son Aureliano's desire for knowledge, as evinced by his interest in his father's laboratory, makes her lament her fate, 'convinced that these extravagances of her sons were as frightening as a pig's tail' (p. 41).

All desire, therefore, becomes suspect since any one of its manifestations might disguise the dreaded incest-urge. A sinister law regulates Ursula's taboo-regime. Every true desire, whether incestuous or not, is never fruitfully satisfied. It is either thwarted, displaced or remains sterile. For example, José Arcadio, the first born, satisfies shadowy longings for his mother Ursula in the arms of Pilar Ternera, who also assuages similar veiled desires in his younger brother Aureliano; she becomes a kind of surrogate mother/lover for the two brothers. Pilar, in turn, will find herself the object of her own son Arcadio's desire, but the latter seeks consolation in his wife Santa Sofía de la Piedad. Pilar's other son Aureliano José harbours sexual feelings for his aunt

Amaranta, who will eventually inspire a similar obsession in her great-great-nephew José Arcadio. Amaranta herself competes murderously with her putative sister Rebeca for the love of Pietro Crespi but Rebeca is later carried away by the blind passion for her putative brother José Arcadio. In another generation, Petra Cotes repeats the role of Pilar Ternera by becoming a surrogate mother/lover to the brothers Aureliano the Second and José Arcadio the Second. In spite of Ursula's taboo-ridden anxieties, we find the spectre of incest stalking the family, criss-crossing the generations to form a web of endogamous passion lurking beneath the surface of legal kinship.

Ironically, the family can only perpetuate itself by continually courting the disaster it most fears. Sexual relations become a potential incest-trap, the begetting of offspring a form of tempting fate. Actual procreation is never the result of mutual love but is achieved instead through surrogates, either with an illicit lover who stands in for a desired relative (e.g. José Arcadio, who desires Ursula but has two sons by Pilar Ternera), or with a legitimate spouse who is a substitute for a desired mistress (e.g. Arcadio who has children by Santa Sofía when he really desires his mother Pilar Ternera, or Aureliano the Second who loves Petra Cotes but has children by his wife Fernanda del Carpio). Genuine desire is not rewarded by legitimate issue; as a rule, children are born either to undesired wives, or to women who have been used vicariously to discharge an unconfessed desire for a family relation. The result is that the legitimacy of the Buendía line is mocked by the emergence of a subsidiary tribe of bastards, mistresses, natural mothers and similar illicit kin that surround the official family and creates in the long run a confusing situation which allows the last two Buendías to commit incest without fully realizing the true nature of their kinship.

The progressive blurring of the distinction between legitimacy and illegitimacy points up the inefficiency of the taboo-regime as a way of controlling the urge to incest. Success is obtained by the repression or displacement of desire, and by a considerable element of sheer luck. In fact, Ursula's order is purchased at the price of the inner devastation of individual lives. Since the Buendías cannot fulfil themselves, they become unhappy with their actual condition and tend to withdraw into a frustrated solitude, repeating the experience of the founding-father. When their initial attempt to assert themselves is frustrated or displaced, they become resigned to a state of sluggish apathy (*desidia*) and live out the rest of their lives either in a self-absorbed nostalgia that disconnects them from historical time, or by distracting themselves in pointless and repetitive activity (*hacer para deshacer*).

In so far as the taboo-regime represses instinct and will, it prevents the characters from realizing a distinctive personality. Unable to attain to the condition of independent characters who consciously direct their own lives, they are marked instead by generic traits or hereditary vices. This subservience to an impersonal family typology is evidenced by the almost bewildering recurrence of names – José Arcadio, Aureliano, Amaranta, Ursula, Remedios and combinations thereof – and of psychological characteristics that overwhelm specific motivation: the Aurelianos are clairvoyant, while the José Arcadios are sexually voracious. In the Buendía family tree, analogies and parallels override particular differences; the experiences of the various generations conform to stock patterns which repeat themselves with such regularity that the linear sequence of historical events appears to be distorted into cycles of time revolving around a still centre of eternity.

And yet, even though the action of *One Hundred Years of Solitude* might appear to express historical time as a series of cyclical recurrences, there is a progressive, linear dynamic to the narrative that belies the typological repetitions generated by the taboo-regime. This dynamic is fuelled by the survival of the founding-father's original desire to rebel against the paralysing fear of the incest-taboo. In every generation there are certain Buendía characters who, albeit confusedly, defy authority in order to break out of the vicious circles of fear that condemn them to conform to type. Struggling to become conscious individuals instead of stock figures, they are prepared to accept the historical present and confront things as they are rather than resign themselves to frustration, solitude and the illusory promise of timelessness afforded by nostalgia.

Let us take the case of that supreme revolutionary leader Colonel Aureliano Buendía. The original motives for his many rebellions are vague. He rebels partly because he is shocked by the deceitfulness of the conservatives (p. 89), and partly because he supports the liberals' wish to accord the same rights to natural offspring as to the legitimate (p. 88). But, apart from his nebulous humanitarian sympathies, 'Aureliano at that time had very confused ideas about the *differences* between conservatives and liberals' (p. 88; my emphasis). His rebellions are, then, a bid to establish this sort of difference, to assert his independence from an order of things which exacts unthinking conformity to a hereditary set of values. The conservatives, it is said, defend the principle of a divine right to rule, the stability of public order and the morality of the family (p. 88). Nevertheless, Colonel Aureliano's confused assault on the established order stirs up the spectre of incest. For example, his illegitimate son Aureliano José, who burns with passion for his aunt Amaranta, is at one point told by a rebel soldier that the war is being fought 'so that one can marry one's own mother' (p. 132). Here one can appreciate the extent to which José Arcadio Buendía's abandonment of his pursuit of scientific knowledge loads the dice against the success of subsequent Buendía rebellions; by simply rebelling against authority, his son Colonel Aureliano assists in the unleashing of incestuous impulses over which he has no control given that he is bereft of the intellectual means to overcome the solipsism that incest represents.

Colonel Aureliano's revolutionary wars, not surprisingly, begin to take on an incestuous quality. The chaotic violence which ravages the country (analogous to the volcanic eruptions of sexual desire that rack his brother José Arcadio) converts the liberals into the mirror-image of their conservative enemies (p. 149); the differences Colonel Aureliano had set out to establish are lost in an all-absorbing, pointless chaos. Faced with failure, Colonel Aureliano now reverts to family type – he 'takes refuge in Macondo to feel the warmth of his oldest memories' (p. 147), and experiences the same apathy that came over his father. And yet, even at this low ebb, he shakes himself out of his nostalgic apathy and resolves to put an end to a war which has turned into little more than a naked struggle for power. Once the war is ended, Colonel Aureliano 'buried his weapons in the courtyard with the same feeling of repentance as his father when he buried the lance that killed Prudencio Aguilar' (p. 152).

The parallels between Colonel Aureliano's rebellion and that of his father, José Arcadio Buendía, are clear, but a crucial difference can be observed in their respective responses to failure. José Arcadio Buendía withdraws from historical reality and seeks refuge in a form of introverted brooding over the past, whereas his son refuses to resign himself to nostalgia and throws himself instead into the compulsive manufacture of little gold fishes. Defeat may have forced the Colonel into a fruitless solitude, but his *attitude* is the very opposite of resignation. He keeps alive his bitterness at historical failure in a rancorous disaffection from the established order of things; political rebellion is replaced by a permanent psychological rebellion, an unwillingness to escape from history into some magical sphere where the problems of his actual situation can be dissolved. Colonel Aureliano Buendía therefore becomes the most highly individualized member of the family; he remains an isolated, eccentric figure who offers an alternative to the stock Buendía response to the impotence of failure.

The significance of the Colonel's defiant stance emerges when Macondo is suddenly linked to the outside world by the arrival of the railway and finds itself at the mercy of a new wave of outsiders who bring with them the technological inventions of the modern age: the cinema, the telephone, gramophones, and eventually the banana industry. Only the Colonel is capable of perceiving the exploitative use to which they are put. The other inhabitants are confused and seduced by the 'intricate hodgepodge of truths and mirages that exasperated the ghost of José Arcadio Buendía under the chestnut tree' (p. 195). These strange artefacts cruelly expose the fatal weakness of the Buendías. Having been deprived of 'the benefits of science', they regard such wonders as products of magic and miracle; so much so, that 'nobody was able to tell for sure where the limits of reality lay' (p. 195). Technology, not surprisingly, is turned against a defenceless Macondo by the sinister Mr Herbert and his teams of scientific advisers. Even so, the impulse to rebel is not yet extinguished. This time, however, the rebellion must be twofold, not just against the magical-real taboo-regime but also against the foreign exploiters who have been able to take advantage of magical realism to the detriment of Macondo.

The internal rebellion against the taboo is carried out by Meme. When she falls in love with the unsuitable Mauricio Babilonia, she meets with the horrified opposition of Ursula herself and her own mother Fernanda del Carpio, an arch-conservative prude whose exalted fantasy-life of aristocratic distinction is a grotesquely exaggerated version of Ursula's preoccupation with the legitimacy of the family. Unerringly, the perverse law that sustains the taboo-regime comes into operation. Any true desire must be repressed, and so Mauricio Babilonia is murdered.

The rebellion against the foreign exploiter falls to José Arcadio the Second, who becomes a ringleader in the strike against the Banana Company. The strike having been put down by a callous massacre of which the only survivor is himself, José Arcadio the Second faces the choice of responding to failure either by emulating José Arcadio Buendía's flight from reality or Colonel Aureliano's stubborn refusal to ignore the facts of history.

The existence of that moral choice is conveyed in the narrative through the device of Melquíades's room, which was built for the gypsy mage when he withdrew into an uncommunicative solitude. There he began to write what will turn out to be a prophetic history of the Buendía family. Melquíades's room can be associated with an esoteric and magical interpretation of historical experience. After the gypsy's death the room is sealed off until Aureliano the Second persuades Ursula to open it up again. It now appears to be bathed in a pure light which keeps it magically free from the dust and cobwebs of time. Still, the state of Melquíades's room varies according to the eye of the beholder. For a character like young Aureliano the Second, who shuts himself up in it and tries to decipher the gypsy's parchments, it is untouched by time, as if it encapsulated that fragment of eternity into which José Arcadio Buendía retired when he resigned his quest for science. By contrast, the unrepentant revolutionary Colonel Aureliano sees it as one would expect it to be, utterly ravaged by the passage of time: 'In the air which had been the purest and most luminous in the house there hung an unbearable stench of rotten memories' (p. 209). What is more, after Fernanda del Carpio takes to storing her innumerable golden chamber-pots in that magical retreat, it comes to be known as the 'chamber-pot room'. For the Colonel, 'that was the best name for it because, while the rest of the family were amazed that Melquíades's room should be immune to dust and decay he saw it simply as a dung-heap' (p. 224).

José Arcadio the Second at first vacillates between the historical and the magical conceptions of time. Two images haunt him: a historical one, namely the smile on the face of a man about to be shot during one of Colonel Aureliano's revolutions; and a more nebulous image, that of an old man in a waistcoat wearing a hat shaped like a crow's wings telling marvellous stories next to a dazzling window, which he cannot place in any period of time. The latter image is of Melquíades but it was 'an uncertain memory . . . as opposed to the memory of the man before the firing squad which had in fact defined the course of his life' (p. 225).

By joining the strike against the Banana Company, José Arcadio the Second opts for historical action, but after the massacre he takes refuge in Melquíades's room. In that magical sanctuary he is able to raise himself beyond the reach of his enemies; he is invisible to the soldiers who are hunting him and who can see only dust and decay when they search the gypsy's room. Having survived defeat, José Arcadio the Second renounces his allegiance to Colonel Aureliano:

Years before, Colonel Aureliano Buendía had told him of the fascination of war and had tried to demonstrate it with countless examples from his own experience. But the night when the soldiers looked at him without seeing him, thinking about the tension of recent months, about the miseries of prison life, about the panic in the railway station and the train loaded with dead bodies, José Arcadio the Second came to the conclusion that Colonel Aureliano Buendía had been either a charlatan or an imbecile. He couldn't understand why so many words should be required to explain what one feels in time of war since a single word would suffice: fear.   (p. 265)

Immured in the gypsy mage's room, José Arcadio the Second escapes the vicissitudes of history:

Protected by the supernatural light, by the sound of rain, by the sensation of being invisible, he found the peace he had not enjoyed for a single moment in his previous life, and the only fear that remained was that he might be buried alive.   (p. 265)

The peace experienced by José Arcadio the Second is, of course, bought at a price – the last nugget of historical consciousness is absorbed into a magical sphere. The last Buendía rebel thus plays into the hands of his oppressors, who now proceed with impunity to erase the massacre from the history books. Given that José Arcadio the Second abdicates his responsibility as a witness to history, the Buendías lose all vestige of objectivity, and, with it, the capacity to discriminate between elementary differential categories such as truth and falsehood. As a result, the town as a whole suffers the fate that had previously befallen the characters individually. It is completely isolated from the external world by rains which are said to presage its eventual destruction, and it sinks into a state of lethargy as it begins to lose its grip on reality.

In the closing phase of the novel the narrative discourse becomes increasingly self-referring and fantastical; magical realism comes fully into its own as the action moves towards the realization of the wholly implausible incest-curse. The fulfilment of the curse, however, is finally possible, not just because the impulse to rebel has been totally crushed, but principally because Ursula's taboo-regime breaks down. After the rains have ceased, Ursula attempts once more to re-impose order by restoring the ancestral home to its pristine condition. Indeed, now that the Banana Company and the other foreigners have departed, Macondo appears to have returned to an earlier point in its history. Ursula is struck by the fact that 'time does not pass . . . it just goes round in circles' (p. 285). But this circular sense of historical time soon proves to be an illusion; it is a false renewal, for Ursula is reaching the limits of her energy, and when she dies shortly afterwards her regime collapses entirely. Neither Fernanda, nor Santa Sofía de la Piedad, nor Amaranta Ursula can retrieve the ancestral home from the ruin that overwhelms it once Ursula passes away.

The traditional system of defence against incest having fallen to pieces, the surviving members of the family exist in an ambiguous new freedom which could, on the one hand, provide the means to transcend the taboo-mentality but which, on the other, could leave them helpless before a resurgence of the fatal urge to incest. Both Aureliano Babilonia and Amaranta Ursula find themselves in a position to overcome the taboo-mentality. Aureliano is originally presented as a potentially messianic figure. He is said by Fernanda to have been discovered in a basket floating in the river like Moses (p. 249), and later, having as a child struck up a friendship with his uncle José Arcadio the Second in Melquíades's room, he is able to relate to the rest of the family the facts of the historic massacre of workers at the railway station, a performance that strikes Fernanda as 'a sacrilegious parody of Jesus among the doctors' (p. 295). Together with the occult and supernatural knowledge he learns from José Arcadio the Second, Aureliano gains possession of historical facts that could bring the Buendías back to an objective awareness of the external world. What he needs is a catalyst that would allow him the discriminatory powers to sift the true from the false, the imaginary from the actual. But Amaranta Ursula's husband Gaston notes that Aureliano 'did not buy books for information but to confirm the accuracy of his knowledge' (p. 323).

Amaranta Ursula, for her part, returns from Europe seemingly unencumbered by superstition and sets about cleaning up the ancestral home: 'With the sweep of her broom she put an end to funereal memories, to the piles of useless bric-à-brac, and to all the paraphernalia of superstition that gathered in every corner' (p. 319). But, again, her husband wryly observes that her return to Macondo is due to her having fallen the unwitting victim of 'a mirage of nostalgia' (p. 320).

The freedom the last Buendías enjoy after the dissolution of Ursula's taboo-regime blinds them to the hereditary flaws that lurk within their natures. Amaranta Ursula's provocatively carefree presence in the ancestral house rouses the latent passions of the hitherto mild and scholarly Aureliano, and so the accumulated momentum of atavistic vices overwhelms the regenerative possibilities of the present. In that disorientating freedom from the taboo, the fundamental law of Ursula's order is decisively broken; desire is neither displaced nor repressed but contrives at long last to possess its true object.

Caught up in the prolonged frenzy of passion that follows, Amaranta Ursula watches 'the ants devastating the garden, sating their prehistoric hunger on the timbers of the house and she saw the torrent of living lava invade the corridors once more' (p. 341). The order that Ursula had striven so hard to uphold is now gleefully destroyed in an orgy of erotic release: 'It was Amaranta Ursula who, with her wild imagination and her lyrical voracity, presided over that paradise of disasters as though she had concentrated into love all the indomitable energy that her great-great-grandmother had devoted to the manufacture of little caramel animals' (p. 341). A vortex of mutual passion isolates the incestuous lovers from their surroundings; they become so engrossed in each other that their separate selves seem to fuse into the selfsame identity: 'As the pregnancy advanced they started turning into a single being, integrating themselves ever more in the solitude of a house which needed only one last puff to blow it down' (p. 345).

The birth of a child with a pig's tail materializes the curse that haunted Ursula throughout the novel. This narrative confirmation of superstitious fear is reinforced when Aureliano cracks the code in which Melquíades's chronicles have been written to see revealed before him a prophetic account of the history of the Buendía family. Nevertheless, it is of no little significance that the unveiling of Melquíades's texts coincides absolutely with the devastation of Macondo by a whirlwind. The prophetic consummation of Macondo's history is a form of self-consumption, for as Aureliano reads the parchments, he is enacting the supreme Buendía vice of nostalgia, figured forth as a gathering wind from the past: 'Then the wind started – warm, incipient, full of voices from the past, murmurings of ancient geraniums, sighs expressing disappointments that preceded the most tenacious nostalgia' (p. 350). Aureliano's reading doubles history back upon itself so that the past is not simply left behind by future events but acquires instead a fatal fascination as it creeps up on and eventually devours the present like a cyclone.

One Hundred Years of Solitude sets forth two distinct modes of reading history:[9] that of Aureliano Babilonia and that of the ordinary reader of García Márquez's novel. Each mode is predicated upon a certain type of consciousness. Aureliano's reading might be termed 'incestuous'; it is devoid of objectivity, of reference to an external reality and to linear time. For, as Aureliano deciphers Melquíades's prophetic chronicles, the time narrated moves ever nearer to the time of present experience, and the closer the events Aureliano is reading about get to the time in which he is living, the smaller the gap between the narrative and the history it purports to record. Eventually, Melquíades's text begins to reflect experience with such immediacy that it becomes a 'speaking mirror' (p. 350). However, the text as 'speaking mirror' is a necessarily transient phenomenon because, if reading is to take place at all, a delay between experience and its narration is inevitable. Aureliano's reflexive reading of his family's history reduces that delay to a point where narrated time and lived time actually meet, and at this point reading becomes impossible because the narrative consumes itself and must disappear. In the last page of the novel one encounters the extraordinary phenomenon of a historical narrative that has become so perfectly self-referring that its sole surviving character reads his own fate while he is in the very process of fulfilling it. The Narcissus figure of Aureliano contemplating himself in the 'speaking mirror' is thus destined to indulge in the ultimate act of self-regard – auto-cannibalism. It is a fate, as it happens, which lends a piquant, not to say prophetic, quality to the nickname 'anthropophagous' which Amaranta Ursula had given him (p. 319).

However, since *One Hundred Years of Solitude can* be read, as the ordinary reader is all too obviously aware, García Márquez's version of the Buendía history must be radically different from Melquíades's.[10] Unlike the magical parchments, the novel does not self-destruct; it manages instead to retain what Melquíades's prophetic texts abolish: the necessary delay between events and their narration. The reader of *One Hundred Years* is, of course, not identical to Aureliano. If Aureliano is an internal reader of the Buendía history who witnesses his own fate in Melquíades's 'speaking mirror', the ordinary reader remains outside the narrated events and is therefore capable of an objective, distanced view of that history. How then does

García Márquez's version preserve that objectivity which that of Melquíades destroys?

The opening towards a sense of objectivity is, in fact, narrated by García Márquez in his own account of the last days of Macondo. In that late phase of the narrative, after Ursula's order has broken down, precisely when Macondo as a whole begins to sink into incestuous self-reference, an entirely new set of characters is introduced: a Catalan bibliophile and his young disciples, one of whom is called Gabriel Márquez, the great-grandson of Colonel Aureliano Buendía's comrade-in-arms, Gerineldo Márquez. Aureliano Babilonia befriends Gabriel and also becomes an admirer of the Catalan. Initially, this Catalan appears to be no more than a modest avatar of Melquíades: 'When Aureliano met him, he had two boxes full of those motley pages which somehow reminded him of Melquíades's parchments' (p. 336). But the Catalan's attitude to the written word is 'a mixture of solemn respect and gossipy irreverence. Not even his own manuscripts were spared this *duality*' (p. 337; my italics). Such duality (as opposed to the obsessive, all-absorbing identification elicited by the 'speaking mirror' of Melquíades's parchments) evinces a sense of irony in the Catalan which will prove to be the salvation of Gabriel and his friends from the destruction of Macondo. For when the Catalan returns to his native village he finds that his nostalgia for his birthplace is eventually contradicted by a growing nostalgia for Macondo:

Confused by two nostalgias confronting each other like two mirrors, he lost his marvellous sense of unreality until he ended up by recommending that they all leave Macondo, that they forget everything he had taught them about the world and the human heart, that they shit on Horace, and that wherever they found themselves they should always remember that the past was a lie, that memory provided no way back, that all the springs they had lived through were irretrievable, and that the most unruly and obsessive love was in any case an ephemeral truth.   (p. 339)

Jolted out of a nostalgic frame of mind altogether by the conflicting pulls of two nostalgias, the Catalan becomes an anti-Melquíades figure who suddenly sees through and repudiates the pattern of consciousness fostered in the Buendía family by the gypsy's occultism. Systematically, he condemns the effects of magical realism: the fascination with the past, the escape from history into memory, the longing to recover a pristine innocence, and the surrender to mindless erotic desire.

This ironic awakening comes too late for Aureliano Babilonia. By this time his incestuous passion for Amaranta Ursula has got the better of him and he has switched his intellectual allegiance back to Melquíades. In doing so, the catalytic effect of his relations with the Catalan, which might have enabled him to salvage the objective truth of the massacre from the welter of nostalgic fantasies he picked up in Melquíades's room, is totally aborted.

By contrast, Aureliano's erstwhile friend Gabriel Márquez takes the Catalan's advice and leaves Macondo. His departure entails a transformation of consciousness from the self-absorbing trammels of magical realism depicted in his visits to the unreal brothel in Macondo to an appreciation of the duality of irony. His journey is from within the fictional world he shared with the Buendías to the world outside the fiction in which the reader of *One Hundred Years* is situated.

Freed from the magical-real consciousness of the Buendías, Gabriel Márquez can look back on his experience and write a history of Macondo to rival the interpretation of Melquíades. But since all narrative is an exercise in retrospection, Gabriel must construct his account in such a way as to reflect Macondo's history without himself falling prey to the siren-song of nostalgia. Taking the Catalan's conflict of nostalgias as a paradigm of liberation from solipsism, Márquez renounces the novelist's traditional allegiance to mimesis and holds up a mirror instead to Melquíades's mirror of the Buendía history. By confronting these two mirrors Gabriel imbues his novel with an ironical duality. The magical realism that informs the consciousness of the Buendías is reproduced in Gabriel's discourse. But it is given the lie by its reflection in the design of the narrative, which orders events in a linear sequence that records the knowledge suppressed by Melquíades's cyclical version of history: the moral capitulation of José Arcadio Buendía, the ravages of Ursula's regime, the lucid defiance of Colonel Aureliano, the difference between technology and magic, the significance of the massacre at the station, José Arcadio the Second's surrender to fear, and so on. In short, the counterpointing of discourse and narrative design registers the existence of a choice before the characters between resignation to illusion on the one hand, and responsibility to historical truth on the other.

The particular originality of García Márquez's technique lies, however, in his having followed through to its ultimate consequences the logic of his magical-real discourse. As the novel describes Macondo's progressive evasion of history, language slips its insecure moorings in reality and drifts away to a limbo where it can arbitrarily realize its own fantasies until it is finally drawn into the void of pure self-reference. And yet, precisely in that state of limbo, Gabriel narrates the manner of his own flight from Macondo, thereby offering the reader a way back to the historical reality that the discourse of the novel has all but abandoned. What is more, in the last sentence of *One Hundred Years* the duality of the novel is made explicit by an unprecedented authorial intrusion. Macondo is described as 'the city of mirrors (or of mirages)'. This parenthetical alternative cracks the surface of the 'speaking mirror' to reveal the underlying choice between illusion and reality; it invites the reader to question the validity of Melquíades's prophecy and to repudiate the apocalyptic ending inscribed in the discourse as nothing more than a pernicious mirage created by those characters like Aureliano Babilonia who have condemned themselves to magical realism and for whom there is, in consequence, no second chance of salvation. By implication, therefore, there may exist a second chance for other natives of Macondo (like Gabriel Márquez and his friends) who have chosen to leave and who have survived the destructive vortex of incest. On this reading, *One Hundred Years of Solitude* ends, if not exactly on a note of optimism, at least with the sense of relief felt after waking from a nightmare.

Notes

1 For a comprehensive review of critical opinion, see Donald L. Shaw, 'Concerning the Interpretation of *Cien años de soledad*', *Ibero-Amerikanisches Archiv*, 3:4 (1977), 318–29.

2 See, for example, Ricardo Gullón, 'García Márquez and the Lost Art of Storytelling', *Diacritics*, 1:1 (autumn 1971); Roberto González Echevarría, 'With Borges in Macondo', *Diacritics*, 2:1 (1972), 57–60; E. Rodríguez Monegal, '*One Hundred Years of Solitude*: the Last Three Pages', *Books Abroad*, 47:3 (1973), 485–9. A more recent exponent is Regina Janes, *Gabriel García Márquez: Revolutions in Wonderland* (Columbia, and London, 1981), pp. 48–69.

3 See, for example, in *Sobre García Márquez*, ed. Pedro Simón Martínez (Montevideo, 1971), the following well-known essays: Mario Vargas Llosa, 'El Amadís en América', pp. 106–11; Ernesto Völkening, 'Anotado al margen de *Cien años de soledad*', pp. 178–206; José Miguel Oviedo, 'Macondo: un territorio mágico y americano', pp. 44–53. The fullest study is Vargas Llosa's *García Márquez: historia de un deicidio* (Barcelona, 1971).

4 See Carpentier's prologue to his novel *El reino de este mundo* (Mexico, 1949). An expanded version appeared in *Tientos y diferencias* (Mexico, 1964).

5 See his remarks in an interview with Plinio Apuleyo Mendoza, *El olor de la guayaba* (Barcelona, 1982), p. 36, where he agrees that the 'rationalism' of European readers tends to prevent them accepting that magical realism is inspired in the fact

that 'everyday life in Latin America shows us that reality is full of extraordinary things'. Nevertheless, he also observes that 'you cannot invent or imagine whatever you like because you run the risk of telling lies . . . Even within what appears to be the utmost arbitrariness, there are laws. You can divest yourself of the fig-leaf of rationality, so long as you do not lapse into chaos, into total irrationality' (p. 31). García Márquez, however, has never explicitly elaborated on the question of the relationship of these 'laws' to historical reality, or on the connection between the fantasy-elements in magical realism and 'the risk of telling lies'.

6 For interpretations that stress the novel's pessimistic fatalism, see James Higgins, '*Cien años de soledad*: historia del hombre occidental', *Cuadernos del Sur*, 11 (1971), 303–14; and Julio Ortega, 'Gabriel García Márquez: *Cien años de soledad*' in *Nueve asedios a García Márquez* (Santiago de Chile, 1969), pp. 74–88.

7 Shaw, 'Concerning the Interpretation of *Cien años de soledad*', p. 324, observed that no critic had yet convincingly explained 'what is, in fact, really wrong with Macondo'.

8 I have translated into English all quotations from *Cien años de soledad* (Buenos Aires: Editorial Sudamericana, 1967). Page references to this edition have been incorporated in the text.

9 So far as I am aware, only Roberto González Echevarría, '*Cien años de soledad*: the Novel as Myth and Archive', *Modern Language Notes*, 99 (1984), 358–80, unequivocally opposes the mythical to the historical elements in the narrative. However, the conclusions he draws from this lead him to a reading which is very different in style and content from my own.

10 Many critics have assumed that the novel is identical to Melquíades's history. For a recent interpretation based on this assumption, see Michael Palencia-Roth, 'Los pergaminos de Aureliano Buendía', *Revista Iberoamericana*, 123–4 (1983), 403–17.

5

Translation and genealogy: *One Hundred Years of Solitude*

ANÍBAL GONZÁLEZ

.

The concept of the *definitive text* belongs only to religion or to exhaustion.   (Borges, 'The Homeric Versions', 1932)

Cela [l'histoire du Babel] inscrit la scène de la traduction dans un espace qui est justement celui de la généalogie des noms propres, de la famille, de l'endettement, de la loi, à l'interieur d'une scène d'héritage.

(Derrida, *L'oreille de l'autre*, 1982)

One of the many fundamental issues addressed in *One Hundred Years of Solitude* is that of translation, and of translation's links with the writing of this particular novel as well as with the novel as a genre. Few critics have failed to observe, of course, that the action in *One Hundred Years of Solitude* is inextricably linked to the process of decoding Melquíades's prophetic manuscript, and that such a decoding involves a translation; but the interpretation of this aspect of the novel has tended to revolve around theories of reading and more general questions about the nature of writing, so that little attention has been paid to the implications of the act of translation itself.[1] Yet, a consideration of what translation implies in the context of *One Hundred Years of Solitude* can provide us not only with insights into this contemporary Latin American classic but also into the role of translation in literary history and in the constitution of the novel as a genre. Starting from a rather simple thematic reading, my purpose in the following pages will be to show how, by foregrounding the topic of translation and relating it to other fundamental topics such as those of genealogy and the incest prohibition, *One Hundred Years of Solitude* suggests that translation is at the very heart of the problematics of the novel as a genre, and that it is one of the key defining characteristics of that most undefinable of literary genres.

Besides the well-known scene at its end (to which I will return), the text of *One Hundred Years of Solitude* abounds with 'scenes of translation' and references to learning and speaking foreign languages.[2] For the moment, I would just like to enumerate some of the more interesting instances of translation, and of allusions to it, in the novel's text, leaving detailed comments for later. The first direct allusion to translation in the novel occurs in the second chapter, when José Arcadio goes to bed with the gypsy girl: 'José Arcadio felt himself lifted up and suspended in the air towards a state of seraphic inspiration, where his heart burst forth with an outpouring of tender obscenities that entered the girl through her ears and came out of her mouth translated into her language'[3]; shortly afterwards, as we know, José Arcadio leaves with the gypsies. In the third chapter we learn that Arcadio and Amaranta, who were brought up in the care of Visitación, the Guajiro Indian woman who had come to Macondo fleeing the plague of insomnia, 'came to speak the Guajiro language before Spanish' (p. 39), and 'went about all day snatching at the Indians' cloaks, stubborn in their decision not to speak Spanish but the Guajiro language' (p. 41). When Rebeca arrives, along with the clicking bones of her parents, she too speaks the Guajiro language, and when Ursula tries to get her to drink some medicine against her vice of eating earth, she replies with 'strange hieroglyphics that she interposed with her bites and spitting, and that, according to the scandalized Indians, were the vilest obscenities that one could ever imagine in their language' (p. 43); however, 'it was soon revealed that she spoke Spanish with as much fluency as the Indian language' (p. 44). Language loss and language reacquisition occur somewhat later on a collective scale, of course, during the plague of insomnia and its accompanying loss of memory (pp. 45–9). An even more significant episode closely related to translation is that of Melquíades's last days, when, already in an advanced stage of decrepitude, 'he would answer questions in a complex hodgepodge of languages' (p. 67). All the while, he is writing his 'enigmatic literature' (p. 68). On one occasion, Aureliano 'thought he understood something of what Melquíades was saying in his groping monologues, and he paid attention. In reality, the only thing that could be isolated in the rocky paragraphs was the insistent hammering on the word *equinox, equinox, equinox*, and the name of Alexander von Humboldt' (p. 68). It is during that same episode that Melquíades makes Aureliano 'listen to several pages of his impenetrable writing, which of course he did not understand, but which when read aloud were like encyclicals being chanted' (p. 68).

Here we have the first of a whole sequence of encounters of the Buendías with Melquíades's cryptic inscriptions, which will culminate in the final decipherment of the manuscript. Another significant episode is that of José Arcadio Buendía's insanity, in which he no longer speaks Spanish but 'a high-sounding and fluent but completely incomprehensible language' (p. 74) that later turns out to be Latin (pp. 77–8). A particularly graphic – so to speak – instance of plurality of languages in the novel is given in the younger José Arcadio's enormous penis, which was 'completely covered with tattoos of words in several languages intertwined in blue and red' (p. 84). In contrast, Pietro Crespi's contribution to the topic of translation in the novel is of a more classical nature: 'he would translate Petrarch's sonnets for Amaranta' (p. 97). It is interesting that the first member of the family who tries to decipher Melquíades's papers is the despotic Arcadio (son of José Arcadio the younger by Pilar Ternera), who, we are told,

never succeeded in communicating with anyone better than he did with Visitación and Cataure in their language. Melquíades was the only one who really was concerned with him as he made him listen to his incomprehensible texts and gave him lessons in the art of the daguerreotype. No one imagined how much he wept in secret and the desperation with which he tried to revive Melquíades with the useless study of his papers.   (p. 100)

The second intense assault on Melquíades's manuscript is that of Aureliano Segundo, who, after reading a book that is obviously the *Arabian Nights* (though the title is never mentioned; p. 161), 'set about deciphering the manuscripts' only to find that 'it was impossible. The letters looked like clothes hung out to dry on a line and they looked more like musical notation than writing' (p. 161). Melquíades then appears to him, and 'tried to infuse him with his old wisdom, but he refused to translate the manuscripts. "No one must know their meaning until he has reached one hundred years of age", he explained' (p. 161). José Arcadio Segundo is the second member of the Buendías' lineage to devote himself to the manuscripts, and the one who makes the most progress in deciphering them before Aureliano Babilonia manages to crack their code. It is he who manages 'to classify the cryptic letters of the parchments. He was certain that they corresponded to an alphabet of forty-seven to fifty-three characters, which when separated looked like scratching and scribbling, and which in the fine hand of Melquíades looked like pieces of clothing put out to dry on a line' (p. 296). Finally, it is Aureliano who discovers that the language in which Melquíades has written his text is Sanskrit (p. 301), but that is still not enough, 'because the text in Spanish did not mean anything: the lines were in code' (p. 307); thus, despite having learned 'English and French and a little Latin and Greek' in addition to Sanskrit (p. 322), Aureliano still lacks the key that will enable him to recognize the text's meaning. That key is not to be found in a text, but in something that looks like a text; the body of his pig-tailed child by Amaranta Ursula 'a dry and bloated bag of skin' (p. 349; in Spanish, 'un pellejo hinchado y reseco') not unlike Melquíades's parchments.[4]

The 'scenes of translation' and the allusions to foreign languages I have just cited strongly suggest that, first of all, the topic of translation forms a thread that runs through the novel and contributes to its coherence: it is obvious that the novel's plot moves inexorably towards that instant when Melquíades's manuscripts are at last translated and the foreordained nature of Macondo's history is revealed; each instance of translation or of foreign language acquisition in the novel is a step towards that goal and a prefiguration of the novel's ending. Secondly, we can see that translation runs parallel in the novel to genealogy: the task of translating the manuscripts is handed down from one generation to the next, to selected members of each generation, in much the same way as Melquíades's ghost appears to those who are fit to deal with the manuscripts' enigma.[5] Nevertheless, thus far I have merely surveyed the question of translation in the novel from a thematic point of view; I shall now consider what is the meaning of translation in the broader context of the novel. Why is translation foregrounded in *One Hundred Years of Solitude*? What makes translation so important? What is its relationship with genealogy and the incest prohibition?

To try to answer some of these questions, it is necessary first to address ourselves to the context of the theory of translation, and specifically to three theoretical pronouncements which are, I think, relevant to any reading of *One Hundred Years of Solitude*. The first of these pronouncements (in chronological order) belongs to Walter Benjamin; in his well-known introduction to his translation of Baudelaire's *Tableaux parisiens* titled 'The Task of the Translator' (1923), Benjamin develops, in his characteristically condensed style, some seminal ideas about translation. It is important to note, first of all, that Benjamin prefers not to speak of 'translation' in an abstract sense, but rather about the work of the translator and what it can reveal about translation and language. For Benjamin, the activity of translation involves a search for – in Benjamin's terms – 'pure language', in other words, language 'which no longer means or expresses anything but is, as expressionless and creative Word, that which is meant in all languages.'[6] Benjamin views the process of translation as a vital component of literary creativity: 'translation is so far removed from being the sterile equation of two dead languages that of all literary forms it is the one charged with the special mission of watching over the maturing process of the original language and the birth pangs of its own'.[7] Benjamin's approach to the problematics of translation is neo-Hegelian, emphasizing as it does a vitalistic notion of language and art, and an idea of translation as a movement towards transcendence. Benjamin sees translation as a process of historical, or to be more precise, philological, research into language which, through the study of 'the central kinship of languages', arrives at a vision of 'the predestined, hitherto inaccessible realm of reconciliation and fulfilment of languages'.[8] Translation, as Benjamin puts it, 'ultimately serves the purpose of expressing the central reciprocal relationship between languages. It cannot possibly reveal or establish this hidden relationship itself; but it can represent it by realizing it in embryonic or intensive form'.[9] As Benjamin notes, this idea that translation demonstrates the kinship of languages is a commonplace of traditional theories of translation; but Benjamin, as we will recall, goes a bit further: he proposes that translation in fact foretells or announces the existence of a 'pure language', a kind of communicative essence freed from the contingent variations imposed upon it by the various tongues and by the author's intentions: 'In this pure language – which no longer means or expresses anything but is, as expressionless and creative Word, that which is meant in all languages – all information, all sense and all intention finally encounter a stratum in which they are destined to be extinguished.'[10] In such a transcendental and messianic idea of translation, religious notions also have to come into play, and indeed Benjamin closes his essay with an evocation of Scripture, of sacred texts, as 'unconditionally translatable', because in them the 'text is identical with truth or dogma'.[11] Yet Benjamin is also aware in his essay that translation's promise of the ultimate reconciliation of languages and the discovery of 'pure language' is simply that – a promise – and that, in practice, translation's linguistic transfer

can never be total . . . Even when all surface content has been extracted and transmitted, the primary concern of the genuine translator remains elusive

. . . While content and language form a certain unity in the original, like a fruit and its skin, the language of the translation envelops its content like a royal robe with ample folds. For it signifies a more exalted language than its own and thus remains unsuited to its content, overpowering and alien. This disjunction prevents translation and at the same time makes it superfluous.[12]

Thus the 'sacred text', with its total coherence between language and content, in which one is inseparable from the other, turns out to be, at the same time, translatable and untranslatable. Because of its fixed meaning, the 'sacred text' seems to offer its own 'authorized translation' between the lines, a translation free from the disjunction between language and content that is produced in other texts by the uncontrolled play of meaning; yet, it is the very fixity of the 'sacred text', its total coherence, which makes it impossible to translate, because it is not possible to 'peel off' – following Benjamin's metaphor of the fruit – the skin of its language to get at its meaning. With its poetic and suggestive metaphors derived from philosophical vitalism and religion, Benjamin's meditation on translation gives poignant expression to the essential double bind in which the act of translation is inscribed. As Jacques Derrida has pointed out in glossing this same essay by Benjamin, translation in general (not only that of 'sacred texts') is caught in the paradox of its simultaneous possibility and impossibility. Texts offer themselves up to be translated, to be transformed into other texts, while at the same time their essential propriety – the system of rules and conventions which governs the differences between languages – places insurmountable barriers to translation's total fulfilment.[13] Derrida's very recent statements about translation, which are based on a deconstructive reading of Benjamin's essay, comprise the second theoretical pronouncement relevant to our reading of *One Hundred Years of Solitude*. Harking back to the Biblical myth of Babel, Derrida shows how translation is linked, in the Western cultural tradition, to the problematics of the proper noun. The myth of Babel tells the story of the attempt by the tribe of Shem (whose name means, in fact, 'Name') to impose their own name, their own language, on the whole universe through the erection of a tower that would carry them to the heavens, only to find themselves having to suffer the imposition by God of a new proper noun which enshrines difference and confusion (Babel). Translation may be seen as a transgressive struggle between proper nouns, or, in more general terms, between two equally 'proper' languages, one of which tries to deny the other's specificity.[14] The name 'Babel' (which was the

Hebrew name for Babylon, meaning 'Gate of God', according to most dictionaries) marks the limits imposed in the myth by a transcendental, sacred authority upon the dissemination of meaning which translation aims to bring about; yet Babel is the gate that translation, in its search for origins and originality, always aims to cross, even at the risk of bringing about confusion and the dispersion of meaning. In this sense, Derrida is more radical in his thoughts about translation than Benjamin: for Derrida, the notion of translation tends to deny the 'sacredness' of any text, and raises the question of how it is that texts become 'sacred'.[15] Translation and the sacredness of texts is the main question addressed by Jorge Luis Borges in his essay on 'The Homeric Versions' (1932), the third and last theoretical discourse I wish to examine. Borges is the most important source for García Márquez's literary ideology, and his thoughts on translation, which parallel those of Benjamin and Derrida, seem to be mirrored (as we shall see) in *One Hundred Years of Solitude*'s use of the topic of translation.[16] In his essay on 'The Homeric Versions', Borges declares that 'no problem is as intimately connected with literature and its modest mystery as that proposed by a translation . . . Translation . . . seems destined to serve as an illustration for aesthetic discussion'.[17] Perhaps more explicitly than Benjamin in 'The Task of the Translator', Borges reminds us here, as he does also in his short story 'Pierre Menard, Author of the *Quixote*', that the notion of translation is intimately linked to the nature of literature, and that translation can serve as an instrument of critical inquiry into the workings of literature. In his comments on several different versions of Homer's *Iliad*, Borges stresses translation's power somehow to 'purify' our understanding of a text by letting us see which elements of the original text are superfluous and which are part of its basic, underlying structure:

The facts of the *Iliad* and the *Odyssey* survive in full, but Achilles and Ulysses have disappeared, as well as what Homer was trying to represent when he named them, and what he really thought about them. The present state of his works resembles a complex equation which sets down precise relationships between unknown quantities.[18]

Through an analysis of the various English versions of Homer's *Iliad*, Borges proposes, in his typically oblique and allusive way, a notion of translation as radical as Derrida's. For Borges, as for Derrida, translation implies a creative breach of linguistic 'propriety' which leads to a questioning of the literary text's integrity and authority. The pleasures – and the perils – of translating Homer, Borges points out, arise from the 'impossibility of separating what belongs to the writer and what belongs to language'.[19] Every attempt at translation, even of works about which more contextual information is known than Homer's *Iliad*, leads to an erasure, a kind of textual razing, a return to the basic building blocks of language and meaning. From this 'zero degree' of signification the new version must arise as if it were another, yet not altogether different work, 'another, yet the same', as Borges says in one of his favourite phrases. For translation to work, then, it must be transgressive; it must hold nothing sacred, least of all the text. As Borges remarks in 'The Homeric Versions', 'To presuppose that every recombination of elements [of a text] is necessarily inferior to its original, is to presuppose that draft number nine is forcibly inferior to draft number H – since there can never be anything but drafts. The concept of the *definitive text* belongs only to religion or to exhaustion.'[20]

It is easy to see where these theoretical discourses about translation and *One Hundred Years of Solitude*'s implicit meditations on the same subject intersect. The plot of García Márquez's novel not only deals explicitly with the Buendías task of translating Melquíades's manuscripts, it also reinscribes that task, 'translates' it, in a broader sense, into the language of kinship (with all that it implies in terms of the incest taboo and the importance of proper names) which configures the other half of the action in the novel in a specular movement that is like a parody of Hegelian dialectics and which leads not to synthesis, but to the novel's collapse into its linguistic origins.[21] The text of the novel itself enacts the same process of genealogical research that the translators in the Buendía family have to perform in order to decode the manuscripts: research into the genealogy of language and into the genealogy of the Buendía family are both similar and complementary endeavours. The association of certain characters in the novel with specific languages already suggests this. As we have seen, in his insanity, José Arcadio Buendía, the founder of the line, reverts to Latin, the language that gave birth to Spanish, and he remains tied to a tree that is both a genealogical and a philological emblem; but there are also new additions, new branches, so to speak, added to the Buendías' linguistic/genealogical tree as the years go by. There are members of the family, as we have seen, who speak Indian languages and others who learn English (like Aureliano Babilonia and Meme; p. 235), plus Papiamento, French, Greek, Latin, and, of course, Sanskrit. Italian is also represented, not only in Pietro Crespi, but also in the last José Arcadio, who returns to Macondo from Italy. Last, but not least, there is the contribution of José Arcadio the younger, who returns from his maritime adventures 'speaking a Spanish that was larded with sailor's slang' (p. 83), but, perhaps more importantly, with his whole body (including his 'unusual masculinity') covered with multilingual tattoos (p. 84). José Arcadio's body-become-text is like an emblem of the family's linguistic cosmopolitanism and it prefigures, of course, the 'dry and bloated bag of skin' covered with ants of the last Buendía. Also, kinship itself becomes another of those languages that must be mastered and decoded before the manuscripts themselves can be understood and this is precisely what happens towards the end of the novel when Aureliano Babilonia's relationship with Amaranta Ursula leads him to seek out his family origins (p. 344).

Let us now take a closer look at Aureliano Babilonia's task as a translator, at how he goes about translating the manuscripts. The first thing he does is to read and learn as much as he can about the world (Melquíades is, as always, present 'like the materialization of a memory', to help; p. 301). The manuscript is still, in Borges's terms, little more than 'a complex equation which sets down precise relationships between unknown quantities'; José Arcadio Segundo had helped to define the equation – so to speak – by counting and classifying the letters of the alphabet in which the manuscripts were written, but it is Aureliano who discovers that the language of that alphabet is Sanskrit (p. 301), and thus he begins to fill in the 'unknowns' in the equation. Sanskrit, is, of course, the *Ursprache* of Spanish and Aureliano's discovery has led him to the origins of the linguistic genealogy of Spanish. Aureliano's task of translation begins, as with every translation (as Benjamin reminds us), with a return to the origins, to the source; but if he now has the linguistic source of the text, the original language (in every sense) of the text, he still has no idea as to what its content might be. That is why Aureliano's readings are so wide-ranging, so encyclopaedic, and at the same time so antiquarian; he obviously assumes that an ancient manuscript written in a dead language can only deal with past events. Later, when Aureliano manages to transliterate (not to translate, though) Melquíades's text into the Spanish alphabet, he discovers that there is another barrier to translation. The text is in code, that is to say, in still another language, and the full translation of the manuscripts depends on Aureliano being able to figure out the relationship, the 'kinship', so to speak, between Spanish and Melquíades's secret code. This is where, finally, the apparently parallel lines of genealogy and translation in the novel converge: Melquíades's code, as we learn in the last pages of the novel and as the manuscripts' epigraph suggests, is the language of kinship itself: '*The first of the line is tied to a tree and the last is being eaten by the ants*' (p. 349). Yet, if we review certain portions of the novel, we shall see that the language of genealogy, of kinship, and the knowledge of languages that makes translation possible had been coinciding all along the text. There are a number of occasions in the text when translation, language learning, and sexual relations are linked. Let us remember José Arcadio the younger's sexual encounter with the gypsy girl, in which translation figured so obviously (p. 36). At the opposite extreme, we find Pietro Crespi's gentle courtship, which is also mediated in part by his translations of Petrarch (p. 97). When Meme Buendía becomes involved with Mauricio Babilonia, it is because of her friendship with the Americans, which led her to learn English (p. 235); let us also recall Aureliano Babilonia's relationship with Papiamento-speaking Nigromanta in which 'Aureliano would spend his mornings deciphering parchments and at siesta time he would go to the bedroom where Nigromanta was waiting for him, to teach him first how to do it like earthworms, then like snails, and finally like crabs . . .' (p. 326). But perhaps the emblem of this link between genealogy, writing, and translation in the text is, as I have said before, José Arcadio's tattooed male member; here the rather hackneyed Freudian symbolism of the writing implement as phallus becomes literalized, and the 'words in several languages intertwined in blue and red' (p. 84) on José Arcadio's penis evoke the confusion of languages at Babel and the Shemites' phallic Tower. And the bond between genealogy and translation can be extended still further. In a broader sense of the word, is not 'translation' one of the consequences of the marriage of José Arcadio and Ursula, when they are forced to migrate from Riohacha after José Arcadio kills Prudencio Aguilar? Are not Colonel Aureliano Buendía's seventeen sons engendered ' on the march', so to speak? Does not Pilar Ternera substitute (translate?) Santa Sofía de la Piedad for herself in the shadows of Arcadio's room to avoid committing incest? And, leaving the Buendías' genealogy aside, are not the gypsies themselves 'translators' of a sort, moving about from here to there across the swamp and, indeed, across the world, bringing to Macondo their version of the outside world? Is not Melquíades himself the translator of a foreign knowledge into Spanish and of the future history of Macondo into Sanskrit? Clearly, when translation is understood in such a broad manner, the concepts of language, writing, genealogy, and translation all collapse into a single, chaotic vortex of dissemination that is reminiscent of the 'biblical hurricane' that erases Macondo from the face of the earth.

The metaphoric equivalent of such a dissemination of the term 'translation' in the novel's plot is, of course, Aureliano Babilonia's and Amaranta Ursula's violation of the incest prohibition. Translation and incest both share a transgressive nature, both are 'improper' acts that imply breaching the barriers between members of the same family or between two languages. As Borges and Derrida point out, translation is a critical, disseminating activity that arises from the questioning of the 'property' or appropriateness of nouns. In this context, we can understand the anxiety with which Aureliano seeks out the origin of his name in the parish archives, not only to make sure he is not Amaranta Ursula's brother but also to ascertain the 'propriety' of his name, of his origins. We can understand his confusion and his outrage when he becomes 'lost in the labyrinths of kinship' and the priest, after hearing his name, tells him not to wear himself out searching, since 'many years ago there used to be a street here with that name and in those days people had the custom of naming their children after streets' (p. 344). Yet Aureliano's name is even more 'appropriate' than he could have ever imagined, since it is not, as he tells it to the priest, 'Aureliano Buendía', but 'Aureliano Babilonia': Aureliano Babel, Aureliano the Gate of God, Aureliano Confusion, Aureliano Translation.

However, we should recall here Derrida's observation about translation's contradictory, aporetic nature, its being at the same time possible and impossible; something always escapes the translator. In Aureliano's case, it is not only those eleven pages (or more, p. 350) that he skips in order to anticipate the ending of the manuscript, but also, quite simply, the manuscript's end itself. Translation is an endless activity, and appropriately, Aureliano, in his reading of the manuscript, is caught in a textual version of Zeno's paradox: he can approach the manuscript's end, but he can never reach or read it, because the text foretells his future and is always one step ahead of him; in order to reach the conclusion, he is forced, ineluctably, to cross a previous span of time (and of text) and no matter how much he skips, he will always have to read again and thus be chained to the text's tyrannical temporality.[22] In much the same way, Aureliano's incestuous union with Amaranta Ursula has chained him irrevocably to his doomed genealogy and, like José Arcadio Buendía, he too ends up tied to a (genealogical) tree, rooted to a spot that is like the eye of the 'biblical hurricane' that razes Macondo. If the 'biblical hurricane' is seen as a figure for interpretation, for criticism at its most extreme (as it is induced by translation), then it is significant that the 'eye' of that vortex, the centre which powers it, is Aureliano's tragic and impossible search for trascendence in the manuscripts, for a principle of perfect and coherent communication akin to Benjamin's 'pure language'. Translation, like incest, leads back to self-reflexiveness, to a cyclonic turning upon one's self which erases all illusions of solidity, all fantasies of a 'pure language', all mirages of 'propriety', and underscores instead language's dependence on the very notion of 'otherness', of difference, in order to signify 'something', as well as the novel's similar dependence on 'other' discourses (those of science, law, and religion, for example) to constitute itself. The novel's proverbial generic indefinition may well be an indication that, of all the literary genres yet invented, it is the one which most closely mimics the rootlessness of language (and the complementary desire to find its roots that it engenders) as it was conceived after modern philology, at the end of the eighteenth and the beginning of the nineteenth centuries, finally debunked the myth of the divine origins of language.[23] The myth of Babel may be one of the founding myths of translation, and indirectly, of the novel, but it is precisely in the novel where that myth is most visibly and consistently denied. More concretely, Aureliano's task as a translator in *One Hundred Years of Solitude* reveals the sterility to which a notion of literature based on literature's own self-sufficiency, on literature's 'solitude', leads. Like 'races condemned to one hundred years of solitude', a literary endeavour that does not take cognizance of its need for 'otherness' and for links with other discourses does not 'have a second opportunity on earth' (p. 351).

One Hundred Years of Solitude's foregrounding of translation as a vital constitutive element of the novel can thus be seen as a Cervantine gesture which tends to unmask the humble origins of the genre; like the *Quixote* and the popular romances of chivalry that the *Quixote* parodies, García Márquez's novel represents its own origins as translation, as that mildly illegal, somewhat treasonous act which violates the propriety of language and the laws of poetics and makes of the novel, metaphorically, a wandering orphan like the *pícaro*, cut off from or at odds with its mother (tongue), always seeking a new master, always seeking to master itself.[24] But perhaps it is not necessary to return to Spain to seek out the origins of *One Hundred Years of Solitude*'s self-reflexive use of translation. Isn't this, after all, already a part of the problematics of writing in America, a problematic that arose with the discovery and conquest of the New World, like a literalized version of the old Medieval topic of *translatio imperii*?[25] It may be enough to remember the example of the Colonial *mestizo* author, Garcilaso Inca, who, by the way, translated Leone Hebreo's *Dialoghi di amore* into Spanish from the Italian, and whose monumental *Royal Commentaries* were, to a great extent, an attempt to translate the elements of Quechua culture into the sphere of European humanistic culture.[26] Translation is also present in the works of the founding figures of modern Latin American culture, from Bello, the philologist, through Sarmiento, the politician and teacher, and Martí, the revolutionary leader and one of the founders of *modernismo*. In the contemporary Latin American novel, translation recurs constantly. We need only recall works such as Carpentier's *Explosion in a Cathedral* (1962), in which one of the protagonists, Esteban, translates the Declaration of the Rights of Man and other documents of the French Revolution into Spanish. The characters' constant wordplay in Guillermo Cabrera Infante's *Three Trapped Tigers* (1964) also involves translation, and translation is explicitly discussed in many of the characters' dialogues. Julio Cortázar's *Hopscotch* (1964), with its international cast of characters and their constant shuttling back and forth between France and Argentina also incorporates translation visibly into its make-up. But it is García Márquez in *One Hundred Years of Solitude* who has more clearly than anyone before him (even Borges) pointed out translation's key role in the constitution of Latin American literature and culture. The topic of translation in *One Hundred Years of Solitude* is a reminder of Latin American literature's 'impure' and conflictive origins. However, Aureliano Babilonia's tragic discovery that he, too, is a translation, far from being an assertion of Latin America's perpetual 'dependence' on some foreign original or 'sacred' text, is García Márquez's way of calling attention instead to *all* literature's origins in translation, in the transport – through violence or exchange – of meaning from other texts and other languages into the literary text.

Notes

1 I should indicate here that I am much indebted, in my understanding of the way the question of writing is treated in *One Hundred Years of Solitude*, to a recent essay by Roberto González Echevarría, '*Cien años de soledad*: the Novel as Myth and Archive', *MLN* 99:2 (1984), 358–80. I have also benefited from an essay by Emir Rodríguez Monegal, '*One Hundred Years of Solitude*: the Last Three Pages', *Books Abroad*, 47:3 (1973), 485–9. Translation, as I will point out later in this essay, is an important topic throughout the history of Latin American literature, but it is worth noting that it has become an especially visible one in a great many contemporary Latin American novels; it appears with particular prominence in works by such diverse authors as Alejo Carpentier, Julio Cortázar, Guillermo Cabrera Infante, Severo Sarduy, Manuel Puig, and, of course, Borges (of whom more will be said in these pages).

2 When I say 'translation' here, I am referring to the ordinary usage of the term as 'interlinguistic translation', to use Jakobson's formulation, and not to any etymological or broadly conceived meaning (there will be moments later in this essay when I will make use of an expanded meaning of the term). Jakobson's well-known tripartite definition of translation (as intralinguistic translation, or paraphrase; as interlinguistic translation, or translation between languages; and intersemiotic translation, or translation between different sign systems) is found in his essay 'On Linguistic Aspects of Translation', in R. A. Brower (ed.), *On Translation* (Cambridge, Mass., 1959), pp. 232–9.

3 Gabriel García Márquez, *Cien años de soledad* (Buenos Aires: Editorial Sudamericana, 1973), p. 36. All quotes will be from this edition. The translation in all cases is mine, although I have consulted, of course, Gregory Rabassa's masterful version, *One Hundred Years of Solitude*, (New York: Avon Books, 1970).

4 See González Echevarría's comments on this scene in '*Cien años de soledad*: the Novel as Myth and Archive', 377–8.

5 In some ways, *One Hundred Years of Solitude* could be seen as a parody of the *Bildungsroman*, or, perhaps more precisely, as a parody of any number of Romantic and Post-Romantic works of literature and philosophy, from Hegel's *Phenomenology of the Spirit* to Vasconcelos's *La raza cósmica*, in which the learning process is seen not only in individual terms but as a collective, racial enterprise: as the accumulation of a collective memory, or, as González Echevarría suggests in the article cited above, an Archive.

6 Walter Benjamin, 'The Task of the Translator', in *Illuminations*, edited and with an introduction by Hannah Arendt (New York, 1969), p. 80.

7 *Ibid.*, p. 73.

8 *Ibid.*, p. 75.

9 *Ibid.*, p. 72.

10 *Ibid.*, p. 80.

11 *Ibid.*, p. 82.

12 *Ibid.*, p. 75.

13 Jacques Derrida *et al.*, *L'oreille de l'autre: otobiographies, transferts, traductions* (Montréal, 1982), pp. 137–8 and *et seq.*

14 *Ibid.*, pp. 135–7.

15 *Ibid.*, pp. 194–7. I am using the term 'dissemination' here in the sense proposed by Jacques Derrida in *La dissemination* (Paris, 1972). For Derrida dissemination is an operation performed by certain texts (or even individual words, such as

'supplement', 'parergon', or 'translation' itself) which consists in making meaning circulate indefinitely through several different domains (science, mathematics, religion, pychoanalysis, etc.) until the boundaries which define meaning in the first place are erased.

16 See Rodríguez Monegal, '*One Hundred Years of Solitude*: the Last Three Pages', also Roberto González Echevarría, 'With Borges in Macondo', *Diacritics*, 2:1 (1972), 57–60.

17 Jorge Luis Borges, 'Las versiones homéricas', in *Discusión* (Buenos Aires, 1957), p. 105. My translation.

18 *Ibid.*, p. 108.

19 *Ibid.*, p. 108.

20 *Ibid.*, pp. 105–6.

21 On kinship as a 'language', see the comments by the most distinguished proponent of such a notion, Claude Lévi-Strauss, in *The Scope of Anthropology* translated from the French by Sherry Ortner Paul and Robert A. Paul (London, 1967), pp. 31–4. There is also a very fine study of kinship systems as languages in *One Hundred Years of Solitude*, done by a critic who is also an anthropologist: Mercedes López-Baralt, '*Cien años de soledad*: cultura e historia latinoamericanas replanteadas en el idioma del parentesco', *Revista de Estudios Hispánicos* (San Juan de Puerto Rico), 6 (1979), 153–5.

22 See González Echevarría's pertinent remarks about temporality and Melquíades's manuscripts in '*Cien años de soledad*: the Novel as Myth and Archive', 375–6.

23 Edward W. Said, *Orientalism* (New York: Vintage Books, 1979), p. 135. I have found very enlightening Ralph Freedman's reflections on the theoretical difficulties raised by the novel as a genre, in 'The Possibility of a Theory of the Novel', in *The Disciplines of Criticism. Essays in Literary Theory, Interpretation and History*, edited by Peter Demetz, Thomas Greene and Lowry Nelson Jr (New Haven, 1968), pp. 57–78.

24 A more historically oriented study of the relationship between translation and the origins of the modern novel would probably have to begin not with the picaresque but with a consideration of the topic of translation in the romances of chivalry. As is known, these were a form of popular literature in sixteenth-century Spain; interest in them was fuelled by the nostalgia for chivalry which pervaded the court of Charles V. Cervantes's parody of the romances of chivalry went so far as to include something that was a topic of every chivalric romance: the claim that the text was a translation into Spanish from a manuscript found far away and written in a foreign, sometimes archaic, language (favourite foreign languages included English, German, Arabic, Hungarian, Phrygian, as well as Greek and Latin). Since the *Quixote*'s writing was motivated, in part, by Cervantes's desire to criticize the romances of chivalry, it is not unjustified, I think, to regard these as important precursors of the modern novel. A good scholarly introduction to the romances of chivalry is provided in Daniel Eisenberg's *Romances of Chivalry in the Spanish Golden Age* (Newark, 1982).

25 On the topic of *traslatio* in the Latin Middle Ages, see Ernst Robert Curtius, *European Literature and the Latin Middle Ages*, translated by Willard R. Trask (Princeton, NJ, 1973), pp. 28–30.

26 Enrique Pupo-Walker, *Historia, creación y profecía en los textos del Inca Garcilaso de la Vega* (Madrid, 1982), pp. 18–20; see also Roberto González Echevarría, 'Humanismo, retórica y las crónicas de la conquista', in *Isla a su vuelo fugitiva. Ensayos críticos de literatura hispanoamericana* (Madrid, 1983), pp. 9–25.

6

The humour of *One Hundred Years of Solitude*

CLIVE GRIFFIN

It is the fate of fine comic writers to be taken seriously. Masters of entertainment like Cervantes and Molière have been woefully misused by those who consider humour and the spinning of a good tale to be worthy of a distinguished artist only when a vehicle for something else. Reappraisals of these two writers have, however, helped to rescue them from critics intent on extracting complex philosophies or literary theories from their comic works.[1] Such reappraisals suggest that García Márquez might similarly be examined with profit first and foremost as a humorist, for there are already clear signs that he is not to escape the fate of his predecessors. *One Hundred Years of Solitude*, the novel which brought him fame and on which his reputation still largely rests, has been called a work of 'deep pessimism', 'an interpretative meditation' upon the literature of the sub-continent, or an analysis of 'the failure of Latin-American history'.[2] Isolated passages of the novel could, at a pinch, be made to support such assertions, but these interpretations will not help us to understand it as a whole nor to account for its remarkable popularity among a heterogeneous readership which has scant knowledge of the history of Colombia or of the recent literary production of Spanish America. Humour, however, can cut across cultural and even linguistic boundaries, appealing to the least and most sophisticated and knowledgeable readers.

To assert from the outset that *One Hundred Years* is funny is, perhaps, to beg the question. Nevertheless, there is ample evidence in the novel that the characters themselves find each other's antics and statements comical as they 'roar with laughter' or 'choke back guffaws'; incidentally, the author also appears to have found the novel's composition a source of considerable amusement.[3] To claim that *One Hundred Years* is humorous is not to sell the novel short, nor is it to deny

81

that it may contain passages which are not funny; indeed, one of García Márquez's strengths is his ability to capture the poignant or even sentimental moment. Rather, it is to recognize that, as Cervantes himself maintained, comic writing can be as difficult to accomplish and as worthwhile to read as any other, and to oblige the literary critic to examine the author's skill as a humorist.

I would maintain that the novel's appeal is largely due to the wide range of different types of humour employed by its author. At one end of the spectrum we have the 'eternal comic situations: beatings, disguises, mistaken identity, wit, buffoonery, indecency' appreciated by readers regardless of their cultural background and literary experience;[4] then there are other kinds of humour which find an echo only among those with particular knowledge of Colombia or of the literature of the sub-continent; and, at the other end of the spectrum, we are treated to the Shandyism and novelistic self-awareness so beloved of modern critics. Nevertheless, however observant the reader, he will inevitably miss, at the very end of this range, the 'in-jokes' which the author claims were inserted for the benefit of a few friends.[5] Europeans and those obliged to read the work in translation will, of course, miss even more. In this essay I shall give an account of this broad spectrum of subjects and techniques which provoke laughter.

Some theoreticians of humour concentrate on the sort of subjects which are 'inherently comical', maintaining, for example, that one universal source of laughter in Western societies is the violation of taboos. The commonest of these subjects concern sexual or other bodily functions. *One Hundred Years* abounds with such scenes. José Arcadio's Herculean strength and stature may be funny enough in itself, but even more so is his minutely described and 'incredible member, covered with a maze of blue and red tattoos written in several languages' (p. 84),[6] a fitting forebear of Aureliano Babilonia's equally astonishing appendage on which, at the end of the novel, he balances a bottle of beer as he cavorts drunkenly round one of Macondo's brothels. Scenes of sexual intercourse cause us to smile either because of their exuberant eroticism, like the seismic orgasms enjoyed by José Arcadio and Rebeca, or because of some of the female characters' ridiculous prudery: Ursula is reluctant to remove her chastity belt and consummate her marriage, and Fernanda obeys a calendar of 'prohibited days' on which she refuses to grant the husband whom she later describes as her 'rightful despoiler' even the frigid submission which characterizes their physical relationship. Deviation provides even more fun: José Arcadio Segundo and the local verger have a penchant for she-asses; Amaranta is a maiden aunt who, even when old, is the object of incestuous fantasies for generations of Buendías; not only is the effete Pietro Crespi thought to be a homosexual,[7] but Catarino is known to be one; there is even a dog in the 'zoological brothel' which is described as 'a gentle pederast who, nevertheless, serviced bitches to earn his keep' (p. 333). Similarly, García Márquez employs lavatorial jokes, describing the complexities of entertaining sixty-eight school-girls and four nuns in a house with only one toilet, or the pungency of José Arcadio's flatulence which makes flowers wither on the spot.

Taboos are not limited to bodily functions. Death and religion are a source of jokes in most societies, the latter being even more piquant in as conservatively Catholic a country as Colombia. In *One Hundred Years* most of the characters either fade away in old age (José Arcadio Buendía, the Colonel, Ursula, Rebeca, and Melquíades) or else their deaths are treated with black humour. José Arcadio's corpse emits such an evil stench that his mourners decide in desperation to 'season it with pepper, cumin and laurel leaves and boil it over a gentle heat for a whole day' (p. 118); the body of Fernanda's distinguished father – appropriately enough a Knight of the Order of the Holy Sepulchre – spent so long on its journey to Macondo that when the coffin was opened 'the skin had erupted in stinking belches and was simmering in a bubbling, frothy stew' (p. 186); a drunken funeral party buries the twins, José Arcadio Segundo and Aureliano Segundo, in each other's graves thus putting the final touch to the running joke about their muddled identities.

Fernanda's stuffy religiosity makes her the butt of numerous comic scenes but, more subtly and with nice irony, the narrator claims that the indelible cross worn by all of the Colonel's campaign sons will guarantee their safety yet, in the end, their murderers recognize them precisely by this sacred sign. A statue of St Joseph revered by Ursula turns out to be merely a hiding place for the gold which enables a renegade apprentice Pope to indulge in orgies with his potential catamites while obsessed by incestuous desires for his great-great aunt.

The final taboo is a linguistic one, for the dialogue of *One Hundred Years* is a convincing representation of the expression of uncultured characters for whom expletives are part of everyday speech. These are frequently used comically to deflate scenes which are in danger of

becoming over-sentimental. For example, the amiable Gerineldo
Márquez's grief at being rejected by Amaranta is reflected by a
sympathetic Nature; he sends his comrade, the Colonel, a poignant
message, 'Aureliano, it is raining in Macondo' only to receive the
reply, 'Don't be a prick, Gerineldo. Of course it's raining; it's August'
(p. 144).

The violation of these taboos is never prurient. The author treats
sex, death, religion and language with a light-hearted candour.
Indeed, as Aureliano Segundo observes when he sees Fernanda's prim
nightdress which covers her from head to foot but has 'a large, round,
delicately trimmed hole over her lower stomach' (p. 182), it is
prudishness which is really obscene. Similarly, euphemism leads only
to pain and ridicule: Fernanda seeks a cure for her medical condition
but, as she cannot bring herself to describe the embarrassing
symptoms openly, the invisible doctors are unable to diagnose her
complaint and she is condemned to a life of suffering.

Renaissance theorists of comedy, understandably enough, did not
identify the contravention of such taboos as a source of humour;
rather, they conjectured more abstractly that it was the provocation of
wonderment and surprise in the reader or spectator which caused
mirth.[8] Such wonderment lies at the heart of much of the laughter of
One Hundred Years where García Márquez has frequent recourse to
exaggeration, fantasy, and the ridiculous. While we are willing to
accept that José Arcadio returns from his travels a grown man, the
exaggeration with which his exploits and appetites are recounted
either leads the reader to reject the novel as nonsense or, as Forster has
it, to pay the extra sixpence at the fair and revel in fantasy and
hyperbole.[9] Just as he laughs at the reaction of the naive inhabitants of
Macondo whose description of the first train to be seen in the town is of
'a terrifying object like a kitchen pulling a village' (p. 192), so the
reader is invited to laugh at his own reaction when his expectations of
the narrative are challenged and he has to suspend his normal
judgement about what is possible in reality and fiction and what is not.
It is with wonderment that he learns of a fantastic character like
Melquíades who frequently returns from the land of the dead but who
grows old there just as people do in the land of the living, of the
appearance of the Duke of Marlborough (the 'Mambrú' of the
traditional Spanish nursery rhyme) at the Colonel's side in the civil
war, or of other equally fantastic situations, often described in
absurdly precise detail, such as the love-making of Petra Cotes and
Aureliano Segundo which increases the numbers of their livestock

overnight. Although the fantasy is often an extension of, or a metaphor for reality, such wonderment provokes laughter. A situation, an event, or a character may start out as entirely credible, but by a logical development *ad absurdum* they become comical. Thus we understand that Fernanda and Ursula, following a well-established tradition among upper-crust Colombian families, should wish José Arcadio, their only legitimate son and great-great-grandson, to enter the church; their ambition only becomes humorous because they are determined that he should not be just any sort of priest and set about grooming him from childhood for the job of Pope. On other occasions, however, the comedy resides in astonishing us by gratuitous details – José Arcadio Buendía can increase his weight at will – or by a challenge to our notions of cause and effect either through the events of the novel or the illogicality of the characters' reasoning: thus, for instance, Francis Drake comes to Riohacha exclusively to set in motion the events of the novel which will eventually lead to the birth of a baby with a pig's tail; when Melquíades's breath begins to smell, he is given a bath.

García Márquez surprises the reader by a constant switching of tone which, like the expletives mentioned above, serves humorously to deflate a carefully constructed mood of seriousness or foreboding. Pietro Crespi is described as the perfect suitor for Amaranta: he is infatuated in a way, it is implied, that only romantic Italians can be; love makes his business prosper; he is loved, in turn, by the whole family. All augurs well for their marriage and happiness. Yet, after this long build-up, his passionate proposal is met with her, 'Don't be a fool, Crespi, I'd rather die than marry you' (p. 98). Similarly, the author carefully creates suspense about the Colonel's reaction to the signing of the Treaty of Neerlandia. We have all the traditional clues that Aureliano will do the honourable thing after surrendering to the government: the Colonel ensures that he has a single bullet in his pistol, he asks his doctor with apparent casualness in what part of his chest his heart is located, he destroys all his papers, and his mother bids him farewell making him promise that his last thought will be of her. As we had feared, he does indeed shoot himself and, the narrator assures us, Ursula realizes with her extraordinary powers of intuition that Aureliano has been killed. It then transpires that he is not dead at all but, rather, consumed with anger: the doctor had tricked him and the bullet missed his heart; in a trice he is planning to lead a new rebellion against the government.

Here it is the unexpected, and this often means the incongruous, which causes wonderment and therefore humour. It has already been observed that poignant scenes are frequently undermined by an incongruous expletive, an inappropriate statement, or a bathetic conclusion to an episode. In other ways surprise is created by exaggeration, by the narrator's ingenuous throw-away comment, or by bizarre reactions to events. The power of the Banana Company to decree that it should rain in Macondo for four years, eleven months and two days is funny because it is an exaggerated and absurdly precise extension of the real power of the multinationals in the Third World. The narrator's comment coming after his detailed account of José Arcadio's popularity with Macondo's whores, his sexual prowess, riotous living, and barbarous manners that 'he didn't manage to settle down in the family' (p. 84) is comical because it is a laconic understatement of the disparity between family life and José Arcadio's behaviour. The detail that Fernanda's only concern after Remedios the Beautiful had been assumed into the heavens while hanging out the washing was that her sheets had disappeared is humorous because it is such an inappropriately mundane reaction to a supernatural event with Christian undertones.

Just as linguistic taboos are violated, so the author causes wonderment in the reader by his use of language. This is often the result of concrete and almost poetic metaphors which are employed to describe abstract moods in an expressive, but decidedly off-key fashion, such as 'the mangrove-swamp of delirium' (p. 63), 'the eggplant-patch of her memories' (p. 236), 'the perfumed and worm-eaten guava-grove of love' (p. 237), 'a quagmire of anguish' (p. 246), and 'a bog of concupiscence' (p. 311), or the telling zeugma like Patricia Brown's 'nights of intolerance and pickled cucumbers in Prattville, Alabama' (p. 340). In a different way, inappropriate words are used for comic effect: when he foresees José Arcadio Buendía's death, Cataure, an uneducated Indian servant, returns to Macondo for, as he puts it, 'the king's exequies' (p. 125). The reader is further surprised by the way in which clichés are treated literally and have unforeseen results. Ursula refuses to be photographed because 'she didn't want to become a laughing-stock for her grandchildren' (p. 49): yet later she becomes quite literally a plaything for her great-great-grandchildren. We are used, at least in fiction, to hearing infatuated men protest to their sweethearts that they will die if their love is not requited: Remedios the Beautiful really does have lethal powers and deals painful deaths to her admirers; and Ursula gives up trying to domesticate Remedios trusting that 'sooner or later some miracle would happen' (p. 204) in the shape of a suitor who would rid the family of her, only for a real miracle to solve the problem when Remedios is assumed into heaven.

However, not all the funny elements in the novel can be neatly accounted for by being categorized as taboo subjects or as the cause of the wonderment Renaissance writers believed to lie at the roots of laughter. Irony is all-pervasive, and García Márquez mixes it with straightforward comedy of situation, character, and language. José Arcadio Buendía strips down and rebuilds a pianola in such a way that the long-awaited party to celebrate the extension of the family home is accompanied, in a scene of high farce, not by Pietro Crespi's melodious waltzes but by a musical cacophony. The traditional exposure of hypocrisy provides comedy of character especially when the butt is somebody as unpleasant as Fernanda. Her first reaction to the news of the birth of her illegitimate grandson is to think of murdering the innocent nun who brought the baby to the family home; she subsequently lies about his origins, sacrilegiously rehearsing the story of Moses found among the bulrushes. It is a nice irony that it is this grandson who will decipher the prophesies about the history of his people. Language is itself a source of humour, from the simple play on words by José Arcadio Buendía 'we need no judge [*corregidor*: literally 'corrector'] in Macondo, because there is nothing in need of correction here' (p. 55) and the constant repetition of epithets until they become absurd – the oriental traders are always referred to as 'the Arabs who exchange trinkets for parrots' (pp. 69, 281, etc.) – to the inversion of a set-phrase – the authorities come to Macondo to 'establish disorder' (p. 55) – and the playful alliteration of gobbledegook such as 'quién iba a saber qué pendejo menjunje de jarapellinosos genios jerosolimitanos [literally 'God knew what bloody concoction of syrupy Hierosolymitan geniuses']' (p. 193). As is traditional in the theatre, accent or verbal pomposity are used to comic effect: so Fernanda speaks a travesty of the language of the Colombian highlands which is ridiculed as an imitation of peninsular Spanish and contrasts markedly with the earthy and laconic Caribbean speech of the narrator and the other inhabitants of Macondo. It is no coincidence that two of Fernanda's surnames are Argote and Carpio, for her 'unnatural' Spanish as well as her anachronistic education, aspirations, and religiosity identify her as a descendant of two of Spain's greatest Golden Age practitioners of elaborate literary styles, Luis de Góngora y Argote and Lope de Vega Carpio. Her language is frequently incomprehensible to the other characters and, it is implied, moribund – her childhood occupation in her cold ancestral home was, appropriately enough, the manufacture of funeral wreaths. On one occasion she describes herself as 'goddaughter to the Duke of Alba, and a gentlewoman of such pure pedigree that she caused presidents' wives greate envy, a noble ladie of the bloode, entitled to sign herselfe with the eleven surnames which graced her Spanish forbears' (p. 274).

These elements of humour would appeal to most readers of *One Hundred Years*. However, many of the novel's scenes depend for a fuller appreciation of their darker and more ironic humour upon a broad acquaintance with the Latin American past and present, and a more specific knowledge of Colombia with its violent history of internal struggles and the extraordinary isolation of its village communities rich in folklore. Characters from this folklore such as Francisco el Hombre are amusingly incorporated into the novel while true episodes from Colombian history are fused with the fictional narrative. Indeed, the story of the strike of banana workers and their subsequent massacre is, paradoxically, less funny to a reader who realizes how close it is to the real events which took place in Ciénaga in 1928 and 1929, and who recognizes the names of real participants in those events, than it would be for a reader who sees it merely as another exaggerated scene from a 'typical' episode in Latin American history.[10] Yet the employment of a *reductio ad absurdum* of local political issues is elsewhere more comical. It is true that Colombian liberals had fought at the turn of the century for, among other things, the recognition of civil marriage; but in *One Hundred Years* a liberal soldier claims that 'we're waging this war against the priests so that we can marry our own mothers' (p. 132). More indirect are the ironic references to the Cuban Revolution which was still the most important political event in the sub-continent when *One Hundred Years* was written. The choice of a character called General Moncada to whom Ursula talks after receiving a message from Santiago de Cuba is not fortuitous, for the Revolution could reasonably be said to have started with Fidel Castro's unsuccessful attack on the Moncada barracks in Santiago de Cuba in 1953. Subsequent events in the novel lead to General Moncada's insight that so much fighting against the military has made Colonel Aureliano Buendía indistinguishable from them. The irony of this comment would not be missed by readers accustomed to seeing Castro, the erstwhile guerrilla, dressed in military uniform and constantly reviewing one of the most powerful armies in the sub-continent. Neither would he miss Moncada's deflation of a typical example of Castro's rhetoric in the scene in which the Colonel visits the General in his cell on the eve of his execution:

'Remember, Moncada, it is not I who is having you shot, but the Revolution.'
General Moncada did not even bother to get up from his bed when he saw the Colonel come in.
'Fuck off, Buendía', he replied. (p. 140)

There is also much in *One Hundred Years* for the more experienced reader of novels with whom García Márquez plays, constantly undermining his expectations. The first sentence of the book is an example of this playfulness:

Many years later, as he faced the firing squad, Colonel Aureliano Buendía would recall that distant afternoon on which his father took him to see what ice was. (p. 9)

Apart from the reader's surprise that one can be taken to 'discover' something as commonplace as ice, this introductory sentence contains two important implications about the subsequent story. First, the Colonel will be executed by firing squad and, second, as is traditional in novels where a condemned or drowning man's life rushes before his eyes at the moment of death, the Colonel relives the experiences of his infancy. The novel is, then, going to be the life-story of this character, beginning in early childhood and ending with his execution. This assumption is carefully reinforced by the author throughout the first few chapters of the novel. We read, for example, that 'many years later, a second before the regular army officer gave the firing squad the order to shoot, Colonel Buendía relived that warm March afternoon' (p. 21 [see also pp. 50, 75 and 87]). A measure of doubt is later cast on the assumption that he is to die in this manner when we hear that 'he lived to old age by making little gold fishes which he manufactured in his workshop in Macondo' (p. 94) and that he survived at least one firing squad but, as this is accompanied by the statement that he never allowed himself to be photographed and we already know this to be untrue (p. 50), we have learnt by this point in the novel to treat such details with healthy scepticism. Our expectations are further confirmed by the fate of his nephew, Arcadio. We are told that 'Years later, when he was facing the firing squad, Arcadio would recall ...' (p. 68); 'She was the last person Arcadio thought of, a few years later, when he faced the firing squad' (p. 82); and 'A few months later, when he faced the firing squad, Arcadio would relive . . .' (p. 101). As in this case the foreshadowing turns out to be accurate and Arcadio does, indeed, meet his end in such an execution, the reader's belief that the Colonel will do so also is confirmed. It is, then, with not a little consternation that when the Colonel's frequently announced 'execution' does occur – not at the end of the novel as expected but less than half-way through – the reader discovers that he is not even killed. In a humorously bathetic scene, the Colonel is rescued at the eleventh hour, much to the relief of the squad who immediately join him in a new rebellion. The first sentence of the novel and its deceptive implications thus teach the reader that the narrator is not to be trusted. Sometimes he (or, possibly, García Márquez himself) is merely muddled: when Aureliano Segundo is said to dream of dying in a night of passion with Fernanda, he surely means Petra Cotes;[11] when he says that the Colonel's seventeen campaign sons are all murdered in a single evening (p. 94), he overlooks Aureliano Amador who escapes, only to be shot in Macondo many years later (p. 317); when he casually mentions that Arcadio and his mistress, Santa Sofía de la Piedad, transfer their love-making to the room at the back of her shop after the school where Arcadio had lived until then was stormed by the government soldiers (p. 102), he misleads the reader yet again, for the lovers never meet after the troops enter Macondo; and when he prefaces his stories with the phrase 'many years later' or 'a few months earlier' he omits to give any clue which would help the reader to discover before or after exactly what these events are meant to have occurred. These examples could be attributed to the forgetfulness of a narrator who is characterized as a spinner of yarns, but on other occasions, as has been seen in the first sentence of the novel, it is clear that the reader is the victim of more wilful deception.

In *Don Quixote* Cervantes had invented a certain Cide Hamete Benengeli who, he playfully told the reader, was the 'author' of the work, the original version of which was written in Arabic; in *One Hundred Years* García Márquez equates his novel with the manuscripts written in Sanskrit by one of its characters, Melquíades. Just as Cide Hamete is at the same time both 'a most truthful historian' and a 'lying Moor', so Melquíades is said to be 'an honest man' (p. 9) but, as we realize from the very first page, is a gypsy and a charlatan: he there explains to the villagers who are astonished by the effects of magnets upon metal that 'objects have a life of their own; it's just a question of arousing their spirit'. García Márquez, like Cervantes before him, deliberately lays false trails. For example, the experienced reader will pick up small details about the Colonel's only surviving son: like his brothers, his fate to be killed before he is thirty-five years old, and he bears an indelible cross on his forehead; not only do his age and the cross suggest Christian symbolism but he is called Aureliano Amador ('Lover') and he is by profession a carpenter. He returns to his father's house only to be rejected in his hour of need by those who claim not to recognize him, one of whom is, ironically enough, the apprentice Pope, that spurious descendant of Peter the denier of Christ. The experienced reader of fiction, then, spots a symbol, his expectations are raised, and then Amador is killed and the carpet is pulled from under the reader's feet as the character in question simply disappears from the novel never to be mentioned again. García Márquez is aware of his readers and sets out to dupe them just as he later claimed, possibly with some measure of truthfulness, to have planted banana skins in *One Hundred Years* for the critics whom he so despises to slip on.[12]

Not only are the reader's expectations dashed, but the author also proves willing to poke fun at himself and his own devices. *One Hundred Years* is built upon predictions of what will happen to the characters in the future: indeed, the phrase 'había de' ('he was to') is one of the most frequent in the book. This is a convention often encountered in novels or stories, but in *One Hundred Years* the narrator's predictions are no more reliable than is Pilar Ternera's cartomancy. Thus the Colonel does not suffer the fate which, according to the first sentence of the novel, awaited him, while Aureliano José, whose destiny was to have seven children by Carmelita Montiel and to die as an old man in her arms, is murdered even before he can meet her. Like an oral spinner of a good yarn, the narrator of *One Hundred Years* is digressive; we do not have a linear narrative of the history of Macondo, let alone of the life of a single character. One may react with anger and frustration to this mockery of the novel's conventions and of the reader's good faith, as the narrator tells what amounts to a shaggy-dog story; yet the popularity of the novel is clear proof of the capacity of readers to treat such inventiveness and mockery with wonderment and laughter.

At the other end of the spectrum of humour from the sexual and lavatorial jokes are the sly references to other Spanish American writers. These would, of course, be appreciated only by a minority of readers familiar with the works concerned. Critics have drawn our attention to the author's predilection for referring to characters invented by other writers: there are Victor Hugues from the Cuban Alejo Carpentier, Artemio Cruz from the Mexican Carlos Fuentes, and Rocamadour from the Argentine Julio Cortázar.[13] The Mamá Grande is even borrowed from another of García Márquez's own works. More important than this mere list of names is the author's knowing wink to the initiated and the effect this has on his own novel. For example, Colonel Lorenzo Gavilán, who comes from Fuentes's *The Death of Artemio Cruz*, says in *One Hundred Years* that he witnessed Cruz's heroism during the Mexican Revolution. Yet the reader familiar with Fuentes's novel knows that Gavilán was duped by Cruz who deserted during an engagement and then contrived to put a good face on his disappearance from the battle-field. García Márquez is careful to stress that Gavilán only *claimed* to have seen Cruz's bravery; this, then, is an 'in-joke' for the reader of modern Spanish American fiction. García Márquez eventually kills off Gavilán during the slaughter of banana workers but, even in the apparently grim episode in which José Arcadio Segundo identifies comrades in a train full of corpses speeding away from the scene of the massacre, García Márquez cannot resist lifting another detail straight from Fuentes's novel: the belt with a silver buckle which was worn by the unnamed comrade whom Cruz could possibly have saved from death but whom he selfishly abandoned at a critical moment of the story.[14] In the second part of *Don Quixote*, 'real' characters rub shoulders with self-confessed inventions leading to a humorous, if bewildering, play of levels of fiction. This same game is played by García Márquez who infuses with deflating comic ambiguity an episode which some have ingenuously regarded as a straightforward denunciation of the United Fruit Company's machinations in the Colombia of the 1920s and 1930s.

Similar ambiguity resulting from literary games can be seen in the treatment of what we might expect to be other serious episodes in the novel such as the death of one of its central characters, Colonel Aureliano Buendía. Just as we saw earlier that an incongruous statement or an expletive might be introduced to puncture a sentimental mood, so here the death scene is undermined by the author's decision to narrate it in a style which is a close parody of that employed in a story entitled 'The Aleph' by the influential Argentine writer, Jorge Luis Borges. Similarly, he had already deflated the execution of Arcadio by a clear literary allusion, this time to another of

Borges's stories, 'The Secret Miracle'.[15] This practice is not a systematic 'meditation upon' Spanish American literature as some would assert. Rather, it has the important consequence of undermining any serious involvement with characters or situations which the novel might otherwise have possessed. *One Hundred Years* thus becomes a cornucopia of adventure and laughter on many levels, but one which, like all great comic works, resists and ridicules any attempt to extract from it a clear message or meaning, and we are tempted as a result to take at face value the author's statement that '*One Hundred Years of Solitude* is completely devoid of seriousness'.[16]

Readers of Borges or of the *nouvelle critique* will have appreciated the passing references to the novel's self-awareness as a fictional work in the course of construction: when José Arcadio Buendía 'looked through the window and saw two barefooted children in the sunny garden, and had the impression that they had come into existence at just that instant' (p. 20) he is of course correct, for this is the first time that the children are focused upon by the narrator. The final joke in *One Hundred Years*, however, comically deflates not just an episode or a character, but the whole novel. At the end of the last chapter Aureliano Babilonia discovers that Melquíades's manuscripts are an account of the history of Macondo including the moment at which Aureliano Babilonia discovers this fact. It is suggested that the novel is, in some way, merely a transcript of Melquíades's predictions although, typically enough, García Márquez does not attempt to wrestle with the logical problems presented by the author's being a character in his own work. The implication is that the reader should ask himself how serious a work can be which is written by a liar, which is a self-confessed piece of fiction – Macondo is constructed of 'mirrors (or reflections)' (p. 351) and its characters suspect that they are unreal (p. 345) – and whose rightful destiny is to be stored away like the manuscripts among disused chamber-pots. In the end Macondo is destroyed by a literary wind which recalls that in *Strong Wind*, a novel by the Guatemalan writer Miguel Angel Asturias. Márquez's novelistic world does not exist after the reader has finished the book. The novel is a way of passing time; it is the spinning out of a yarn – a process already seen in miniature in the cyclical tale of the capon which the villagers tell each other to while away nights of insomnia (p. 46). *One Hundred Years* is an entertainment which does not transcend the enjoyment of reading it, and it does not pose serious questions upon which the reader is invited to meditate at length. On the contrary, it is a kaleidoscope, or spectrum, of comic narration in which the over-earnest reader or critic is the final butt of the author's jokes for, as Aureliano Babilonia discovers, 'literature was the best toy which had ever been invented to pull people's legs' (p. 327). To take it all too seriously would be about as fruitful as a discussion of 'the various mediaeval techniques for killing cockroaches' (p. 327).

Notes

EO = Plinio Apuleyo Mendoza, *El olor de la guayaba* (Barcelona, 1982)

1 For example, W. G. Moore, *Molière: A New Criticism* (Oxford, 1949), P. E. Russell, 'Don Quixote as a Funny Book', *Modern Language Review*, 64 (1969), 312–26, and the latter's *Cervantes* (Oxford and New York, 1985), *passim*.
2 Donald L. Shaw, *Nueva narrativa hispanoamericana* (Madrid, 1981), p. 215; David Gallagher, *Modern Latin American Literature* (London, 1973), pp. 147 and 162.
3 *EO*, p. 111.
4 Moore, *Molière*, p. 99.
5 *EO*, p. 104.
6 All page references are to the Editorial Sudamericana 1975 edition. The translations are my own.
7 Pietro Crespi is also given a comically inappropriate name: it recalls Pedro Crespo, one of the best-known figures from Spanish drama of the seventeenth century where he is the major character in Pedro Calderón de la Barca's *El alcalde de Zalamea*; Crespo, far from being an effete Italian, was a forceful and cunning Spanish peasant.
8 Russell, 'Don Quixote', p. 321.
9 E. M. Forster, *Aspects of the Novel* (Harmondsworth, 1977), pp. 103–4.
10 Mario Vargas Llosa, *García Márquez: historia de un deicidio* (Barcelona, 1971), pp. 16–20. Regina Janes, *Gabriel García Márquez: Revolutions in Wonderland* (Columbia and London, 1981), pp. 11–12.
11 P. 166; the English translation, *One Hundred Years of Solitude*, translated by Gregory Rabassa (London, 1978), p. 159, 'corrects' this slip.
12 *EO*, p. 104.
13 Gallagher, *Modern Latin American Literature*, p. 146.
14 Carlos Fuentes, *La muerte de Artemio Cruz* (Mexico City, 1973), pp. 73–9. Originally published in 1962.
15 Compare *Cien años de soledad*, p. 229, with Jorge Luis Borges, 'El aleph', in *El aleph* (Buenos Aires, 1952), pp. 151–2; compare *Cien años*, pp. 107–8 with Borges 'El milagro secreto' in *Ficciones* (Buenos Aires, 1971), pp. 165–7.
16 *EO*, p. 104.

7

On 'magical' and social realism in García Márquez

GERALD MARTIN

Although you have every right not to believe me after putting up for so long with my sly tricks and falsifications, I swear to you by the bones of my mother that what I am now about to show you is no illusion but the plain and simple truth . . .'   (García Márquez, 'Blacamán the Good, miracle-salesman')

What interested me in my novel was above all to tell the story of a family obsessed by incest, and which, in spite of every precaution taken for several generations, ends up having a child with a strange pig's tail.

(García Márquez on *One Hundred Years of Solitude*, 1968)

The true history of Latin America is as yet an almost totally blank book, save for a few phrases recorded in such equivocal terms that no one troubles to try and understand them . . . Through misinterpreting their past, Latin Americans construct false projects for the future, and every step they take in the present in accordance with those projects, vitiated by that initial falseness, only serves to sink them deeper in their sickness, as in a circle from which there is no way out.   (H. A. Murena, *The Original Sin of America*)

They wanted nothing to do with that series of conflicts, revolts, alternations between dictatorship and anarchy. In past history they found nothing constructive, nothing they aspired to be. And yet, in spite of everything, the Latin American was making history, not the history he would have wished for, but his own history. A very special history, with no negations or dialectical assimilations. A history full of contradictions that never came to synthesis. But history for all that. The history that we Latin Americans, halfway through the twentieth century, must negate dialectically, that is, assimilate.   (Leopoldo Zea, *The Latin American Mind*)

Beyond this general collapse of Reason and Faith, God and Utopia, there are no intellectual systems old or new to be erected, capable of appeasing our anguish or relieving our dismay: there is nothing before us. We are finally alone. Like all men . . . Out there, in the open solitude, transcendence also awaits us: the hands of other solitary beings. We are, for the first time in our history, the contemporaries of all men.

(Octavio Paz, *The Labyrinth of Solitude*)

A few long weeks ago, already in the iron grip of disenchantment and waves of *déjà vu* (this is written from Portsmouth a year after the war in the South Atlantic which has rekindled the dying embers of so many national myths), I chanced again on some earlier meditations on distant 'South America' recorded by Lord Byron in 1809: 'Europe's decrepitude', he lamented, 'is increasing; everybody here is the same, everything repeats itself. There the people are as fresh as their New World, and as violent as their earthquakes.'[1] We Europeans, one reflects, have always viewed Latin America, like Africa, through all the twists and turns of a long historical relationship (it will soon be 1992), as alternately the earthly paradise or the heart of darkness, their inhabitants as noble or ignoble savages, according to the opportune requirements of the moment. Although awareness of the stratagems involved has increased markedly since the appearance of works by Fanon, Memmi, Césaire and Fernández Retamar (*Caliban*), and especially now that Said has studied 'Orientalism' and Todorov the conquest of America from the standpoint of 'Otherness', a majority of readers of fiction in this country remain curiously and conveniently innocent of them. But it is only such ideological self-awareness which, in my opinion, can provide the framework essential for any serious investigation into the deceptively transparent writing of Colombia's Gabriel García Márquez.

The 1982 Nobel Prize winner has repeatedly declared that nothing of importance happened to him after the death of his beloved grandfather, the Colonel, when he was eight years old, so that his novels are suffused with the emotions and memories of those early years, and therefore, one might add, by a nostalgic quest – many years later – for that lost time. It was at a similar age that I, almost a century and a half after Byron, infant inhabitant of a grey post-war London, first began, on the basis of two or three postage stamps of volcanoes and cactuses, the *Wonder Book of the Amazon Jungle*, and the Hollywood trail down Mexico way, to invent a world for myself, the multicoloured new world of Latin America. My nostalgia was for a reality I had never known, and what I invented was something rather like the exotic literary phenomenon critics now call 'magical realism'. Needless to say, I knew nothing of the fabulous imaginings of the Spanish *conquistadores*, the innocent primitive engendered by the Enlightenment, or the *Volksgeist* conceived by the Romantics; nor of the metamorphoses involved as such concepts lived on into the Surrealist 1920s. Indeed, I was a distinctly reluctant, if bemused witness to the age of decolonization, shortly before the next – now 'Third World' – nativist tide began to flow in the 1960s, with its grotesque reflections in Western hippiedom and psychedelia. Yet, when I began to study Latin America at university in those early sixties, it seemed that all I had invented was really true: here indeed was a comic opera world of fantasy and magic, generals and doctors, beggars on golden stools. I recall the impact upon me of one of the first texts I read, Sarmiento's archetypal *Facundo: Civilization and Barbarism*, in which I learned – and I wanted to believe it – that in 1833, in a province of 400,000 inhabitants, only three had voted against the tyrant Rosas; or that the same Rosas's mother had insisted, to the end of her days, on the family servants ministering to her on their knees (part III, 2). I did not suspect that magic had turned to reality for Rosas, that he had ceased to be colourful when, at the end of his life long ago, he came to die in faraway Hampshire.

In 1965, the year in which Parry reported on the lost Seaborne Empire, I bought the now famous Latin America number of *Encounter* (funded by the CIA), and, in a hallucinatory article on *la violencia* by Malcolm Deas,[2] was persuaded that Colombians were every bit as bizarre and hyperbolic in reality as García Márquez, two years later, would show them to be in his fictional *One Hundred Years of Solitude*. Like Latin Americans themselves, though without the same bitter contradictions, we roar with laughter at the ridiculous egocentricity of these fictional characters, these South Americans: but our own ethnocentricity is no laughing matter. Later that year I too finally travelled to Latin America, as I had done so often in my imagination; and slowly, incredulously, began to realize that I did not, after all, believe in fairies, and that even fantasy and magic have their own histories, their own secret motivation.

One Hundred Years of Solitude, despite the occasional carelessness and repetitiveness of some of its writing, can justly lay claim to being, perhaps, the greatest of all Latin American novels, appropriately enough, since the story of the Buendía family is obviously a metaphor for the history of the continent since Independence, that is, for the neocolonial period. More than that, though, it is also, I believe, a narrative about the *myths* of Latin American history. If this is where its true importance lies, it is also the reason why so many readers have become lost in its shimmering hall of mirrors. And if each reader inevitably interprets the novel according to his or her own ideological

preconceptions, one must be sceptical of some of the unconscious
motives behind its astonishing success in the still imperialistic English-
speaking world, where, after all, very few Latin American novels have
gone before.

It is instructive in this, as in other ways, to compare and contrast
García Márquez with Borges. However 'Argentine' Borges may or
may not be (and one would not wish to reopen this largely tautological
debate), he went into production, to put it crudely, with a top-quality
luxury product aimed implicitly at the European consumer. It proved
a highly marketable finished commodity, albeit a minority one.
García Márquez's work shows every sign of having been manufactured for the home market, Latin America, and yet it has been just as
acceptable to European and North American – which is to say,
'universal' – taste. He became the first truly international best-seller in
Latin American publishing history.[3] If, as I believe, part of the novel's
achievement is a socialist – though not a 'social realist' – reading of
Latin American history, the most likely explanation for its sensational
success in, say, Britain and the United States is that its subtle
ambiguities make it as possible for readers to despise or sympathize
with its Latin American characters as it would be in life outside the
novel. None of this is so surprising. Almost four hundred years after
Cervantes wrote *Don Quixote*, critics continue to assure us that it is
about some eternal or frozen distinction between reality and illusion,
rather than – as seems evident to me – about a nostalgia (deeply felt by
its author but all the more strongly satirized for that in its characters)
for a mythologized aristocratic world-view in an age of mercantilist
relations. *One Hundred Years of Solitude*, it is arguable, was born of a
nostalgic longing for certain pre-capitalist rural relations in an age of
rapid urbanization and the implantation of industrial capitalism.
Perhaps the most 'limpid' and transparent works are, in reality, the
most opaque.

This is why, although it is tempting to write in an abstract and
sophisticated manner about the works of García Márquez, it is not the
approach that I intend to take. Certainly he is a master of magic and
mystery, and his writing is so consistently *enjoyable* that one frequently
forgets that to believe, even temporarily, in illusions is to settle for a
world that is undecipherable and unknowable. But this is surely not
the job of criticism. My view is that the essential point of departure for
any comprehensive analysis of *One Hundred Years of Solitude* must be an
examination of its perception of the relation between ideology and
consciousness, and between lived reality, historiography and litera-

ture. More precisely, whilst a number of the novel's central themes
and achievements are not in doubt (though we shall be forced to
reiterate them), I believe that García Márquez criticism as a whole
has suffered from three basic errors, particularly with reference to
studies of *One Hundred Years of Solitude*:

(1) Critics have failed to perceive that history is not only devoured
by myth, as is so frequently claimed,[4] but that *every myth also has its
history*. This novel is not about 'history-and-myth', but about the
myths of history and their demystification.

2) They fail to differentiate correctly between the perspective of the
novelist and that of his characters, an elementary distinction with
infinitely complex ramifications in this most subtle yet apparently
straightforward text.

(3) They largely ignore the context, historical and literary, in
which the novel was written and published.

An approach based on these three perceptions can guide us to a
more satisfactory reading of the novel, in particular to a convincing
interpretation of its ending, and can explain to us García Márquez's
standpoint on 'time' and 'magic', history and society. It can also help
to demystify critical terminology itself and perhaps dispel the optical
illusions of such pernicious – even racist – ideologies as those which
underpin the concept of 'magical realism'.

Donald Shaw, in an invaluable review of responses to *One Hundred
Years of Solitude*, indicates what for him is its basic critical problem: 'the
fact that the novel appears to function on three different levels of
meaning: one related to the nature of reality, a second concerned with
universal human destiny and a third connected with the problems of
Latin America'.[5] He later argues: 'What is important, however, is that
such pathways towards the understanding of the novel should not be
followed separately, as has mainly been the case hitherto, but explored
simultaneously with the fullest recognition of their implications for
one another.'[6] I agree with Shaw that the three dimensions (ontological, epistemological, historical) are each of comparable importance in
this as in all great works of artistic fiction. Where I would differ is in my
belief that García Márquez's apparent underlying tragic vision is not
necessarily in contradiction with a revolutionary standpoint on Latin
American development. Indeed, the view that I would propose is that
in *One Hundred Years of Solitude*, García Márquez momentarily found a
means of reconciling his rather evident philosophical pessimism (of a
'Leopardian' materialist variety, to echo Timpanaro) with his

determinedly optimistic conception of the march of history. It is
perhaps through this tension that the novel has attained its undeni-
able classic status.[7] Clearly, though, as Shaw argues, everything
ultimately rests on one's interpretation of the apocalyptic conclusion,
and I shall return to this problem below.

Although the topic under discussion here – how magical and how
realist is García Márquez? – is relevant to all his fictional production
(not excluding some of his journalism),[8] *One Hundred Years of Solitude*
(1967) remains the pivotal work, and by far the most complex. In
Leafstorm (1955), *In Evil Hour* (1962), or, quintessentially, *No One
Writes to the Colonel* (1958), the basic narrative conventions are those of
critical realism, with implicit but perfectly straightforward economic,
social and political (that is, historical) explanations for the psychological motivations of each of the characters (Angel Rama speaks of 'a
pronounced social determinism').[9] Any picturesqueness in them is no
more than eccentricity born of ex-centricity. In the much later *The
Autumn of the Patriarch* (1975), on the other hand, the weakness for
hyperbole – what J. Mejía Duque has called 'the crisis of dispropor-
tion'[10] – and the temptation of the *tour de force* between them sweep
almost all grasp on historical reality away, and it is worth recalling
that the novel was written in Spain, where García Márquez was living
during the last seven years of the Franco regime. In this novel he
appears – doubtless it is the price of playing to the gallery – to become
lost in the same ideological and linguistic labyrinths into which he had
unintentionally lured so·many other unsuspecting writers with the
glittering success of *One Hundred Years of Solitude*. That work, it seems to
me, remains the only text of his in which the mix of real and fantasy
elements is both perfectly fused and, analytically – as I interpret it –
perfectly separable.[11]

Dualisms, even manichaeisms, of every kind, while entirely
explicable in terms of Latin America's colonial experience, are
frequently the bane of its literature and criticism. Angel Rama, in his
early article on García Márquez, noted 'an oscillation in the author
himself with regard to the plane on which any given explanation
should rest: whether on the social or the metaphysical level'.[12] By the
time of *One Hundred Years of Solitude*, however, the technical sleight of
hand had become almost invisible, and most critics began to
emphasize the blend of myth and history, fiction and reality, and to
view with approval the apparent impossibility of distinguishing
between them. Julio Ortega insisted that 'the play of reality and

fantasy is never dual in this novel';[13] José Miguel Oviedo declared that the novelist had 'mixed the real and the fantastic in so perfect and inextricable a fashion that no one can tell where the frontier between them may lie';[14] and Ernst Völkening commented admiringly that García Márquez was blessed with 'the uncommon gift of seeing both sides of the moon at one and the same time'.[15]

This, then, is the novel which, perhaps more than any other, has been taken to confirm the historical demise of social realism in Latin American fiction and to herald the arrival of the linguistic, experimental or post-Modernist novel. Such social realism, as most critics now agree, dominated the period from about 1915, the moment of Mariano Azuela's *Los de abajo* (*The Underdogs*) and other novels of the Mexican Revolution, to about 1945, when writers like Asturias, Borges and Carpentier came into view. But to see things this way seems to me an over-simplification of Latin American literary history and a misreading of *One Hundred Years of Solitude* itself, which contains a greater variety of carefully encoded material relating to the positivistic orders of social psychology, political economy and the history of ideas than almost any other Latin American novel that comes to mind. Angel Rama's verdict on García Márquez's early works, already disconcerting to most readers, seems to me to be equally applicable to *One Hundred Years of Solitude* itself: 'I do not believe any other novelist has so acutely, so truthfully seen the intimate relationship between the socio-political structure of a given country and the behaviour of his characters.'[16] The main reason why so many readers have missed these otherwise obvious facts is that García Márquez presents most aspects of reality from the standpoint of his characters, while he himself, as narrator, adopts a perspective based – largely but not entirely ironically, in which lies much of the difficulty – on the mainly metaphysical views of the *pensadores* ('thinkers'), those ideologists who dominated Latin America's interpretation of its own history until after the Second World War. Sarmiento's struggle between civilization and barbarism, Rodó's exaltation of Ariel against Caliban, the sick continent diagnosed by Bunge and Arguedas, Keyserling's swamp-like dawn of creation and *tristeza criolla* (creole sadness), Martínez Estrada's view of Latin Americans as victims of a historical mirage, Mallea's incommunicability, and – above all – Murena's original sin thesis:[17] these and many other weird and wonderful theories of American history jostle for supremacy throughout the novel, only to find

themselves circumscribed, at the last, by a conception which coincides
closely with the rather more lucid kinds of perspective that emerged in
Mexico after 1945, namely Paz's assertion that Latin Americans were
now the contemporaries of all men and Zea's thesis that it was time, at
long last, to break out of the labyrinth of solitude and assimilate the
history of the continent. Seen like this, there is perhaps more to García
Márquez's work than the echoes of Faulkner, Borges and other such
literary influences so widely debated by some critics.

If this conception of *One Hundred Years of Solitude* is accepted, all the
hallowed references to Vico, Hegel and Croce, all talk of circularities
and eternal returns become redundant. It is for this reason that for me
the most convincing interpretations of the novel's apparent dualism
have come from critics with a sociological approach, above all Agustín
Cueva, who argues that García Márquez 'is not seeking to put
forward an irrationalist philosophy but merely to recreate a representation of a world that he knows is over and done with'.[18] Cueva shows
that the work is a synthesis of elements belonging to two different
genres, the epic and the novel, a line later followed by Todorov, who
likewise brings out the clash between an individualist and a collective
view of the world.[19] Similarly, Sergio Benvenuto, in a brilliant short
study, affirms that 'living contradiction is the only appropriate
language for this incredible intersection of universal culture and local
unculture'.[20]

To those who know Latin America, the culture traits in the text are
unmistakable, though each is almost impossible to extricate from its
anecdotic materiality; to those who do not know the continent, the
novel is more abstract, and the incidents are recognizable as vehicles
of universal experiences or truths distorted by Latin American
eccentricity. Thus almost everything is at once familiar but
unidentifiable inside this literary 'aleph': we see the world from genesis
to apocalypse, from Renaissance to Baroque, from independence to
neocolonialism; or from use values to exchange values, transparence
to opaqueness, childhood innocence to adult guilt, lines and circles to
labyrinths. The result has been called magical realism. The problem is
that the same term is used, consciously or unconsciously, as an
ideological stratagem to collapse many different kinds of writing, and
many different political perspectives, into one single, usually escapist,
concept.[21] Like the Surrealist movement from which it ultimately
derives, magical realism might in part be seen as an unconscious –
irony of ironies! – conspiracy between European or North American

critics eager to get away, in their imagination, to the colourful world of
Latin America, and certain Latin American writers desperate to take
refuge, in their writing, from the injustice and brutality of their
continent's unacceptable reality. This makes detailed analysis of
every case particularly important. There is a world of difference
between the view that tacitly assumes that reality itself is or may be
fantastic, or that the imagination is autonomous (Borges, Lezama
Lima, sometimes Cortázar) and a perspective which takes seriously
the religious beliefs or myths, the fantasies or illusions of the fictional
characters, whether by reproducing them 'anthropologically' or by
critically demystifying them (Asturias, Carpentier, Rulfo, Roa Bastos
and – in this but not all cases – García Márquez). If the term must be
used, it is best confined to the latter kind of writing, in which,
essentially, there is a dialectic between pre-scientific and scientific
visions of reality, seen most clearly in works which combine the
mythological or folk beliefs of the characters with the consciousness of
a twentieth-century observer. Although García Márquez is by no
means always clear about the distinction in all his fiction, I believe
that *One Hundred Years of Solitude* at least is entirely coherent in this
regard and that it is to this in large measure that it owes the
unparalleled breadth and depth of its critical and popular success.
Our difficulty is that the two levels are really separable only on the
abstract plane of analysis, so seriously does the omniscient narrator
take the beliefs of his characters. García Márquez uses a battery of
complementary literary techniques – above all, caricature, hyperbole, bathos and condensation of every kind – to unite the two levels in
each and every anecdote of his narrative.

The fact remains that a majority of critics and general readers
appear to admire the novel precisely because, in their view, it conjures
up a magical reality. Let us therefore examine this. In order to
demonstrate such a view – and herein lies the contradiction – one has
to know what reality is. So herewith an elementary hypothesis:
whatever contemporary reality may be, it is determined and defined
by the metropolitan centres of culture in Europe and, above all now,
the United States. As Marx and Engels noted, 'The ruling ideas of
each age have ever been the ideas of its ruling class...' Latin America
can therefore be viewed, by definition, as a home of irreality, where
people are larger or smaller than life: there for my entertainment,
specimens in the national-geographical catalogue of planetary
showbiz safaris (in short, less than human). Critics accordingly praise

the novel for its further confirmation that life is a dream, whereas it is, to say the least, plausible that what the novel is saying is that *Latin American life* is a dream – the 'unreality' and 'unauthenticity' imposed by almost five hundred years of colonialism – and that when a dream becomes a permanent living nightmare it is probably time to wake up.[22] The official history which 'Europe' has projected is that of rationalism, capitalism, progressive development and linear chronology. However contradictory and repressive this history may seem to any European, it is, for the typical Latin American, organic and coherent by definition; whereas his own history is fragmented, discontinuous, absurd ('time itself underwent jolts and accidents, and thus could splinter and leave an eternalized instant in a room').[23] It is his fate actually to be one of the despised inhabitants of a 'banana republic', victim of a 'comic-opera regime' or a 'tin-pot junta'. He is a 'mimic man'. Or so 'we' would have him think.

In *One Hundred Years of Solitude* nothing ever turns out as people expect; everything surprises them; all of them fail; all are frustrated; few achieve communion with others for more than a fleeting moment, and the majority not at all. Most of their actions – at first sight like the structure of the novel as a whole – are circular (*hacer para deshacer*: 'doing in order to undo'). Ploughers of the sea, they are unable to make their lives purposive, achieve productiveness, break out of the vicious circle of their fate. In short, they fail to become agents of history for themselves: like the characters of Rulfo's *Pedro Páramo* (1955), they are the echoes of someone else's history, the last link in the centre–periphery chain.[24] The only explanation possible is that they are living out their lives in the name of someone else's values. Hence the solitude, central theme (together with the quest) of Latin American history: it is their abandonment in an empty continent, a vast cultural vacuum, marooned thousands of miles away from their true home. Conceived by Spain in the sixteenth century (the stranded galleon, the buried suit of armour), the characters awaken in the late eighteenth-century Enlightenment (magnet and telescope as symbols of the two pillars of Newtonian physics), but are entirely unable to bring themselves into focus in a world they have not made. Influences from outside (the gypsies) are sporadic, piecemeal, throughout the notional hundred years of the novel, which is the span from the Independence era to the early 1960s, when it was being written.

Of course the characters are supposed – by themselves, at least – to be living in 'our' world. Times of the day, days of the week, statistics of every kind are to be found everywhere in the novel, but are no more helpful or meaningful than the more obviously illusory temporal references such as 'many years later' which appear with equal frequency, from its very first sentence. The characters all believe that their actions are purposive, but whenever they follow their logical chain to its conclusion they find that they have come in a circle. Yet, despite the historical immobility which lies at its heart, the narrative literally teems with actions (part of its revival of the 'forgotten art of story-telling', to use Gullón's phrase).[25]

One Hundred Years of Solitude is the domain of the verb. The actions of which the verbs tell are individualistic, usually to the point of an extraordinary egotism – at least on the part of the male characters – and such individualism, given its relation to liberal ideology, might seem to suggest that they were genuinely historical, occurring only once in time and contributing more or less consciously to the movement of human history. But, once the reader is immersed in the narrative, each action begins to remind him of many other actions, since their inner meanings, like the names of the characters, constantly recur and refer, giving such apparently Borgesian concepts as the labyrinth and the mirror an inescapably material reading. Thus the very individualism and self-centredness of the characters is an obsessively repeated ritual. The fountain-head of this form of unreality is the first José Arcadio Buendía. It is he, progenitor of the novel, who, soon after the start, initiates the pattern of bemused contemplation, self-absorption and withdrawal. The Aurelianos, by contrast, are actively selfish and individualistic, seekers of power rather than knowledge. Ursula, who has been much studied, is the paradigm of the commonsensical mother figure, symbol of an entire epoch of family relations, but herself comes to believe that everything is circular (that the present is subordinate to the past), a conviction which brings her death and prompts the death of many others. Curiously enough, she makes her discovery, as we shall see, at precisely the moment when history, and the consciousness of modernity, has finally broken through to Macondo.

At this point, then, the Buendía line is doomed. I take this to mean that neocolonialism is at an end, remembering that the novel was written during the early years of the Cuban Revolution. There seems little doubt that the morbid fear of the birth of a child cursed with a pig's tail is a condensed metaphor for the combined ideologies of original sin and biological determinism (so that, again, esoteric or essentialist arguments about the nature and meaning of the incest theme seem to me beside the point, and appear to have given García Márquez almost endless amusement). The former circumscribed the whole of life in the colonial period, and was overlain by the latter after Independence, as an explanation of Latin America's continuing backwardness and a positivist justification of the rule of Europeanized minorities. (If we take the term *estirpe* – stock, lineage – literally, we have merely been lured into the same ideological misreading as the characters themselves: it is a historical era that is over, not a biological line). The impact of Darwin and Spencer produced the ideologies of Bunge and Arguedas in the early twentieth century, at a time when the European powers and the United States were still extending their colonial possessions. The reflection of these overlapping religious, philosophical and scientific theories in the self-image of the characters brings about an immensely subtle tragicomic fusion of fatalism and individualism. Most of the characters are aware that others have weaknesses and are doomed to failure, yet none of them know this about themselves. The secret last analysis of every situation reverts to racial or metaphysical explanations. If you call a child Aureliano, he will turn out like 'an Aureliano'. There is no escape; and no second chance. Problems of underdevelopment, dependency or imperialism never occur to these characters (they have occurred to the author, but, like Borges's Pierre Menard, his genius lies in having apparently managed to 'forget' them.) They are blissfully unaware of historical reality and know nothing of the world which has determined their destiny. Their only thoughts or memories are about things which relate to the structure of the novel; which is therefore the very fabric of their perceived social history. This explains the exoticism, for them, of phenomena which to us are quite normal – it is to our discredit if we can still find this surprising or amusing – as it also explains the often cited dreamlike quality of the Banana Company massacre narrated in the later part of the text.

Seen in this light, the novel seems less concerned with any 'magical' reality than with the general effect of a colonial history upon individual relationships: hence the themes of circularity, irrationality, fatalism, isolation, superstition, fanaticism, corruption and violence. The judgement as to whether these traits are inherent or produced by history is as much a political as a philosophical or scientific determination.

Even among critics who would follow me this far in the argument, there is little agreement about the meaning of the conclusion. Whilst not wishing to over-simplify it, I believe that it, too, is more straightforward than most readers have imagined. An old-fashioned biographical approach, as followed by Vargas Llosa in his pathbreaking critical study, can give us the first clue.[26] A number of critics have recognized the strike against the Banana Company and the ensuing massacre as the central shaping episode of the entire novel, though few have realized just how much this is the case. It is the theme of proletarian struggle, however, which is the secret thread that can guide us out into the light at the end of the labyrinth. García Márquez was born in 1928, the very year in which the historic massacre took place. It is at about the same time that Meme Buendía's son, the illegitimate Aureliano, is born in the novel. His mother had been forbidden to see Mauricio, his father, because, as an apprentice mechanic in the company workshop and one-time employee of Aureliano Triste, he was from an inferior class. Mauricio's surname is Babilonia, conceivably because the proletariat, which he represents, will bring about the historical destruction of 'Macondo', which is less a place than the name García Márquez gives to an era. Interestingly, Mauricio looks like a gypsy (p. 242), which suggests that as a migrant manual worker, a member of the *hojarasca* ('trash') so despised by García Márquez's own family when he was a child, he is a vehicle of the same kind of internationalist consciousness and impact (what the Mexican government now calls 'exotic influences') as the real gypsies led by Melquíades in the earlier sections of the novel. Mauricio is permanently crippled in an accident at the end of chapter 14, shortly after Meme becomes pregnant, and appears no more. But, at the beginning of chapter 15, the arrival of his illegitimate son is made to coincide explicitly with the author's own prophesy of doom for Macondo: 'The events which were to deal Macondo its mortal blow were already on the horizon when they brought Meme Buendía's son home' (p. 249).

These apocalyptic 'events' are *historical* ones. It is of course Aureliano Babilonia himself who will eventually decipher Melquíades's parchments on the final page. All the disasters to come had in fact already been presaged by a previous textual moment, at the end of chapter 11, through a familiar image of progress: 'the innocent yellow train that was to bring so many insecurities and uncertainties, so many joys and misfortunes, so many changes, calamities and nostalgias to Macondo' (p. 193). The decision to bring the yellow train, inaugurating the final stage in the penetration of Macondo's introversion and self-centredness, was taken by Aureliano Triste, the man who turned the magical ice into a commodity, which we can construe as representative of the embryonic local bourgeoisie: 'they remembered him well because in a matter of hours he had managed to destroy every breakable object that passed through his hands' (p. 191). The train in its turn brings the multinational Banana Company, United States imperialism, and eventual disaster, a perfectly logical sequence of events carefully explained by the author himself, all of which has little to do with pigs' tails.

The Banana Company brings temporary prosperity around the time of the First World War, but as profits are threatened in the late 1920s the workers begin strike action. José Arcadio Segundo, great-uncle of the baby Aureliano Babilonia, and at first a foreman in the company, becomes a trade union leader and plays a leading role in the conflict. He is one of the few survivors of the massacre, and insists on repeating his eye-witness account of the death of more than three thousand demonstrators until the day he dies. Indeed, his last words – to none other than Aureliano Babilonia, in Melquíades's old but ageless room – are: 'Always remember that there were more than three thousand and that they threw them in the sea' (p. 300). At which the narrator comments: 'Then he collapsed over the parchments and died with his eyes open.' The massacre had been denied both by the locals and by the authorities: 'In Macondo nothing has happened, nor is anything happening now, nor will it ever' (p. 263). Then all history and all memory were comprehensively blotted out by the rain which lasted four years, eleven months and two days, and which recalls the previous 'plague of insomnia' in chapter 3, provoked on that occasion by the suppression of Indian history. Now proletarian history was to be erased. In this instance, however, despite assiduous efforts by Colombia's official historians to make even the memory of the murdered strikers 'disappear', it was not to be so easy. The massacre was perpetrated by troops under General Carlos Cortés Vargas at the Ciénaga (Magdalena) railway station on 5 December 1928, in direct connivance with the United Fruit Company. More than thirty thousand workers were on strike in the zone and it appears that at least four thousand were at the Ciénaga demonstration when the troops opened fire. The conservative government of Miguel Abadía Méndez (1926–30) reported that a mere nine strikers were killed and, like all succeeding regimes, set about suppressing the true story. After some tempestuous parliamentary debates in September 1929, almost nothing of importance concerning these events appeared in Colombia in the forty years up to the publication of *One Hundred Years of Solitude*.[27] The rest is silence.

After the interminable rain, Ursula's own 'one hundred torrential years' come to an end, and with it her morality and her view of the world, the cement that has held the family together until these final chapters. When she dies, Macondo's decline accelerates, and the doom of the entire Buendía family rapidly approaches. Nevertheless, as García Márquez reveals, all is not forgotten. First José Arcadio Segundo, then Aureliano Babilonia, keep the memory of the workers' struggles and their suppression alive, at the same time as they themselves strive to decipher the broader historical panorama encoded in the parchments in Melquíades's room. José Arcadio's first memory was of seeing a man executed by firing squad as a child, and as we decode his own life we perceive clearly that he is one of the few characters who has struggled in any way sincerely against injustice. He it is, then, who leads the strike; who begins to decipher the parchments, or 'true history', of the Buendía family; and who, as his legacy, educates young Aureliano Babilonia:

In reality, although everyone took him for a madman, José Arcadio Segundo was at this time the most lucid member of the household. He taught little Aureliano to read and write, initiated him in the study of the parchments, and instilled in him so personal an interpretation of the meaning of the Banana Company for Macondo, that many years later, when Aureliano finally went out into the world, people would think that he was telling some hallucinatory story, because it was so radically opposed to the false version accepted by the historians and confirmed in the school textbooks.   (p. 296)

Nothing, surely, could be clearer. After José Arcadio Segundo's death, Aureliano Babilonia remains in Melquíades's room, continuing his own education and the deciphering of the parchments, sometimes aided by the ghost of Melquíades himself. The room, needless to say, is that timeless space of memory, domain of history and literature (García Márquez in his writer's solitude), marked by 'the diaphanous purity of its air, its immunity against dust and destruction' (p. 264), until, that is, Melquíades himself dies and time pursues its work in his room also. Aureliano, meanwhile, obsessed by the parchments, takes no interest in what is going on around him and makes only occasional excursions to buy reference works at the old Catalan's bookshop (the political aftermath of the Spanish Civil War and its impact in Latin

America). At length, having deduced that the manuscripts are written in Sanskrit, he manages to translate the first page, only to discover that they are poems and still in code. Finally, firmly 'fortified within written reality', he emerges into the real world and makes four new friends at the bookshop, thereafter dividing his time between books and brothels: 'Only then did it occur to him that literature was the best game ever devised for pulling the wool over people's eyes' (p. 327).

One of his new friends, Gabriel, is none other than the author, and his fiancée, Mercedes, is none other than the author's wife. Gabriel leaves for Europe to become a writer after winning a competition. This would be in 1954, in the midst of *la violencia*, when Colombia as a whole was indeed, like Macondo, in an advanced stage of social decomposition. It is to Gabriel that Aureliano, now left behind, had felt closest, for a very important reason. Both knew the story of the strike: 'Aureliano and Gabriel were linked by a sort of complicity, founded on real events in which no one else believed and which had so affected their lives that both were adrift in the wake of a world that was gone, and of which only their own nostalgic longings remained' (p. 329). Once again, could anything be clearer? García Márquez leaves the novel for Paris, but he also remains through the medium of Aureliano, who is so closely linked to him and to José Arcadio Segundo through their shared interpretation of the history of Macondo and of the Buendía family. Moreover, Aureliano is the character who eventually deciphers the parchments (the novel, his own life, Latin American history) on the very last page.

In that hypnotic final section we have the famous metaphor of dialectical decline, which is the Buendía family's historical spiral as understood by Pilar Ternera: '. . . the history of the family was a system of irreparable repetitions, a turning wheel which would have gone on spinning until eternity were it not for the progressive and irremediable wearing of the axle' (p. 334). Needless to say, the family members themselves had perceived no spiral, only cycles of futility: ' "I know this off by heart", shrieked Ursula. "It's as though time were going round in circles and we'd come back to the beginning again" ' (p. 169). 'Once more she shivered at the realization that time did not pass, as she had just acknowledged, but merely went round and round in circles' (p. 284). Then, on the penultimate page, García Márquez explains not so much the nature of the family history as the inner theory of his novel: 'Melquíades had not arranged events in the order of man's conventional time, but had concentrated a whole century of daily episodes in such a way that they coexisted in a single instant' (p. 350). Again, the statement is not a philosophical speculation on the nature of time or the problems of literature, but a historical interpretation of reality in terms of what Cueva calls the 'great structural heterogeneity of Latin American social formations'.[28] This sudden focusing of the literary–structural problems involved in conveying uneven development through the classic bourgeois vehicle of the novel brings us at last to the central question of authorship and readership with which the novel ends.

It is the younger generation, that of García Márquez himself (Aureliano Babilonia and Gabriel), which finally comes to read and write the real history of the continent. They do so precisely by deciphering the magical reality and labyrinthine fantasies of the previous one hundred years of solitude, this very novel, which is their world, and in which so many other characters have been bewitched and bewildered. Hence the mirror/mirage (*espejos/espejismos*) ambiguity on the last page. There we find Aureliano Babilonia – and the author reminds us of his surname – 'deciphering the instant he was living, deciphering it as he lived it', or, as Zea would no doubt argue, negating the past dialectically in order to become, in Paz's phrase, 'contemporary with all men'. Thus he breaks out of false circularities, meaningless repetitions, the prehistory before the dawn of proletarian consciousness. Aureliano's reading literally puts an end to one hundred years of solitude, to *One Hundred Years of Solitude*, and turns the reader who is reading about him back out into the history outside the text.[29] The only remaining question is whether this is a logical outcome to the structural conception of the novel as a whole, or whether García Márquez has merely imposed it in a moment of inspiration, in order to escape, Houdini-like, from the implications of his own pessimistic philosophy. I think not, precisely because, as has been said, this is not so much a literary narration of Latin American history as a 'deconstructionist' reading of that history. Once the characters become able to interpret their own past, the author is able to end on an optimistic note. The apocalypse of the Buendías is not – how could it be? – the end of Latin America but the end of neocolonialism and its conscious or unconscious collaborators.

To those who complain that the novel does not *say* this, we can only ask: What other significance is there in the chain of memory from the Banana massacre through José Arcadio Segundo, Aureliano

Babilonia, the fictional and the real Gabriel García Márquez, and the reader himself? Yet, if this reading is already Cervantine enough ('from Cide Hamete Benengeli to Melquíades the gypsy'), there is a further dimension to unfold. For the new novelists of the 1960s, the two key signs of the impending transformation of Latin America were the Cuban Revolution and the *boom* of the Latin American novel itself.[30] Cuba was perceived by Latin American socialists – and even, for a time, by liberals – as the material conversion of the workers' struggle into historical reality. Looking back from this vantage point, many years later, its seems obvious that the *boom*, which was announced by Julio Cortázar's *Rayuela* (Hopscotch) in 1963, reached its apotheosis with *One Hundred Years of Solitude* in 1967; and that the novel as text is perfectly aware of its own literary–historical signifi-cance, one whose implicit claim is that the *boom* itself is a proof of the end of neocolonialism and the beginning of true liberation. The celebrated 'inter-textual' references to Alejo Carpentier's *El siglo de las luces* (*Explosion in a Cathedral*, 1962), Carlos Fuentes's *La muerte de Artemio Cruz* (*The Death of Artemio Cruz*, 1962), *Rayuela* itself and Mario Vargas Llosa's *La casa verde* (*The Green House*, 1966), are clear signs of this (as compared with, say Borges, whose textual references are overwhelmingly to literatures outside Latin America). The sense of euphoria in the novel, and particularly in its final pages – one can almost hear García Márquez shout *Eureka!* – is palpable. It communi-cates to us the excitement of a writer who has at long last solved his artistic problems by deciphering his own life history, who is aware that in the process he has written a classic, and, not only that, is also conscious that his work will appear at the perfect culminating moment in the political and literary history of his continent, encapsulating that history and his own biography at one and the same time.[31]

To this extent one should perhaps revise the impression of a novel whose two levels, magical and realist, mythical and historical, are entirely inseparable, since after the massacre and the death of Ursula they slowly but surely begin to come apart. The opening of the novel – 'diaphanous', 'recent', bathed in light – is an evocation not only of Latin America's mythical innocence after Independence but of the magical childhood world García Márquez inhabited in Aracataca with his grandfather, the colonel.[32] The endless civil wars in the novel between liberals and conservatives bring no enlightenment, only disillusion and despair. Nevertheless, as the novel wears on and García Márquez himself as narrator gradually metamorphoses from child into adult (finally becoming fully himself only on the last page of the book), the characters slowly, reluctantly come to understand, among other things, what it is that Latin American colonels are generally paid to do, and innocence comes to an end. Whereas at the start of the text the characters are mainly optimistic and forward-looking, by the time the narrative is half-way through they begin to hear the music, not of hope and destiny, but of nostalgia for the past and for innocence itself. Once Ursula loses her residual faith in the purpose and coherence of the present, she dies, and once she has died the solid unity – or mystification – of myth and history is broken. The rest of the novel condenses the decipherment of Colombian history which García Márquez and his generation (especially the Grupo de Barranquilla) carried out in the wake of the 1948 *Bogotazo* (he was twenty years old at the time), when the workers' movement was again denied its place in national life, and on through the dark years of *la violencia*.[33] It seems clear that he was able to do this precisely by having distanced himself from these realities, escaping at last from Colombia, Aracataca, his family 'demons' (to quote Vargas Llosa). This is one more illustration of the truth that Latin American authors can best achieve greatness not through a national, still less a cosmopolitan, perspective but from a continental standpoint: by conceiving themselves as Latin Americans.

Seen in this multiple light, *One Hundred Years of Solitude* is clearly a demystification, though apparently one so labyrinthine in itself that most readers have managed to get themselves as lost in its winding corridors and spiralling stairways as most Latin Americans, including the Buendías, in the 'esperpentic'[34] history which it reconstructs.[35] My belief is that the major works of the boom were largely misread by critics, and that the writers themselves were misled by critical reaction to their texts into misinterpreting them, and thereafter – from about 1968 – into giving the public what they mistakenly thought it wanted. No misreading could be more serious for Latin American literary history than the 'mythreading' of its most celebrated work, *One Hundred Years of Solitude*.

Notes

1 L. Zea, *El pensamiento latinoamericano* (Mexico, 1965), p. 36, quotes Hegel's similar view: 'America is the land of the future . . . It is a country longed for by those who are weary of Europe's historical museum'.
2 M. Deas, 'Politics and Violence: Aspects of *la violencia* in Colombia', *Encounter*, 25:3

(1965), 110–14. The article is invaluable for readers of *One Hundred Years of Solitude*.

3 García Márquez's stamp is already clearly visible in other 'Third World' novels, such as Salman Rushdie's *Midnight's Children*, whose ending is an evident salute to *One Hundred Years of Solitude*: 'because it is the privilege and the curse of midnight's children to be both masters and victims of their times, to forsake privacy and be sucked into the annihilating whirlpool of the multitudes, and to be unable to live or die in peace' (London, 1982, p. 463).

4 A. Dorfman, *Imaginación y violencia en América Latina* (2nd ed., Barcelona, 1972), sees in *One Hundred Years of Solitude* 'an immense expanse of time, in which the individual is swallowed up by history and history is swallowed up in turn by myth' (p. 152).

5 D. L. Shaw, 'Concerning the Interpretation of *Cien años de soledad*', *Ibero-Amerikanisches Archiv*, 3:4 (1977), 318–29 (p. 319).

6 *Ibid*, p. 327.

7 In this sense *One Hundred Years of Solitude* reminds me of Carpentier's *Los pasos perdidos* (*The Lost Steps*, 1953), in which the author draws strength from his own weakness: the central theme becomes his own penchant for rhetoric which, as it immobilizes reality, reveals the inadequacy both of Latin American historiography and literary language in their attempt to capture this new continent's reality. Likewise García Márquez is able to transfer to his characters his own weakness for hyperbole and fabulation, in order to subject it to a critique from the standpoint of his more conscious socialist perspective.

8 Part of the problem with García Márquez – ironically enough, in view of my interpretation of *One Hundred Years of Solitude* – is that he really does appear to have more difficulty than most men in telling literature from reality, fiction from truth. His journalism is full of what I would call *Blacamanismos*, and he can even turn a Salvador Allende into a potential character from one of his own novels: '. . . fate could only grant him that rare and tragic greatness of dying in armed defence of the anachronistic booby of bourgeois law' (*New Statesman*, 15 March 1974, p. 358).

9 A. Rama, 'Un novelista de la violencia americana', in P. S. Martínez (ed.), *Recopilación de textos sobre Gabriel García Márquez* (Havana, 1969), pp. 58–71 (p. 62).

10 J. Mejía Duque, '*El otoño del patriarca*' o la crisis de la desmesura (Bogotá, 1975).

11 My initial impression of *Chronicle of a Death Foretold* (1981) is that we are back in the realm of *No One Writes to the Colonel*, although the pessimism is more pointed: the townsfolk themselves now share a collective guilt which used to be blamed on the 'outsiders'.

12 Rama, 'Un novelista', p. 63.

13 J. Ortega, *La contemplación y la fiesta* (Caracas, 1969), p. 125.

14 J. M. Oviedo, 'Macondo: un territorio mágico y americano', in *Nueve asedios a García Márquez* (3rd ed., Santiago de Chile, 1972), pp. 89–105 (p. 97).

15 E. Völkening, 'Anotado al margen de *Cien años de soledad*', in *Nueva novela latinoamericana*, ed. J. Lafforgue (Buenos Aires, 1969), vol. 1, p. 168.

16 Rama, 'Un novelista', p. 64.

17 I feel that Murena's neglected work, *El pecado original de América*, first published in 1954, has had an immense impact upon García Márquez's vision in *One Hundred Years of Solitude*. Even if this hypothesis is incorrect, a comparative study of the two texts would be illuminating. Another similarly suggestive work by García Márquez's compatriot, Germán Arciniegas, shows that cultural historians also can believe in their continent's magical reality: see the final chapter, 'Appointment with Necromancy', of his *Latin America: a Cultural History* (London, 1969).

18 A. Cueva, 'Para una interpretación sociológica de *Cien años de soledad*', *Revista Mexicana de Sociología*, 36 (1974), 59–76 (p. 67). No reader of *One Hundred Years of Solitude* can overlook this brilliant study.

19 T. Todorov, 'Macondo à Paris', in J. Leenhardt (ed.), *Littérature latino-américaine d'aujourd'hui* (Paris, 1980), pp. 316–34.

20 S. Benvenuto, 'Estética como historia', in *Recopilación de textos*, pp. 167–75 (p. 169).

21 One of the principal students of the phenomenon, E. Anderson Imbert, perceives the dangers of this confusion and then falls into the trap himself. See his '*El realismo mágico*' *y otros ensayos* (Caracas, 1976); also A. Flores, 'Magical Realism in Spanish American Fiction', *Hispania*, 38 (May 1955); and, above all, an invaluable recent study, J. Weisgerber, 'Le réalisme magique: la locution et le concept', *Rivista di Letterature Moderne e Comparate*, 35:1 (1982), 27–53.

22 This, on the whole, is the view taken by Rama, Benvenuto and Cueva in the works already referred to, and by Jean Franco in various studies: significantly for literary history, it is also the view taken in the 1960s by Carlos Fuentes in his 'Macondo, sede del tiempo' (in *Recopilación*, pp. 119–22), and by Mario Vargas Llosa in his 'El Amadís en América' (*Recopilación*, pp. 113–18).

23 *One Hundred Years of Solitude*, p. 296. All references are to the 2nd edition, Buenos Aires, Sudamericana, 1968.

24 C. Blanco Aguinaga's excellent article on this topic, 'Realidad y estilo de Juan Rulfo', in J. Lafforgue (ed.), *Nueva novela latinoamericana* (Buenos Aires, 1969), pp. 85–113, is well known; it is all the more curious, then, that in his study 'Sobre la lluvia y la historia en las ficciones de García Márquez', in his *De mitólogos y novelistas* (Madrid, 1975), he completely misreads the conclusion of *One Hundred Years of Solitude*, failing to see that García Márquez has treated exactly the same phenomenon as Rulfo in almost exactly the same way. Juan Masoliver, 'Los cien engaños de García Márquez', *Bulletin of the Society for Latin American Studies*, 31 (October 1979), 22–37, takes a more judiciously critical but equally stringent view.

25 R. Gullón, *García Márquez o el olvidado arte de contar* (Madrid, 1970).

26 M. Vargas Llosa, *García Márquez: historia de un deicidio* (Barcelona, Barral, 1971). This remains the fundamental source work on García Márquez.

27 A recent documentary anthology, *1928: La masacre en las Bananeras* (Bogotá, n.d.), reprints the parliamentary debates of 1929, and in particular the protests of two politicians, Jorge Eliécer Gaitán and Gabriel Turbay, together with a number of eye-witness accounts, including the vital contribution of none other than the parish priest of Aracataca, Father Francisco Angarita (in a letter dated 16 July 1929). In the introduction the editors claim, like García Márquez in his novel, that 'the official version of Colombian history has tried by every means to omit or distort this bloody episode' (p. 5). Turbay himself had underlined the policy of censorship in a speech on 3 September 1929 when he referred to the 'tragic and horrifying secret of the endless chain of ignominious acts committed during the apocalyptic march of the military through the banana zone'. Fifty years later H. Rodríguez Acosta, in his *Elementos críticos para una nueva interpretación de la historia colombiana* (Bogotá, 1979), would still be making the same point: 'This episode of Colombian history has been repeatedly ignored by our historians because to reveal it would damage the reputation of the ruling class' (p. 203).

28 Cueva, 'Para una interpretación sociológica', p. 59. Cueva's brilliant study fails, in my opinion, to recognize that García Márquez's critique of imperialism is always far more radical than his critique of capitalism itself. This is a feature of the entire *nueva novela* as a historical phenomenon.

29 G. Brotherston indicates this effect in *The Emergence of the Latin American Novel*

(Cambridge, 1977), noting that it ' "opens" the novel to include and involve the reader, as Umberto Eco has defined that process' (p. 135).

30 Thus Mario Vargas Llosa: 'This seems to me a symptom, the sign of great historical changes to come in Latin America... All the great eras of the novel have taken place just before some social apocalypse', quoted in H. Cattolica, 'Vargas Llosa: Europa y el escritor latinoamericano', *El Escarabajo de Oro*, 33 (March 1967), 20–32.

31 In this regard one could draw illuminating comparisons between *Cien años de soledad* and Asturias's *Hombres de maíz*. See my critical edition of the latter, *Hombres de maíz* (Edición Crítica de las Obras Completas de Miguel Angel Asturias, vol. 4, Klincksieck, Paris, and Fondo de Cultura Económica, Mexico, 1981). *One Hundred Years of Solitude* in fact appeared in the year in which Asturias was awarded the Nobel Prize. The two writers, who probably had more in common with one another than with any other Latin American authors except perhaps Rulfo and Guimarães Rosa, evidently recognized their implicit filiation and engaged in a brief and rather vulgar polemic which did neither much credit. Asturias, belatedly crowned, feared the young pretender, and García Márquez, newly acclaimed, was bent on parricide. (Specifically, he vowed that with his new project *El otoño del patriarca*, he would 'teach' the author of *El señor Presidente* 'how to write a real dictator novel'.)

32 M. Vargas Llosa, 'García Márquez: de Aracataca a Macondo', in *Nueve asedios*, pp. 126–46: 'Aracataca was living on its memories when he was born: his fictions, in turn, would live off his memories of Aracataca' (p. 128).

33 This historical thread in fact coincides with that of the life and death of Jorge Eliécer Gaitán, who in 1929 was the principal critic of the government's role in the Banana massacres ('We know to our sorrow that in this country the government points its murderous machine guns at the fatherland's own sons and its trembling knees to the ground in the face of yankee gold'), and whose assassination, as presidential candidate for the Liberal party, led to the 1948 *Bogotazo* and the horrific period of general violence that followed over the next two decades, of which García Márquez's novels *No One Writes to the Colonel* (1958) and *In Evil Hour* (1962) show only the blood-chilling icy tip.

34 Valle-Inclán's term for his grotesque and distorting dramatic vision of Spanish history.

35 There are many novels in Latin America after 1945 about characters whose quests – whether conscious or unconscious – show the reader the way out of the historical labyrinth and at the same time flatter him, to quote Borges on Herbert Quain, that he is 'more perspicacious than the detective'. Examples are Asturias's *Hombres de maíz* (*Men of Maize*, 1949), Marechal's *Adán Buenosayres* (*Adam Buenosaires*, 1948), Carpentier's *Los pasos perdidos* (*The Lost Steps*, 1953), Rulfo's *Pedro Páramo* (1955), Fuentes's *La muerte de Artemio Cruz* (*The Death of Artemio Cruz*, 1962), Cortázar's *Rayuela* (*Hopscotch*, 1963), José Lezama Lima's *Paradiso* (1966), and Vargas Llosa's *La casa verde* (*The Green House*, 1966), all of them Modernist, 'Ulyssean' works completed before the onset of 'Post-Modernism' in the Latin American 1970s. For further consideration of these issues, see my ' "Boom", Yes; "New" Novel, No: Further Reflections on the Optical Illusions of the 1960s in Latin America', *Bulletin of Latin American Research*, 3:2 (1984), 53–63; 'The Literature, Music and Art of Latin America from 1870 to 1930', *Cambridge History of Latin America*, vol. 4 (1986), pp. 443–526; and 'James Joyce and Latin American Fiction' (University of Calgary Press, 1987).

8

Aspects of narrative structure in *The Incredible and Sad Story of the Innocent Eréndira and her Heartless Grandmother*

MARK MILLINGTON

I am going to begin with beginnings. Each story in *ISS*[1] begins with an arrival – a space or a consciousness is invaded by an unknown presence. But the nature of the invading presence differs: in 'Constant Death' and 'Blacamán' it is human (Onésimo Sánchez and Blacamán respectively); in 'Very Old Man' it is part-human (the bird-man); in 'Drowned Man' it was formerly human (Esteban's corpse); in 'Sea' and 'Incredible Story' it is a natural phenomenon (the smell of roses and a wind respectively);[2] and in 'Last Journey' it is an object (the ghost ship). But in four of the stories the source of the invading presence is the same: in one way or another, the sea is associated with the arrival in 'Very Old Man', 'Sea', 'Drowned Man' and 'Last Journey', and in the first two of these the invading presence returns to the sea at the end.[3] And in all of the stories the arrival has the same extraordinary effect – it becomes the focus of widespread, sometimes all-absorbing, attention – and in each case the arrival represents the inception of a series of events that will occupy the remainder of the story. The effect of the arrival is to disrupt – it introduces instability into a pre-existent situation, and that instability produces interest and also movement. The interest stimulated by the new arrival centres on a common reaction in several stories: the need to discover the meaning of the disruption. But the invading presence also seems to produce a release of energy in the characters and so to create a new pattern of life. In both respects the arrival is a beginning – a point of inception.

The fact that in certain stories the characters need to interpret the arrival, to establish the meaning of the invading presence, is a sign of the destabilizing character of the event. The diversity of the interpretations and the confusion felt is most graphically apparent in 'Very Old Man'. Here the desire to understand is powerful but the capacity to comprehend minimal: the bird-man is variously seen by the villagers as a nightmare, a shipwrecked sailor, an angel and a circus animal; and their confusion is shared by the chain of ecclesiastical interpreters extending up to the Vatican, which is notable for its failure to produce even a conjectural interpretation. The same overloading of interpretative skills is evident in 'Drowned Man', where the desire to establish whether Esteban is human is simply swept aside by unquestioning awe in the face of his extraordinary beauty. In both of these cases (and in the other stories with inanimate invasions) the new arrival sets up no dialogue with the community that is invaded – the bird-man and Esteban simply arrive and are observed. They provide no self-explanation, and that accounts, in part, for the disputes that arise as to their nature and even existence (examples of the latter are in 'Sea' and 'Last Journey'). In each case, the interpretations are attempts to accommodate the unknown within everyday frames of knowledge. Given the nature of the new arrivals, the interpretations are not surprising, though they are certainly not definitive either. They also provide a valuable means of assessing the workings of characters' minds, that is, their capacity for rational thought, and this factor is crucial for the reader's response, in potentially stimulating an ironic view of characters.

More important than the question of characters' interpretations is the new direction that their lives take. The change results from the instability that the new arrivals produce, since characters are stimulated to undertake action, and action means change. It is not that any specific response is demanded, any inescapable action forced upon them, but that a field of possibility is opened up. In the case of 'Blacamán' the arrival of Blacamán in the narrator's life effects a transformation: it means leaving home, trying to be a clairvoyant, fleeing from the US marines, suffering at the hands of Blacamán and finally discovering his real gifts for healing the sick and resurrecting the dead, in other words, a multifarious field of new experience. In 'Very Old Man' the bird-man's arrival involves Pelayo and Elisenda willy nilly in trying to cope with the sheer physical problem of crowds of onlookers, and that problem leads to their financial triumph, the building of a luxurious house and a new job for Pelayo: life is transformed. In 'Last Journey' the strength of the general disbelief in the narrator's story about the ship provides the motive for his proving himself and achieving maturity[4] – the ship's intrusion (into his consciousness alone at first) stimulates his resourcefulness and leads him to act decisively. Again, a new direction is taken. Even in the less obvious case of 'Constant Death', a similar structure of new movement is apparent. In this case, the point of view is partially with the new arrival, Onésimo Sánchez, whereas in most stories it is with those intruded upon; but there is also a prior intrusion into Sánchez's consciousness before the start of the story, namely the information that he is about to die. The conjunction of the two new 'arrivals' is what counts, for Sánchez's presence in Rosal del Virrey brings contact with Laura, but the presence of the awareness of death stimulates him to act in a way that is largely contrary to his past behaviour. So the intruding presences again lead to particular forms of innovatory action.

The structure so far isolated, therefore, involves various kinds of invasion or arrival, which sometimes stimulate interpretation but which, above all, destabilize a pre-existent situation and lead to the inception of new movement, new courses of action. And the remarkable feature of the new movement in *ISS* is that the individuals involved, who first perceive the intruding presence, are frequently joined by the whole community – a broad expansion takes place, which makes the disequilibrium a shared and festive event. There is a multiplication of interest which often extends beyond the bounds of the local population. The fair motif is central to this expansion. In 'Very Old Man' the bird-man's arrival initially affects only Pelayo and Elisenda, but overnight there is a large influx of people from the neighbourhood (pp. 12–13) and subsequently of huge crowds of people from far and wide who stretch in a line over the horizon waiting to see the prodigy (p. 15). This influx brings with it a variety of fairground performers from around the Caribbean who temporarily transform the community – life undergoes a process of carnivalization.[5] A similar kind of response follows on the news of Esteban's arrival in 'Drowned Man':

Some women who had gone to fetch flowers in the neighbouring towns returned with other women who didn't believe what they had been told, and these others went for more flowers when they saw the dead man, and they brought more and more, till there were so many flowers and so many people that it was almost impossible to walk. (p. 55)

And likewise in 'Sea' three outsiders go away and return with a great crowd of people who bring with them a variety of fairground acts and festivities; their arrival poses the same problems as in 'Drowned Man': 'The men and the woman who came to Catarino's store went away one Friday, but they came back on the Saturday with a crowd. More came on the Sunday. They swarmed everywhere, looking for something to eat and somewhere to sleep, till it was impossible to walk along the street' (p. 32).

These influxes are experienced from the standpoint of the places which are invaded, but a reverse perspective exists in 'Blacamán' where the protagonists are the invading fairground performers. Indeed, 'Blacamán' opens by exploiting and extending an archetypal fairground frame: Blacamán stands on a table selling a patent medicine and verbally and physically performs his way to success. The narrator joins him in his exploits and ultimately becomes a showman whom the crowds flock to see – the fair becomes a permanent way of life for him. 'Constant Death' draws on the same frame; in this case, the fair or carnival is Sánchez's election campaign. The trappings of the campaign create the same fairground atmosphere as in Blacamán's performance. Standing on his platform, Sánchez presents his case to the people in a euphoric and histrionic verbal *tour de force*, while his helpers build an illusion of a secure future – in effect, a promise that carnival will take over permanently.

[These phrases] were the formulas of his circus. Whilst he spoke, his helpers threw into the air handfuls of small, paper birds, and the pretend animals took on life, fluttered over the wooden platform, and went away out to sea. At the same time, others took out of the wagons theatrical trees with felt leaves and set them up behind the crowd on the ground of saltpetre. Finally they put together a cardboard façade showing imitation redbrick houses with glass windows, and with it blocked from view the squalid slums of real life.

(p. 61)

Nelson Farina's description (in French) makes the point about Blacamán's and Sánchez's similar techniques incisively: ' "Shit . . . he's the Blacamán of politics" ' (p. 63).

The same perspective is apparent in 'Incredible Story'; again the viewpoint is with the travelling performers – the carn(iv)al[6] entertainment provided by Eréndira – and again there is a process of expansion as Eréndira and her grandmother gain experience and money (they buy a circus tent, p. 134), and as they are joined by lottery-ticket sellers, a photographer, a band and foodstalls. Eventually their presence in a town seems to convert it into a single, huge brothel and gambling den; the queue waiting for Eréndira,

. . . comprising men of varied race and diverse condition, seemed like a snake with human vertebrae that was dozing across plots of land and squares, through many-coloured bazaars and noisy markets, and emerged from the streets of that deafening city of traders in transit. Every street was a public gambling house, every street a bar, every door a refuge for fugitives.

(p. 145)

The process of carnivalization and the capacity for extension could scarcely be more vivid.

This move into expansion and carnivalization amplifies the localized effects of new arrivals; it is a consistent structural motif throughout *ISS*, but there is no precise repetition of detail in each story; it is a general rhythm and developmental strategy.

It is appropriate to move from that general framework of development to the specifics of the structural relations between the events in the narrative thread. In some stories there is not a strong sense of necessary connection. It is clear that the narrative line may not depend on strict relations of causality. The sequence of narrated events can be fairly contingent, though chronological time *is* predominant. This is most noticeable in 'Incredible Story' and 'Sea', which are fairly episodic, and where the cause and effect relations between events are therefore rather weak. What narrative coherence there is may derive from other factors. In 'Sea', especially, there are many discrete phases and minor sequences – either involving new situations, or new characters in repeated situations. Exemplifying the former are the multiple and somewhat haphazard facets of Sr Herbert's 'philanthropic' activities, and exemplifying the latter the different responses of Tobías and Petra to the arrival of the smell of roses. In addition, the lack of a constant protagonist in 'Sea' reinforces the episodic quality. The story is dependent for coherence on the stability of time and place reference, and on two general situational contexts, which appear in succession in the story but have no causal connection: the response to the rose smell, and the revelries of the carnival.

'Incredible Story' lacks the coherence provided by a single setting, but it does have a fairly constant trio of protagonists. Even though the specifics of situation change rapidly from one section to the next, often with no causal link between them (sections six and seven being exceptions), there is an implicit, underlying problem that is constant: will Eréndira ever be free of her grandmother's tyranny? But this may come through as a clear, cohesive thread only at a late stage – it is not foregrounded until the end of section six – and that deferral contributes to the episodic character of the story. Similarly 'Blacamán' has no tight narrative line – one episode is not linked closely to the next – and that is emphasized by the summarizing narration, in which a general description of events bypasses the specifics of sequential narrative.

Clearly the sheer demands of writing involve a certain line, one which reading inevitably retraces at a basic level of contact, but the episodic character of some stories is made yet more apparent by considering two other factors which, conventionally, provide cohesion. The first is that characters rarely have overt or identifiable goals or plans of actions – and there is no inner discourse or monologue to make any plain. (Again, the quality of characters' minds is made apparent negatively.) That particular absence is obvious in 'Incredible Story', where, as I have suggested, the long-term problem, 'Will Eréndira ever be free?', is clearly alluded to only near the end. 'Last Journey' is remarkable as an exception, in that the narrator declares his basic aim in the first line and the whole story is built around showing how it is achieved. The second factor is the lack of any mystery or tension to resolve; this kind of element would provide a strong sense of direction and a high level of coherence, that is, coherence with clear relevance to the semantic core of a story, as against the second order coherence of time, place, and character. Mystery or tension might provide tighter relations in the narrative sequence, but there is little use of either.

Given that some of the stories do not rely heavily on strong causal links to sustain forward movement, it is interesting to consider how endings are achieved. If there is little causal emphasis, what relation can an ending have with what precedes it? Is there any evidence to suggest that the endings in *ISS* act as points of culmination or resolution? And, if not, how does each story create a 'sense of an ending'? The key factor here is departure. Most of the stories rely on departures to provide a 'sense of an ending', that is to create an impression that a 'natural' cycle has been completed: the departure terminates what the arrival inaugurated, which is something that readers can accept by drawing on cultural knowledge and without needing an explanation of how or why it came about. 'Very Old Man' ends with the growth of the bird-man's feathers which creates the possibility of flight and departure. The ending of 'Sea' depends on departures too, implicit ones: the rose smell seems to vanish, Sr Herbert bids farewell and the crowd of people which overwhelmed the town goes away also. But these departures are not culminations; they are no more than an indication that the carnival is over. Both

'Constant Death' and 'Incredible Story' end with deaths – that is, departures of a sort – but in neither case is it a culmination or resolution; in 'Constant Death' the death of Sánchez simply fulfils a doctor's prognosis;[7] and in 'Incredible Story' the grandmother's death provides no liberation for Eréndira and Ulises, at least in no obvious way, since Eréndira disappears and abandons Ulises. In both stories, therefore, the death/departure is a satisfactory termination without providing a definitive step forward or insight.

'Drowned Man' and 'Last Journey' offer a different, more causal structure. 'Drowned Man', it is true, does end with a departure – Esteban is thrown back into the sea, he is given a second burial – but, as well as representing the end of a cultural cycle (the preparation of a body for burial), it also marks a moment of crucial insight for the villagers. The whole story is based on the single task of preparing the body for burial – this gives it a tighter integration than most of the other stories – and therefore the ending, the burial, is a culmination, is a climax directly related to the preceding events and given extra weight by the coincidental resolution of the villagers to change their outlook on life. Similarly, 'Last Journey' has a climactic ending (this time with no departure motif) which is the direct outcome of a particular resolution brought to fruition. By contrast, the ending of 'Very Old Man' (not untypically) seems to be underdetermined; it is pointless to ask why the bird-man's feathers grow and why he flies away, since there is no cause other than the need to provide a narrative ending.

This type of ending leaves us with a global structure as a basis for most of the stories: arrival–reaction and expansion–departure. But the symmetry of this structure is deceptively attractive. It is deceptive because it provides a neat representation which fails to take into account an important aspect of the stories: their elusiveness. It is not that this structure is wrong, simply that it does not tell us enough. Above all, this pattern seems 'closed', where the stories are teasingly 'open' – that is, they are thematically reticent while foregrounding elements of a highly imaginative and problematic sort. There is a need, therefore, to question any simple, closed representation. One way to modify the neatness of the first representation is by looking at the reversals which contribute to the instability of the stories; and one way to begin trying to make sense of their openness – without reducing the stories to statements of what they are 'about', which would impose closure from 'outside' – is to examine the fair motif.

The reversals in *ISS* consist of transpositions of a limited number of initial ideas into new configurations. This is a consistent trend and 'Blacamán' will serve as a first example of it. The crucial reversal here concerns power. Blacamán's initial position of authority over the narrator is inverted by the end of the story – where Blacamán was strong and cruel, the narrator becomes so. And this is emphasized by the repetition of certain details: at the end the narrator gives a public performance by the sea at Santa María del Darién (pp. 92–3) just as Blacamán does at the very start (pp. 83–5), and he uses exactly the same forms of words as Blacamán.[8] Clearly there is a comprehensive reversal here, and it is inseparable from repetition; there is a repetition of forms with variation of agents or characters; in other words, substantial repetition of detail is accompanied by strategic variation, and both repetition and variation are crucial to the existence of the reversal. Here we find some of the paradoxical complexity of *ISS*: the narrative line depends on forms of repetition, the repetition involves strategic variation, and strategic variation helps constitute reversal.

'Last Journey' also depends on interlocking repetitions and reversals. And this is not simply a matter of people's believing the narrator at the end where they do not do so for the bulk of the story. Belief/disbelief *is* an important polarity, but there are also others: not seeing/seeing, dark/light, silence/sound, illusion/reality. Now the story is advanced by annual repetitions of the same events: the town and the narrator's mother do not see the shipwreck, but the narrator does; the narrator believes that the silent shipwreck is real, but others believe it is an illusion. These polarities are reinforced by the unexpected effects of darkness and light: though it arrives at night the ship shows no light as it passes the lighted buoys in the bay, and it is visible to the narrator only when the lighthouse throws no light on it (p. 73). But the final repetition introduces multiple variations and repetitions: the positions of light and darkness are inverted – the lights on the ship suddenly blaze as the lights on the buoys go out; the ship produces normal noises (from engines and passengers); and the whole town sees the shipwreck – it happens as a real, shared experience. So the experience is repeated again, but only partially; the shipwreck is broadly the same for the narrator (only light and sound differ), but it is totally different for other people – in other words, it takes place. There is a reversal, and one which abolishes the polarities which seemed to define the initial conflict; there is a repetition with major variations, the elements being thrown into a new configuration, displaced not enough to obscure the repetition of a general framework, but enough to resemanticize it. Again there is a slightly paradoxical structure since the narrative thread relies on repetition, and that repetition contributes to the existence of reversals, and both repetition and reversal seem to run counter to the notion of narrative thread, suggesting a process of return or folding back rather than of forward movement.

The sheer variety of the reversal/repetition structures will be evident by looking at a final example. At the start of 'Constant Death' the positions of the two main characters are as follows: Onésimo Sánchez, the senator seeking re-election, is a man with power, an insider from the legal point of view, a man with a certain future, namely imminent death; Nelson Farina is a man with a guilty past because of death (he has murdered his wife) and this makes him an outsider legally speaking, a man with an uncertain future. Preceding the events in the story is a past of interaction between Farina and Sánchez – Farina has repeatedly petitioned Sánchez for a false identity card to put him on the right side of the law, and he has been unsuccessful; by contrast, Sánchez has himself repeatedly petitioned the town's voters for their support in elections and been successful. This pattern of polarities in the past is a crucial point of reference for the events in the story. The events repeat and vary those of the past. This time Sánchez is dogged by recent news of his own impending death, it dominates him as death has formerly dominated Farina, and it alters the course of his day-to-day life: his decision-making is affected and also his attitude to others; this is a reversal of his former position. But there is also repetition here in so far as Farina petitions Sánchez again, tempting him with his daughter, Laura, and this time he is successful since he acquires legal, insider status and a safe future, a reversal of his former position. Sánchez acquires Laura, but their relationship causes scandal – they are social outsiders as Farina was before. So the positions are reversed, though the basic detail and points of reference (death, legality, past/future) are repeated. The narrative has moved forward, but it has done so by going back. In this story and others the attractiveness of reversals for the structure is surely that they obviate the need to introduce external or new factors – the focus of a story is tightly delimited to a working out or exploitation of given material, and that circumscribes and minimizes the scope of a story: a first principle of the genre. Moreover, reversals also provide a strong sense of balance – the process of reconfiguration achieves a clear impression of completeness, of a movement finished, of an absolute realignment not susceptible to further modification. Clearly this reinforces the 'sense of an ending' in some stories as an addition to the departure motif discussed on pp. 122–3.

There remains the question of *ISS*'s thematic reticence. How might some thematic focus be located? This is an especially acute question in so far as *Big Mama's Funeral* shows a consistent focus on human confrontation, on the nature of human resourcefulness, and even (implicitly) on psychology; with the exception of 'Big Mama's Funeral', that collection shows little of the festive expansiveness of *ISS*, which is nearer the status of 'pure fiction'. But to talk of 'reticence' is not another way of describing 'emptiness', that is, a way of saying 'these stories are simple *divertissements*'. The apparently closed, linear pattern – arrival–reaction and expansion–departure – in its sheer visibility can suggest the need to probe more deeply into the stories; that linear pattern may be visible in inverse proportion to the 'visibility' of meaning – in this case, to isolate structures is clearly not to have exhausted the stories. Derrida states this point with clarity in an early essay: 'the relief and design of structures appears more clearly when content, which is the living energy of meaning, is neutralized'.[9] The word 'expansion' which I have used might give further pause for thought, suggesting as it does an openness which formal analysis may overlook. The idea of openness is precisely what the fair motif tends to foreground.

The fair motif is, or accompanies, an intrusion into the narrative space in *ISS* – it constitutes or reinforces a radical disequilibrium in life patterns; in this way it represents a potential opening or transformation. And in that connection the fair motif can be examined in the light of what Bakhtin calls popular-festive forms or carnivals. Bakhtin's theorization is useful:

Carnival is a pageant without a stage and without a division into performers and spectators. In the carnival everyone is an active participant, everyone communes in the carnival act. Carnival is not contemplated, it is, strictly speaking, not even played out; its participants *live* in it, they live according to its laws, as long as those laws are in force, i.e. they live a *carnivalistic life*. The carnivalistic life is life drawn out of its *usual rut*, it is to a degree 'life turned inside out', 'life the wrong way round' ('monde à l'envers').

The laws, prohibitions and restrictions which determine the system and order of normal, i.e. non-carnival, life are for the period of carnival suspended; above all, the hierarchical system and all the connected forms of fear, awe, piety, etiquette, etc. are suspended, i.e. everything that is determined by social-hierarchical inequality among people, or any other form of inequality, including age.   (pp. 100–1)

Carnival celebrates change itself, the very process of replaceability . . .

(p. 103)[10]

The stress here is on newness, on the potential for change, on living in a radically different way from before, if only for the duration of the festivity. In that perspective the fairs or carnivals of *ISS* are recognizable as stimuli for change ('Sea' and 'Very Old Man') or as ways of life ('Blacamán' and 'Incredible Story').

But the key question is: 'How much really changes or is transformed in *ISS*?' The answer is that there is some variation. In 'Very Old Man' there is real transformation; the fair builds on and exceeds the arbitrary arrival of the bird-man and it helps Pelayo and Elisenda to gain new social status by allowing them to earn money from the curiosity the bird-man is. Here the change outlasts the festivity. Sánchez in 'Constant Death' arrives accompanied by the trappings of a fair and again life's normality is pushed aside and things are transformed; the special, carnivalesque circumstances aid the reversal in fortunes of Farina and Sánchez. But there is also a passage in the story showing another, temporary, transformation, the rare contact between the man of power and the people. Sánchez ostentatiously moves among them dispensing limited largesse in order to win their support. Here is an important transformation, as the people's power – their vote – is solicited and a utopian future is promised. Sánchez is briefly in need and the people's needs are satisfied by his bestowing gifts. This passage is entirely in the spirit of the carnival defined by Bakhtin.

In 'Blacamán' the narrator's life is transformed by Blacamán's carnivalesque existence – his talent for resurrection is discovered and that brings him wealth and apparently satisfaction too. The intrusion of Esteban in 'Drowned Man' stimulates carnivalesque activity which leads to the long-term transformation of the villagers' attitudes – they become industrious and productive as never before. By contrast, in 'Incredible Story' the characters are the fair, but no clear transformation is effected; and in 'Sea' the fair takes over people's lives but only temporarily. And this last case is perhaps the most interesting since in some details it comes closest to Bakhtin's description; for in 'Sea' the fair covers a certain period of time and then disappears leaving things as before, and this pattern is clearly that of the real carnivals that Bakhtin describes. In Bakhtin's theory the promise of social reorganization, of new futures, of hierarchies levelled is not sustained. In *ISS* there is no clear social implication to the transformations effected, but these transformations *are* sustained in several cases – the fair/carnival is not simply an institutionalized release of frustration, a circumscribed, annual event; openings are responded to and the carnival impulse is not always lost. And this impulse does alert the reader to a certain thematic focus and consistency throughout, without providing definite propositions or monopolizing attention.[11]

I will end by attempting to analyse the structure of the narrative space created in *ISS*. I want to suggest a way of understanding the kind of narrative world that exists in *ISS*; that is, by trying to establish the nature and consistency of the relations that hold between the actual world and the narrative world, I want to propose an analytical approach to the comprehension of the stories' narrative space.

In discussing the way all discourse is comprehended, Teun van Dijk has stressed the importance of knowledge frames[12]. He defines these as follows:

Frames are knowledge representations about the 'world' which enable us to perform such basic cognitive acts as perception, action, and language comprehension.   (p. 19)

We propose that frames define units or chunks of concepts which are not essentially, but *typically*, related. Some intuitive examples may clarify this point. Conceptually, there is no immediate or essential relation between the concept of 'table' and the concept of 'cereal', nor between 'soap' and 'water', nor between 'waitress' and 'menu'. They are distinct and do not presuppose each other. Yet, they are organized by the frames of 'breakfast', 'washing' and 'restaurant', respectively. They usually denote certain normal courses of events or courses of actions involving several objects, persons, properties, relations, and facts . . . It is in this sense that frames are higher-level organizing principles. They unify concepts of various types and at various levels of representation under the constraint of typicality and normality.
                                                        (p. 21)

. . . Frames . . . are conventional and general. Most members of a society or culture have approximately the same set of frames.   (p. 22)

Van Dijk points out that these frames act as a crucial part of our horizon of expectation and comprehension in processing all discourse (including literature), and it is clear that they complement whatever conventions may hold within any specific discourse. The reliance of discourse on knowledge frames is evident in its capacity to be comprehended without recourse to totalizing explanation. Discourse is efficient and concise; it can elide information precisely because it can rely on triggering knowledge frames in its audience – it can rely on shared experience.[13] This is a basic assumption which is operative in discourse processing by default; that is, unless there is any indication to the contrary, it seems that normal knowledge frames are operative.

This basic assumption is apparent in innumerable details of *ISS*: the reader can be relied upon to attach the appropriate frame to single actions that in global terms form part of, for instance, having breakfast, making love, or attempting murder. Similarly, global action need only be alluded to for a knowledge frame to fill it out: playing draughts, selling a patent medicine, attempting to corrupt a politician. These bits of knowledge are trivial because they correspond to a possible or actual world of experience, and the input of information by the reader is, therefore, effortless, even unconscious, whatever the specific detail of the narrative.

But the key point is that much of the force of *ISS* derives from the deviation from knowledge frames. If one defines a 'possible world' as one that is constructed and comprehended in terms of knowledge frames of the actual world (in specific combination or permutation), then it is evident that *ISS* constructs only partially possible worlds; it blurs or subverts the normal structures of the actual world. Some examples of blurring or subversive phenomena or actions which are 'facts' within the stories will make the point more clearly. In 'Very Old Man' the spider-woman has an explanation for her condition: she is not a fairground curiosity; her condition is real just as that of the bird-man himself is real, and this blurs the normal distinction between the fairground and the real world. In 'Sea', Tobías goes swimming with Sr Herbert, but what happens beneath the surface exceeds the limits of the actual world; it is not just that they spend a large amount of time under water without breathing equipment and that they can hold subaquatic conversations too, but that they see people living there and flowers growing. Sr Herbert explains these things to Tobías, but the explanation cannot satisfy the reader's actual world knowledge. In 'Very Old Man', a cultural knowledge frame is subverted when it becomes obvious that the supposed angel displays only one feature characteristic of an angel: he has wings. Otherwise he is physically unimpressive, withdrawn, passive, fails to understand Latin and is ultimately a domestic nuisance.

There are more remarkable cases in which physical laws within our knowledge frames are overridden with no attempt at explanation. Where the first two examples above involve the infringement of physical laws there is an implicit recognition of this in so far as pseudo-explanations are provided. This is not so with the paper butterfly which knocks into the wall and becomes part of the wallpaper in 'Constant Death' (pp. 65–6); nor with the oranges that grow with diamonds inside them in 'Incredible Story' (p. 135); nor with the narrator of 'Blacamán' who brings back to life a rabbit (p. 90) and then Blacamán too, repeatedly (p. 94); nor with Eréndira's grandmother who has green blood (p. 161) and who fails to succumb to a massive dose of rat-poison (pp. 155–8).

These details help to define the position of the stories relative to the actual world; often the knowledge frames of the actual world are indispensable in reading, but there are also significant deviations from or transgressions of this ensemble of structured knowledge. So, in part, *ISS* is aligned with and, in part, sits athwart actual knowledge frames. And the area of discrepancy does sometimes extend to the conscious actions and the minds of characters. Not only is there no rational critique of events by characters from within the stories – that is a viewpoint potentially equivalent to that of the reader – but the characters frequently add to the number of deviations. So Tobías is satisfied by Sr Herbert's dubious explanations in 'Sea' (p. 42); Blacamán thinks that he can cure his bad luck by mortifying the narrator of 'Blacamán' (pp. 89–90); the army officer in 'Incredible Story' shoots at the clouds to make it rain (p. 122); in 'Constant Death' Sánchez takes his analgesics before feeling pain in order to feel relief first, thus reversing rational practice (p. 60); and, perhaps above all, Eréndira freely decides to return to her grandmother in 'Incredible Story', having been saved from her exploiting grasp and having enjoyed her new life, and with no guarantee of better treatment in the future (p. 130). Here characters' minds, thoughts, actions and motivations run counter to frames of knowledge about or models of rationality in the actual world.

In this way the narrative space seems rather idiosyncratic. And so a final question must be posed concerning the position of narrators. The narrators' position could theoretically provide a gauge of events or behaviour; it could align the global point of view with that of the reader and his/her knowledge frames; it could constitute an internal reference point of critical distance. In fact, the question of the narrators' position is quite complex. In the first place the authority and mediation of the narrators in *ISS* is more or less uniform. This is the case regardless of whether the narrator speaks with a first or a third person voice, though the latter is more common.[14] So there is no lack of

authoritative set-pieces on characters or context: the narrator of
'Constant Death' knows Sánchez's secret about his imminent death
(p. 60) and has the knowledge to begin the story with a summary of its
main points (p. 59); the narrator of 'Incredible Story' can identify the
importance of the wind in section one and anticipate the disaster it will
create (pp. 97 and 99); in section four of the same story the narrator
can sketch in the pertinent details of the campaign to persuade
prostitutes to marry (p. 128); and in 'Sea' the narrator can give
information about the dead Petra, floating in the Bay of Bengal,
knowledge which no character possesses (p. 32). This authority and
mediating power – plus the capacity to name and classify, and the
control of chronological progress – doubtless create a certain
consistency and clarity. But the question is to see how that authority
and mediation are used. Do they carry out the task of distancing
critique mentioned above? The answer is that they do not. The
narrators' authority is partial; it is used to register scenes and to fill in
certain contextual gaps, but it is not used to justify, explain or question
what the characters do or what phenomena are. So, for example, in
'Incredible Story' the close vigilance of Ulises by his parents during
the orange picking (p. 131), the placing of the picked oranges in the
safe (p. 133), and Ulises's need to pick three oranges before running
away from home (p. 134), are not explained by the narrator. It
happens that Ulises shows Eréndira that the oranges contain
diamonds (p. 135), but while this gives a certain retrospective
clarification, it actually adds more confusion to the situation. On
occasions such as this, the narrators' silence, the lack of authoritative,
rational discourse, is an important feature. The narrators do not
rationalize; they do not analyse; they rather present events as if they
were 'simple facts', even if these 'facts' deviate substantially from our
knowledge frames. This is curious in so far as their authority seems to
imply a capacity for rationalizing distance; but, in fact, the narrators'
viewpoint is closer to the characters than to the reader. Very often the
'seeing eye' of narration is that of one aligned with a character's
viewpoint or with an amalgamation of characters' viewpoints.[15] And
this is hardly surprising since the narrative structure, the relations
between narrative world and actual world, would be inconsistent and
simplified if the narrators cut through the complexities of the other
features I have described. The gaps and uncertainties are crucial and
exist in terms of the relation actual/narrative worlds. To have recourse
to such labels as fairy stories or children's stories to describe *ISS* would

be to seek security and closure by removing the stories into an unworldly, 'purely literary' frame of reference (if such a concept is anything more than wishful thinking). The fissures in our knowledge frames that are created, and the consequent uncertainty potentially stimulated in our reading, are surely consistent with the basic thrust of the fair or carnival motif: namely, to open up and transform.

Notes

1 Gabriel García Márquez, *La increíble y triste historia de la cándida Eréndira y de su abuela desalmada*, (Buenos Aires), Sudamericana, 1976: (5th ed.). Abbreviations used:
   The Incredible and Sad Story . . .: ISS
   'A Very Old Man with Enormous Wings': 'Very Old Man'
   'The Sea of Lost Time': 'Sea'
   'The World's Most Beautiful Drowned Man': 'Drowned Man'
   'Constant Death beyond Love': 'Constant Death'
   'The Last Journey of the Ghost Ship': 'Last Journey'
   'Blacamán the Good, Miracle Seller': 'Blacamán'
   'The Incredible and Sad Story . . .': 'Incredible Story'
2 In the case of 'Incredible Story' it might be argued that there is a second arrival of equal significance when Ulises appears in section three; it is not just that he has such striking looks, but also that the relationship that develops between him and Eréndira is crucial to the story's structure.
3 It is also worth noting that in the remaining three stories the sea is not absent; in 'Blacamán' the opening and final paragraphs are set by the sea; in 'Incredible Story' there is gradual progress, from section five into section six, towards the sea, and moreover Ulises promises Eréndira the sea; and in 'Constant Death' the whole story is set in a coastal town.
4 The reference to his 'new, deep, man's voice' (p. 73) is an obvious sign of newly gained maturity.
5 See below pp. 126–8 for a more detailed treatment of this carnivalization process.
6 The etymology of the word 'carnival' seems to suggest that it derives from Latin – 'carnem levare', to put away flesh or 'carne vale', farewell to flesh – the Roman carnival being celebrated just before the fasting of Lent. The word is now loosely interchangeable with the word 'fair'.
7 This ending may be a piece of ironic play with Francisco de Quevedo's sonnet, 'Amor constante más allá de la muerte' ('Constant Love beyond Death'): not only does García Márquez invert Quevedo's title, but where the sonnet ends with a declaration that the poet's love can survive even death, the story ends by showing the unavoidably destructive effect a corrupt politician's death has on his love.
8 The interlocking of positions is emphasized by the references to good and bad in the story. At an early stage the narrator establishes a distinction between himself and Blacamán: 'That's how he was Blacamán, the bad, because the good one is me' (p. 86). And yet the title of the story refers to Blacamán as 'the good', which leads one to transfer 'the bad' to the narrator as well, especially as he is as much a torturer in the end as Blacamán was at the beginning.
9 Jacques Derrida, 'Force and Signification', in *Writing and Difference*, translated by Alan Bass (London, 1981), p. 5.
10 Mikhail Bakhtin, *Problems of Dostoevsky's Poetics*, translated by R. W. Rotsel (Ann Arbor, 1973).

11 The carnival motif is recurrent throughout the work of García Márquez: in the atmosphere and political repercussions of the cockfight in *No One Writes to the Colonel*; in the gypsy intrusions in *One Hundred Years of Solitude* which so transform Macondo and the world-view of José Arcadio Buendía; in the solidarity and collective festivities of the people in *Autumn of the Patriarch*; and in the marriage celebrations and the collective greetings of the bishop in *Chronicle of a Death Foretold*.

12 Teun van Dijk, 'Semantic Macro-Structures and Knowledge Frames in Discourse Comprehension', in *Cognitive Processes in Comprehension*, ed. M. A. Just and P. A. Carpenter (Hillsdale, NJ, 1977).

13 The word 'shared' conceals a problematic situation. In dealing with a Latin American text the European or North American critic faces the perennial difficulty of deciding how to align him-/herself with the Latin American context. To what extent is there a shared context, even in Latin America? And who is the probable audience for *ISS*, since it is clearly not people like those in the stories? There are no simple answers to these questions, but it remains of vital importance for critics to be aware of these issues and so of the precarious nature of their enterprise.

14 Only in 'Blacamán' is the first person voice used throughout; in 'Incredible Story' a first person voice does emerge briefly at the start of section six (pp. 145 and 148), but the bulk of the story is in the third person.

15 For the crucial distinctions between narrative voice and narrative viewpoint see G. Genette, 'Discours du récit', in *Figures III* (Paris, 1972), pp. 203–6. English translation, *Narrative Discourse*, translated by Jane Lewin (Ithaca, 1980).

9

Language and power in *The Autumn of the Patriarch*

JO LABANYI

Language and power are closely linked. We use language to persuade, that is, to manipulate others into acquiescence. We call a statement true if it has power over us. The authority of language derives from the notion of authorship, the assumption that language is the direct expression of a central, unified voice. The statement which does not have a clear relationship to the voice that speaks it does not have authority. Reported speech is less authoritative than direct speech because its relationship to its source has become adulterated. Writing, as Derrida has shown, is frequently regarded as an extreme form of reported – and therefore adulterated – speech.[1] As a novel about power, *The Autumn of the Patriarch* is inevitably concerned with the expression of power via language, and particularly via the written word. It is a disconcerting novel, because it depicts a dictator who is not directly responsible for his commands, but becomes their prisoner. García Márquez's creation of a powerless tyrant looks, at first sight, politically naive. The novel can be read, however, not as an attempt to exonerate dictators of their crimes, but as an exploration of the relationship between power and language. This relationship is shown to work in two directions. On the one hand, language is the patriarch's principal instrument of power. On the other, it is his increasing delegation of power to language that brings about his downfall. García Márquez shows that language can undermine power as well as enforce it.

The power of speech is referred to at the beginning of the novel. 'We did not have to force an entry, as we had thought, because the main door seemed to yield to the mere force of the human voice' (p. 7).[2] The patriarch's authority resides in his voice: 'he spat out a lethal blast of authority with his words' (p. 73). But, for most of the novel, the patriarch exercises his power via reported speech. His voice is not heard directly, but his commands are relayed at second hand from an invisible centre of power. He is a dictator in the literal sense of the word, someone who dictates his words to others. To be more precise, the 'autumn' of his reign is inaugurated by the transition from direct to reported speech. Decadence sets in when he ceases to be a presence and becomes a legend, heard but not seen. The dependence of the patriarch's authority on hearsay is underlined by the repeated ironic use in the novel of the phrase 'we saw', when what is meant is that the people see only what legend has told them.[3] They see the dead patriarch not as he actually died, but as the prophecy had said he would. They have no way of checking the authentic identity of the corpse, because they can measure what they see only against a remote chain of verbal accounts:

Only when we turned him over to see his face did we realize there was no way of recognizing him . . . because none of us had ever seen him and although his profile was on both sides of all the coins . . . we knew they were copies of copies of portraits which were deemed unfaithful at the time of the comet, when our parents knew who he was because they had been told by their parents, as they had been told by theirs.   (p. 8)

Seeing has been replaced by hearing.

The patriarch's reliance on reported speech strengthens his power in the sense that his existence via second-hand verbal repetitions leads to the attribution to him of a superhuman ubiquity. What this really means is that he is nowhere, except in the form of words. In effect, the replacement of the patriarch's presence by hearsay adulterates his authority, inasmuch as it leads to a usurpation of his voice: 'On many occasions it was held that he had lost his voice from so much speaking and had ventriloquists posted behind the curtains pretending he was speaking' (p. 49). The first chapter of the novel specifies that the patriarch's 'autumn' begins with his recourse to a double, who replaces him on most of his public appearances. García Márquez points out that the one area where the double is not able to provide an exact replica of the original is that of speech: ' "That's me damn it", he said, because it was, indeed, as if it were he, except for the authority of his voice, which the double had never learnt to imitate properly' (p. 14). The linguistic nature of the usurpation is emphasized by the fact that the double has a name (Patricio Aragonés), while the patriarch has none. The patriarch's voice has passed to a substitute; language has become independent of its source.

The patriarch's recourse to reported speech creates a power vacuum, as authority comes to reside increasingly in the words themselves rather than in the voice from which they originate. The more he conceals his presence, the more absolutely his commands are obeyed, to the extent that they begin to be obeyed without him even voicing them: 'all in accord with an order he had not given but which was an order of his beyond any doubt my general because it had the imperturbable firmness of his voice and the incontrovertible style of his authority' (p. 178). The mere thought that it would be preferable for his wife and son to be dead rather than live daily with the fear of their death leads to their murder. 'It was like a thunderous command not yet articulated when his aides burst into his office with the ghastly news that Leticia Nazareno and the child had been torn to pieces and devoured by the dogs' (p. 199). Language, having become independent of its master, has turned against him.

From this point on, the patriarch's role as the absent centre of command makes him increasingly dependent on the reports of the outside world that he receives from his informers. Since these reports reflect back at him the commands he had previously issued, he becomes trapped in a series of mirror-reflections: 'a captive monarch . . . dragging his heavy feet through the dark mirrors' (pp. 215–16). In the same way, he comes to rely on information extracted under torture which, again, reflects back at him what he wants to see. The ironic leitmotif 'we saw' is paralleled by the equally ironic 'he saw'. Like the people, the patriarch does not see reality but hears his own legend. 'He had seen this and many other things in that remote world although not even he could be sure whether they really were memories or tales he had heard' (p. 173). By the end of the novel, the patriarch has become symbolically deaf to the outside world – 'deaf like a mirror' (p. 131) – able to hear only the noise of the silence inside his own head.

The ironic confusion of seeing with hearing is at its most amusing when the patriarch notices outside his window the three caravels of Christopher Columbus which his informers have told him about. In this scene, something important has happened: the three caravels are derived indirectly from a written text – Columbus's diary – from which García Márquez quotes to reinforce the point. Seeing here has become confused not just with hearing but also with reading. The patriarch is forced to rely on second-hand oral reports, because at this stage in the novel he is still illiterate. The absurd logic of this scene implies that, if the written word has the authority with which the patriarch credits it, then he has been living all this time in an undiscovered – indeed non-existent – world. The patriarch's 'invention' of the nation in his patriotic speeches – 'The fatherland is the best thing that's ever been invented, mother' (p. 22) – pales into insignificance in comparison with the ability of the written word to 'invent' the whole continent of America, himself included. The patriarch is, of course, ironically unaware that he is indeed the creation of a written text, that his invention by García Márquez means that he exists only in words.

A key point in the novel, when the patriarch is for the first time confronted directly with the power of the written word, is the recital given by the poet Rubén Darío. The recital makes such a strong impact because the written word is combined with the speaking voice of the author. Darío's reading of his poem 'Marcha triunfal' (from which García Márquez again quotes) reveals to the patriarch a verbal power which transcends that of any mortal ruler and whose authority is absolute:

> He saw the heroic athletes ... he saw the ranks of warlike youths [fighting for] the eternal splendour of an immortal fatherland greater and more glorious than any he had ever imagined . . . he felt impoverished and diminished . . . dazzled by the revelation of written beauty.   (pp. 194–5)

What attracts the patriarch in Darío's poetry is his attempt to create an eternal, universal poetic language that transcends the limitations of human existence. For the patriarch, writing has the value of memory; it is an attempt to perpetuate through repetition that which otherwise is condemned to oblivion. After the recital, he takes to 'writing the verses on the lavatory walls, trying to recite the whole poem from memory' (p. 195). His second-hand repetitions inevitably fail to reproduce the power of the author's original rendition. The futility of the attempt to immortalize reality via the written word is underlined by García Márquez's ironic application to the decaying palace of the euphemisms and mythological references which characterize Darío's poetic language: 'in the calid Olympus of the cowshit in the dairy' (p. 195). The choice of Darío as the patriarch's literary mentor is appropriate, not only because of his reputation as the doyen of Spanish American letters, but also because a major theme of his later poetry is the fear of death.

The early part of chapter 5, where Darío's recital is narrated, describes the efforts of Leticia Nazareno to teach the patriarch to read and write. Even at the beginning of his 'autumn', while still illiterate, the value attached by the patriarch to the ability of writing to preserve human life could be seen in his choice of two ministers, 'his private doctor and another who was the nation's best calligrapher' (p. 37). The adulteration of authority that began with the transition from direct to reported speech is completed with the patriarch's initiation, in the later part of the novel, into writing. The delegation of his power to the written word leads to his mythification, in the sense that the manifestations of his existence become increasingly remote from their source. An image of the mythical prestige of the written word, as the trace of an absent voice, can be seen in the description, in that chapter in which the patriarch discovers writing, of the patriarch's footprint: 'In that imprint/trace [Sp. *huella*] we saw power, we felt the contact of its mystery with a greater sense of revelation than when one of us was chosen to see him in person' (p. 187). The religious terminology used here is no accident. The discovery of writing allows the patriarch to play God. He refuses to admit God to his presence – ' "let no one into the house, come what may, he ordered . . . not even God, if he turns up" ' (p. 264) – because he has learnt his secret, that omnipotence depends on absence. Only if the speaker is invisible do his words attain the status of Scripture. From now on, the patriarch stops appearing in public altogether. It is not for nothing that he recognizes in the church his main rival for power. At the same time, he is bound to be an agnostic, since he knows that God is all powerful because he does not exist except in terms of written texts.

The patriarch's scepticism about the existence of God, however, logically leads him to have doubts about his own identity as the mythical product of words: 'One night he had written my name is Zacarías, had reread it by the fleeting glare of the lighthouse, had read it over and over again, and with so many repetitions the name ended up looking remote and alien' (p. 132). The written word, as the repetition of an absent original, does serve as a form of memory, but the memory becomes detached from its source. The patriarch's last years are spent recording his own power in graffiti in the palace lavatories and hiding away written reminders to himself which he cannot remember writing. The written word does not give him eternal life, but condemns him to living in terms of memories of the past. His activity as head of state becomes limited to the commemoration of anniversaries.

The patriarch looks to the written word not only to immortalize himself but also to preserve his links with the outside world: 'At that time his only contacts with the reality of this world were a few loose fragments of his most important memories', written appropriately in the margins of the volumes of official records (p. 132). Here again, writing fails him. The written word does not connect him with the outside world, but becomes a substitute for it: 'He checked the truths stated in the documents against the misleading truths of real life' (p. 161). Writing mythifies not only its author but also its subject matter, inasmuch as it supplants, and ultimately suppresses, the original it represents. By the end of the novel the patriarch is relying for information entirely on his own censored newspapers. His written reminders to himself are rendered worthless, despite their permanence, by the fact that he forgets what they refer to. His last act before dying is to return to its hiding place the note he had written recording 'some anniversary or other of the illustrious poet Rubén Darío', whose identity he has now forgotten (p. 267). Writing perpetuates neither its author nor the outside world, but only itself. The patriarch's obsession, in his later years, with writing traps him in an unreal world beyond the looking glass, where 'the light of the mirrors has been turned inside out' (p. 234). 'In the trail of yellow leaves of his autumn he became convinced that he would never be master of all his power, that he was condemned to know life the wrong way round/from the other side [Sp. *por el revés*]' (p. 270). The written word does not hold a mirror up to reality, but turns reality into a mirror-image.

The image of the trace – the 'trail of yellow leaves of his autumn' – is an apt metaphor for writing.[4] The displacement of the patriarch's power from speech to writing converts it into a trail of words referring back to an absent source. The implication is that, like myth, writing separates man from a source with which at the same time it seeks to re-establish contact. Writing is a circular, counter-productive process, in that it causes the problem it sets out to solve. The patriarch's recourse to written expressions of his authority aggravates the power vacuum he is trying to overcome. He attempts to secure a papal edict grounding his power in his genealogical origins by canonizing his mother, but the papal envoy's efforts to trace his ancestry reveal only that he is the son of an unknown father and a mother of uncertain name and reputation, who used to make a living by painting birds (falsifying nature). The people also attempt to establish an authoritative account of the patriarch's life by piecing together vestiges of a past that becomes more elusive the more they inquire: 'it would have been all too easy to let oneself be convinced by the immediate signs', 'neither in that room could we find any clue', 'every trace of his origins had disappeared from the textbooks' (pp. 48–50). The patriarch's power becomes reduced to the peripheral trace of a remote and intermittent central source of light: 'the flurry of dust of the trail of stars of the gold spur in the fleeting dawn of the green flashes of the shafts of light of the turns of the lighthouse' (p. 69). At the end of the novel, with the sale of the sea to the United States, the patriarch orders the lighthouse – his metaphorical centre of power – to be put out of action. With this symbolic act, designed to conceal the power vacuum left by the absence of the sea, he destroys the last remaining vestiges of his power, and dies. The loss of the sea can be seen not only as an allegory of imperialism, but also as a metaphor for the loss by the 'ship of state' of its foundations. Prior to the sale of the sea, the palace is described as a ship that has broken free of its anchor and is floating in the air: 'The house of power [. . .] looked like a steamboat sailing in the sky' (p. 185). A similar image is used to describe the effect on the patriarch of his discovery, at Darío's recital, of the written word: '[it] lifted him clean out of his place and time and left him floating' (p. 194). The patriarch dies drowned in his own efforts to immortalize himself in words, 'a solitary corpse floating face down in the lunar waters of his dreams' (p. 13).

The image of the trace which has lost touch with its source, repeatedly applied to the patriarch, invites comparison with the description of the comet, which returns every hundred years, as a 'trail of radiant dust of astral residues and dawns prolonged by tar moons and ashes of craters of oceans prior to the origins of time on earth' (pp. 83–4). The implication is that the comet, as part of nature, is in touch with a source to which it can return, in order to renew itself. The patriarch, by contrast, loses contact with his origins through his delegation of power to words, and his attempts at repetition – again through words – lead to exhaustion. When he orders a repeat of the comet, he gets an eclipse. The transition from speech to writing cuts him off from nature. The loss of the sea provides an appropriate image of the final phase of this process of alienation.

The notion that writing is the trace of an absent source is reinforced by García Márquez's use of narrative perspective. It is important that the novel should start with the end, the patriarch's death. The patriarch is thus an absence throughout the novel. It is also important that García Márquez should, within the flashback that is the whole novel, narrate chronologically only the events of the patriarch's 'autumn'. The heyday of his power, when he was still a presence, becomes a flashback within a flashback, narrated via a double chain of hearsay. By making it clear that the text of the novel refers back to an absent source, García Márquez shows how writing is untrustworthy because it mythifies reality. The distance of the written word from its source undermines its authority. The patriarch's most authoritative acts are narrated in the least authoritative way.

Conversely, the moments in the novel which appear to give a direct, authoritative insight into the patriarch's mind, unmediated by hearsay, are those which reveal his inner doubts. When we are given a description of the thoughts he silently addresses to his mother – 'thinking dearest mother Bendición Alvarado, if only you knew that this world is too much for me, that I want to run away but I don't know where to, mother, away from all this misery, but he didn't even show his private sighs to his mother' (p. 25) – we assume that the omniscient author is speaking, since no character can see inside the patriarch's head. We again assume the omniscient author is responsible for the narration of the patriarch's dream of Manuela Sánchez (pp. 70–1) and of his encounter with death (pp. 268–9), particularly since he is locked alone in his bedroom at the time. In these last two instances, the illusion of objectivity is heightened by the fact that the patriarch's mental states are narrated as if they were events. But, in fact, all the apparently omniscient insights into the patriarch's mind are contained in a narrative which, in each chapter, clearly starts as the uninformed collective voice of the people who discover the patriarch's corpse. What looks at first sight like an authoritative/authorial account of what the patriarch is really like is, it seems, hypothetical speculation on the part of the uninformed collective narrator, in other words, another part of the legend. By tricking the reader into thinking that what he is reading is the work of an omniscient author, and subsequently making him realize it is the product of an unreliable intermediary narrator, García Márquez calls into question the authority of the written word. Just as the patriarch discovers that he is not in control of the words that are designed to perpetuate his power, so the reader discovers that there is no omniscient author in control of the text he is reading.

What is more, the text is the product not of one unreliable intermediary narrator, but of a bewildering profusion of intermediary narrators, all of them unreliable. It is impossible to know at how many removes we are from the original version; all we know for sure is that the version we have is adulterated. The collective voice that narrates the beginning of each chapter, and which we therefore presume is responsible for the whole text, contains within it a multiplicity of individual voices which report events at second hand, and in turn are reported at second hand. Whenever we have something that looks like a factual account we suddenly come across a term of address which shows that it is a story told by one character to another. The intercalation 'my general' appears throughout, revealing that what we have been reading is a second-hand report made to the patriarch. In the same way, the intercalation 'Sir' reveals that what looks like objective narration is spoken by the patriarch's mother, who constantly uses this term of address. To add to the confusion, it is not always clear whether she is speaking to an interviewer or to God, since the Spanish *Señor* could also be translated as 'Lord'. The frequent interruption of the narrative by the expletive 'damn it' (Sp. *carajo*), or the interjections 'mother' or 'poor man', likewise indicates that the patriarch is speaking, despite the absence of any other indication to that effect. The army chief is always referred to as 'my old pal General Rodrigo de Aguilar', raising the possibility that the patriarch may be speaking even when this seems unlikely. There are several moments when we are made aware that what we are reading is spoken by a character, without being sure who the speaker is. The end of chapter 4 is addressed to the patriarch as 'general', despite the fact that he is also referred to in the third person – 'and yet he forgot her, he was left alone in the dark searching for himself in the salty water of his tears general' (p. 168) – but it seems unlikely that this is spoken by Leticia Nazareno who is the only person present (and who is also referred to in the third person). The episode with the three caravels of Columbus again provides the most amusing example of this ambiguous use of narrative voice, with the patriarch's informers slipping anachronistically into the language of Columbus's diary that ought to be reserved for the newly arrived conquistadors (p. 45). This kind of narrative inconsistency makes it impossible to attribute the text to anyone in particular.

Not only do all the apparently factual accounts in the novel turn out to be reported speech, but so do all the passages which appear to be narrated as direct speech. The first-person narrative voice which characterizes direct speech is usually taken, despite its partiality, to give an authoritative account of events second only to that of the omniscient author, inasmuch as it gives an eye-witness description,

unmediated by an external narrator. In *The Autumn of the Patriarch*,
nothing can be regarded as authoritative, because everything is
mediated. The absence of any punctuation indicating speech in the
passages narrated in the first person is a clue to the fact that what we
have is a disguised form of reported speech. The first time in the novel
that direct speech appears, it is made quite clear that it is really
reported speech: 'Someone had told how I saw the sad eyes' (p. 8). In
subsequent examples, we have to wait for some time before discovering that what we have been reading is not genuine direct speech. The
first-person account by Francisca Linero of her rape by the patriarch
ends with the sentence, 'They were images of his power which reached
him from afar' (p. 100), implying the whole story is a dramatization of
legend. We frequently find an inconsistent mixture of direct and
reported speech, suggesting that nothing is uncontaminated by
hearsay. The patriarch issues orders to his servants in what starts as
direct speech but lapses into reported speech: 'Take that door away for
me and put it over there . . . the belfry clock was not to strike twelve at
twelve but at two' (p. 12). The first and third persons that correspond
to direct and reported speech respectively occur in the same sentence:
'They had intimidated them with all manner of threats and that was
why we did it' (p. 39); 'Bendición Alvarado spurned the crown jewels
which make me feel like the Pope's wife' (p. 52). This technique is used
most effectively in the patriarch's repeated invocations of 'his mother
of my life', 'his mother of my soul', 'his mother of my death' (pp. 137–
9), implying that what looks like a direct rendering of the patriarch's
words is in fact relayed to us indirectly. The patriarch's voice is absent
even when it appears to be present. Conversely, the people's voice is
present even when it appears to be absent, inasmuch as all the
individual voices in the novel are presented indirectly via popular
legend.

The most extreme case of this confusion of direct and reported
speech occurs, appropriately, in the episode in which the patriarch's
informers reconstruct the efforts of the papal envoy to reconstruct the
patriarch's origins. Within the illusion of direct speech that is the
informers' report to the patriarch we have the illusion of direct speech
of the informers' earlier conversations with the envoy:

. . . my general, if you could only see him in the midst of the human debris of
the weatherbeaten sloops . . . packed with their cargo of teenage whores for
the glass hotels of Curaçao, bound for Guantánamo, father . . . remember

how strange we felt when the boat had left . . . the distant drums, life, father, this god-awful life, boys, because he talks like us my general.   (p. 149)

The confusion of distinct conversations taking place at different times and places leaves the reader unsure where he stands. A similar effect is produced by the use of a number of anonymous first-person-singular voices – an ex-dictator (pp. 21, 42), a fortune-teller (pp. 95–6), the revolutionary (p. 107), a schoolgirl (pp. 220–3), a prostitute (pp. 226–7), a palace decorator (p. 227), a leper (p. 251) – whose identity cannot be established with any precision. It is, of course, important that the major individual voice in the novel – that of the patriarch – should belong to this category of anonymous narrators. On several occasions, these first-person-singular voices fade into the anonymous first-person-plural voice of the collective narrator, so that we begin to think that the collective narrator perhaps comprises the sum of the individual voices, rather than being a separate group of people recording their stories at a remove.

The reader is reluctant to abandon his assumption that the first-person-plural narrator who relates the beginning of each chapter is responsible for the whole novel, because the existence of a frame-narrator gives at least some coherence to the text, by locating it within the framework of a single perspective. But the collective narrator turns out, on inspection, to be even more inconsistent than the individual voices it appears to contain. The very existence of a first-person-plural narrator confronts us with a disconcerting mixture of the apparent authority of the first-person voice and the plurality – and probable divergence – of a collective voice. The authority of this first-person-plural narrator is undermined in the opening pages, which show that the 'we' who is speaking is superstitious and ignorant. The initial impression that the text emanates from a fixed source, given by the fact that at the beginning of each chapter the collective narrator is clearly identified as the people who find the patriarch's corpse, is quickly dispelled as the 'we' that narrates the subsequent passages starts, like the patriarch's palace, to drift free of its anchor. It is not that we cannot attribute the text to a source, but that this source constantly shifts. The impression that the text is floating, ungrounded in a fixed source, is reinforced by the fact that this shifting first-person-plural narrator is always anonymous. First of all we find that the 'we' frequently refers to the patriarch's subjects at the time of events, such as the landing of the Marines (p. 51) or the appearance of the comet (p. 84), which the 'we' of the opening pages has told us took place many years before their birth. Then the 'we' begins to pass, at increasing speed, from one group of characters to another. The successive identities assumed by the first-person-plural narrator include the following (in order of appearance): the national baseball team (p. 40), the ex-dictators of other Latin American countries (p. 42), the witnesses of Columbus's landing (pp. 44–5), successive generations of army generals (pp. 60, 126–7, 196–7, 207), marauding pirates (p. 95), various army officers (pp. 109–11, 248), government advisers (p. 170), merchants (p. 188), the audience at Darío's recital (p. 193–4), schoolgirls (p. 202), economists (p. 224), security guards (p. 226), cadets (p. 240), lepers and cripples (p. 251), the police looking for Columbus (p. 258), palace servants (p. 264). To add to the confusion, the patriarch sometimes uses the royal 'we'.

Our first reaction is to explain this proliferation of first-person-plural narrators in the same way as we had initially explained the first-person-singular narrators, as being voices contained within the narrative of the 'we' who, at the beginning of each chapter, find the patriarch's corpse. But the view that the people who find the corpse provide a narrative frame to the novel appears to be contradicted by the fact that on two occasions, at the beginning and end of the novel, the people who find the corpse are referred to in the third person. The first time, this can be explained by the fact that the reference includes the different group of people who previously found the corpse of the patriarch's double, even though 'we' plus 'they' normally adds up to 'we': 'but not even then did we dare believe in his death because it was the second time they had found him in that office' (p. 20). But when at the end of the novel we read, 'although those who found the body were to say that it was on the office floor' (p. 269), no such explanation is available. Either there is no frame-narrator, or else the people who find the corpse are characters in someone else's story. If there is a frame-narrator, it can only be the 'we' who narrates the last two pages of the novel. This final 'we' appears to represent a different group of people from the 'we' that starts each chapter, because the people who find the corpse are uninformed and submissive, whereas the first-person-plural narrator of the closing pages utters a clear rejection of everything the patriarch stands for. This is the one authoritative statement in the novel. All we know about this final 'we' is that they live 'on this side of reality in the world of the poor' (p. 270). If they are responsible for reporting the stories of all the other narrators in the novel, the fact that they are entirely absent until the last two pages means that they do not provide the coherence of a genuine frame-narrator, like Scheherezade in the *Arabian Nights*, whose presence is made clear at the very beginning in order to ground the ensuing proliferation of narrative voices in a single perspective. There is, in fact, no evidence to suggest that the narrator of the end of the novel is responsible for the rest of the text. The reader has to face the disquieting fact that the story he has been reading is, like an Escher drawing, depicted from an entirely inconsistent, indeed impossible, perspective. The fact that the collective narrator can be identified only as the sum of all the individual points of view confronts the reader with the optical illusion of a narrator that is the voices it appears to report. The impossible nature of the narrative voice is underlined at the end of the novel, when the patriarch's dead mother and death itself speak in the first person. The implausibility of the voice that speaks destroys the authority of what is said.

The critic Julio Ortega has suggested that García Márquez's use of a collective narrative voice represents a vindication of democracy, since the dictator is placed in the power of the masses who narrate his story.[5] This is an attractive interpretation, but it presents problems. The most noticeable feature of the collective narrative voice is that, with the exception of the last two pages, it shows remarkably little political awareness. Indeed, it is often highly hagiographic in tone. García Márquez is not suggesting that the patriarch's tyranny is justified by popular support, for the point is that the collective voice of the people is unreliable. The fact that it is anonymous, uninformed and inconsistent means that it cannot be seen as an alternative source of authority. I would suggest that García Márquez's use of narrative perspective does not represent a vindication of popular power, but an attempt to subvert the concept of language as an instrument of power. The absence in the novel of a central, coherent narrative voice is a warning to the reader that he should not look to the text for an authoritative account of events. García Márquez's writing is subversive because it is unashamedly fictitious. He is not mythifying dictatorship, but using language ironically in order to expose the ways in which it mythifies reality. By using language to undermine its own mythifications, he demonstrates that the unreliability of fiction, when used critically, can be a strength as well as a weakness. His use of an anonymous, uninformed and inconsistent narrative voice suggests that writing has an advantage over speech precisely because it is not the voice of authority.

García Márquez has, on several occasions, talked of his self-identification with the patriarch as a prisoner of power. By this, he is referring not only to the power that comes with fame but also to that of the creator. To quote one interview:

> On the one hand, as you say, the solitude of fame is very like the solitude of power . . . on the other hand, there is no profession more solitary than that of the writer, in the sense that at the time of writing no one can help you, no one can tell you what you want to do. When you are faced with the blank page, you are on your own, totally on your own.[6]

The writer, like the dictator, chooses to play God but, at the same time, if he succumbs to the temptation to do so he is lost. García Márquez's depiction of a dictator who becomes the prisoner of the power of words shows an understanding of the pitfalls that await the writer who lets his power go to his head. García Márquez's delegation of responsibility for the text of his novel to an anonymous, unreliable collective voice can be seen as an act of authorial self-effacement. It is also an affirmation of the value of human error and limitation. In its one authoritative pronouncement at the end of the novel, the collective narrator rejects the dictator's search for divine status, in favour of 'this life which we loved with an insatiable passion that you never even dared imagine for fear of knowing what we knew so well that it was brief and cruel, but there was no other' (pp. 270–1). The patriarch's concern with language as an instrument of power leaves him speechless when it comes to expressing his love for Manuela Sánchez. 'He overwhelmed her in silence with those crazy gifts with which he tried to tell her what he could not say in words, because the only way he knew of expressing his deepest desires was through the visible symbols of his monstrous power' (p. 79). The language of *The Autumn of the Patriarch* lays no claim to authority. García Márquez opts for the more modest aim of depicting human fallibility.

Notes

1 See J. Derrida, *Of Grammatology*, trans. Gayatry Chakravorty Spivak (Baltimore and London, 1976). A lucid analysis of Derrida's ideas on language can be found in Jonathan Culler's article in *Structuralism and Since*, ed. J. Sturrock (Oxford, 1979), pp. 154–80.

2 All references given in the text are to the first edition of *El otoño del patriarca* (Barcelona, 1975). The translations are my own.

3 The ironic references in the novel to seeing have been pointed out by Seymour Menton in his article 'Ver para no creer: *El otoño del patriarca*', in *García Márquez*, ed. P. Earle (Madrid, 1981), pp. 189–209.

4 The metaphor of the trace is also used by Derrida to describe language. García Márquez's view of language, however, differs from that of Derrida in an important respect. Derrida rejects the view that writing is a decadent form of speech inasmuch as it is the indirect expression of a voice which is absent, as opposed to speech which is assumed to be the direct expression of the speaker's voice. For Derrida, both speech and writing are the trace of an absent source. García Márquez retains the traditional notion of the decadence of writing with regard to speech.

5 See J. Ortega, '*El otoño del patriarca*, texto y cultura', in *García Márquez*, ed. P. Earle, pp. 214–35.

6 Plinio Apuleyo Mendoza, *El olor de la guayaba* (Barcelona, 1982), p. 127.

10

Writing and ritual in
Chronicle of a Death Foretold

CARLOS ALONSO

> Gloomy Orion and the Dog
> Are veiled; and hushed the shrunken seas.
> (T. S. Eliot, 'Sweeney
> Among the Nightingales')

If one were to take to the letter *Chronicle of a Death Foretold*'s avowed generic filiation as reportage, one would have to acknowledge immediately that the narrator's performance in its entirety constitutes nothing short of a scandal. For, as is made evident through the novel, the investigator was a member of the community in which the events took place, a circumstance that puts in check the objectivity that his rhetorical posturing demands. Even if the narrator takes pains to establish early on that he was asleep when tragedy struck, his 'participation' is implicitly recognized in the text when he himself refers to Santiago Nasar's death as a crime 'for which we all could have been to blame'.[1] As if to underscore this fact, the novel is quite careful in establishing the complex web of relationships that tied the narrator to all the protagonists of the tragic plot.[2] In addition, the narrator time and again expresses his agreement with a given witness's opinion in a formula that arises from shared communal experience. ' "One night he asked me which house I liked the most", Angela Vicario told me. "And I answered, without knowing what he intended, that the prettiest house in town was the farmhouse belonging to the widower Xius." *I would have said the same*' (p. 49, my italics).[3] Nevertheless, cloaked by the dispassionate and measured tone that the inquest seemingly imposes on him, the narrator affords us few details about his person or motivations. Thus, the investigative framework of the novel may serve paradoxically to nurture the secret at the core of the events, since of all the ambivalent, mysterious and contradictory figures in *Chronicle of a Death Foretold*, none is more perplexing than the narrator of the story himself.[4]

Moreover, when examined further from this generic perspective, *Chronicle of a Death Foretold* would appear to be an exercise in futility.

After all the repeated interviews, corroborations and painstaking archival research, the narrator cannot produce any new concrete facts on the circumstances that determined the death of Santiago Nasar. Indeed, when considered in the light of the original official investigation, there seems no justification for the narrator's report on his new inquest since it repeats the failure of the preceding one. If he manages not to fall prey to the despondence and frustration that were repeatedly expressed by the civil magistrate in his report, the result is yet the same: the intervening years have not disentangled the 'ciphered knot' (p. 33) around which the narrator weaves the weft of his own interpretative enterprise. This failure must be recognized even if we take the object of the investigation to be not the discovery of the truth but rather the determination of how such a publicized death could have taken place irrespective of the town's purported desire to prevent it. For what we are left with in the end is a series of coincidences, moments of personal weakness and false assumptions whose heterogeneity precludes the possibility of an overarching explanation or understanding of the crime. The only significant fact not available to the hapless first magistrate, the final reconciliation between Bayardo San Román and Angela Vicario some twenty years after the murder, does not illuminate unambiguously the tragic events and has exasperated more than one critic for its apparent lack of consequence.[5] Nevertheless, the investigative framework of the novel forever seems to imply the imminent uncovering of some hitherto unknown datum that will bestow coherence upon the fateful events of that distant February morning. In particular, the repeated intimations of Santiago Nasar's innocence encourage the belief that the identity of the person responsible for Angela's dishonour will finally be revealed. And yet, the novel constantly thwarts all expectations of revelation through what seems a perpetual game of deferrals, extremely detailed but inconsequential information and contradictory affirmations. In fact, one could characterize the narrator's discourse with a phrase used in the text to describe Bayardo San Román's speech: 'He had a way of speaking that served more to conceal than to reveal' (p. 37). These textual circumstances should have rendered superfluous the critical obsession with the referential status of *Chronicle of a Death Foretold*, manifested in the myriad attempts to confront the events depicted in the novel with a similar incident in Colombian *petite histoire*.[6] Such a concern, and the critical enterprise that it has engendered, however, are symptomatic of a widespread critical conceit regarding the entire *oeuvre* of García Márquez, one that would characterize his work as devoid for the most part of the meta-literary concerns that characterize contemporary Latin American literature.

The difference between the rhetorical specificity of the novel and the text's failure when viewed from this perspective is significant, and should perhaps alert us to the fact that the development of the text is guided primordially by a performative rather than by a logical or teleological drive.[7] Only from such a performative perspective can the narrative be said to *mean* something, given the evident inconsequence of its self-designated hermeneutic project. In other words, we are led to the realization that the logic that underlies the production of the text appears to be at odds with the logic inaugurated by the novel's avowed rhetorical model. This *décalage*, this differing of the text from itself, will constitute the space and subject in and on which the present commentary on the novel will dwell.

If the text makes entirely problematic its relationship to the *generic* application of the term 'chronicle', an interpretation of the word that is attuned to its *etymological* charge proves no less of a misnomer, given the novel's non-linear chronological structure. It is not my intent, however, to detail the multiple ways in which the temporal displace-ments of the narrative render ineffective rigorous chronological succession in the novel. I would propose, on the other hand, to arrive at an examination of the performative dimension described above by exploring initially the paradoxical and yet relentless presence of repetition in the fabric of a text that invokes for its self-definition the rubric of 'chronicle'.

It could be argued that the superfluity of the narrator's investiga-tion *vis-à-vis* the original inquest is emblematic of the narrative as a whole, inasmuch as it signals the overwhelming occurrence of repetition in the entire text. It would perhaps be more accurate to propose that instances like it attest to the untrammelled and unproblematic status of repetition in *Chronicle of a Death Foretold*. If the novel in its entirety can be perceived as a re-enactment of the preceding inquiry, it is also true that the text itself is assembled from instances of repeated information. At the most general level, *Chronicle of a Death Foretold* is constituted by an orchestrated collage of quotations, paraphrases and summaries.[8] In this regard, Raymond Williams has established in very precise terms that 'The narrator-investigator's total "record" of his chronicle consists of nine citations from the written record and a total of 102 quotations from the thirty-seven characters.'[9] But, more importantly, the novel itself can be shown to be organized through a succession of internal repetitions and restatements, whose cumulative effect is to give the text an overall sense of redundancy and familiarity. This aspect of the text determines, for instance, that the last pages of the novel should constitute a thoroughly anticlimactic moment. The depiction of Santiago Nasar's death with which the book closes has been rendered at that point entirely superfluous by the text's own dialectics. All its circumstances and gruesome particulars are thoroughly known at that juncture; we anticipate and recognize each thrust of the murderers' knives, since they and the damage inflicted by them were first inscribed in the autopsy report before they ever scarred the body of Santiago Nasar. This mechanism is what deprives the murder scene of its potentially ghastly impact. At the same time, the detachment that it produces renders it impossible not to notice the painstaking manner in which the description endeavours to account for each of the blows that had been previously detailed in the post-mortem examination. This quality becomes apparent when the two passages are confronted with each other:

Seven of the numerous wounds were fatal. The liver was almost sliced by two deep cuts on the anterior side. He had four incisions in the stomach, one of them so deep that it went completely through it and destroyed the pancreas. He had six other lesser perforations in the transverse colon and multiple wounds in the small intestine. The only one he had in the back, at the level of the third lumbar vertebra, had perforated the right kidney . . . The thoracic cavity showed two perforations: one in the second right rib space that reached the lung, and another quite close to the left armpit. He also had six minor wounds on his arms and hands, and two horizontal slashes: one on the right thigh and the other in the abdominal muscles. He had a deep puncture wound in the right hand.   (pp. 98–9)

The knife went through the palm of his right hand and then sank into his side up to the hilt . . . Pedro Vicario pulled out his knife with his slaughterer's savage wrist and dealt him a second blow almost in the same place . . . Santiago Nasar twisted after the third stab . . . and tried to turn his back to them. Pablo Vicario, who was on his left with the curved knife, then gave him the only stab in the back . . . Trying to finish the task once and for all, Pedro Vicario sought his heart, but he looked for it almost in the armpit, where pigs have it . . . Desperate, Pablo Vicario gave him a horizontal slash on the abdomen, and all his intestines exploded out. Pedro Vicario was about to do the same, but his wrist twisted with horror and he gave him a wild cut on the thigh.   (pp. 152–4)

Examples like these could be garnered almost at random from the text. It might be argued that repetition is unavoidable in a narrative of this sort, where the overlapping of strands of evidence and accounts has a confirmatory value. But, given the generic ambiguity and intractability of *Chronicle of a Death Foretold* as well as the performative intention identified earlier, perhaps a more meaningful realization awaits us.

I should like to propose that the intricate web of repetition and restatements in the text seeks to duplicate effectively at the level of the narrative the same structure of foreknowledge that characterized the events leading to the assassination of Santiago Nasar. Surely, as the narrator affirms in reference to Nasar's murder, 'there was never a death so publicized' (p. 69). The town's collective knowledge of the crime-to-be, and its unbearable guilt, is built on discrete instances of individual foresight: Hortensia Baute sees the knives dripping blood before they have performed their murderous task (p. 83); Santiago's hand feels like a dead man's to Divina Flor (p. 21); Pedro Vicario says that warning Santiago will not make any difference in the final outcome: 'Don't bother . . . No matter what, he's as good as dead already' (p. 133). And later, when reminded that Santiago usually went about armed, he shouts, 'Dead men can't shoot' (p. 141); to Margot, the narrator's sister, Nasar already had the countenance of a dead person some time before the murder actually took place (p. 143). And, when asked for the whereabouts of Santiago Nasar, the narrator's brother Luis Enrique answers inexplicably, 'Santiago Nasar is dead' (p. 92).[10] The same sense of foreknowledge that surrounded the murder of Santiago Nasar is incorporated by the narrative in its own coming into being through the pervasive presence of repetition in its structure. This parallelism advances the proposition that there exists a very significant relationship linking the events that led to the murder of Santiago Nasar to the text of *Chronicle of a Death Foretold*, the narration that recreates those same events. The novel appears to posit a homology between the way the crime takes place and the manner in which the narrative about the crime is constructed. In this fashion, the organization of the text would seem to recall the process that many years earlier had culminated in the assassination of Santiago Nasar. The recognition of this analogy will allow us to explore comprehensively the powerful and totalizing role of repetition in *Chronicle of a Death Foretold*.

Given the homology just described, one could adduce that the narrative would like to project itself as a re-enactment of the murder of Santiago Nasar. More exactly – and as I will argue below – the text would endeavour to constitute a sort of ritual repetition of the crime. There are in fact many characteristics of the novel that would attest to this ritual dimension.[11] To begin with, one would have to point out the 'sacral' nature of the text's discourse. It is this aspect of the novel that clashes most violently with the rhetorical conventions of the model to which *Chronicle of a Death Foretold* ostensibly belongs, particularly the hermeneutical demands imposed by the genre: it is ultimately not a matter of understanding or accounting for the murder of Santiago Nasar, but of re-enacting it. This explains why the text of the novel is rife with instances of apparent redundancy, digressions and extraneous information, all of which are nevertheless deemed essential for the textual reconstruction of the sacrificial *mise en scène*. Take, for instance, the following passage:

My brother Luis Enrique entered the house through the kitchen door . . . He went to the bathroom before going to bed, but he fell asleep sitting on the toilet, and when my brother Jaime got up to go to school he found him stretched out face down on the tile floor and singing in his sleep. My sister the nun . . . could not get him to wake up . . . Later, when my sister Margot went in to bathe before going to the docks, she managed with great difficulty to drag him to his bedroom. From the other side of sleep he heard the first bellows of the bishop's boat without awakening. Then he fell into a deep sleep . . . until my sister the nun rushed into the bedroom, trying to put her habit on as quickly as she could and woke him up with her frantic cry: 'They've killed Santiago Nasar!' (pp. 93–4)

The fragment does not provide any privileged information regarding the murder of Nasar; and, given the particulars of the account provided, it would be difficult to claim that it describes a character's 'participation' in the events. But from within a conception of the text as ritual repetition there is no meaningless or wasted action; no fleeting gesture is unworthy of being consigned to writing. Given the conventionality and rigidity that characterize it, ritual language has by its very nature this levelling effect that can be identified in the novel, paradoxically, as the apparently indiscriminate bringing together of data. There has been no attempt to sort out what is meaningful from what is extraneous in the information gathered; on the contrary, the pertinence and significance of every fact or event seems to be underwritten by its very presence in the narrative. Almost as if to call attention to this aspect of the text, there is a series of patent contradictions that plague the various depositions, and which are left to stand as such in the narrator's account. The most glaring of these leads to the inability to establish with any degree of precision something as elementary as the state of the weather during the morning of the crime.[12]

In this ritual re-enactment it is not surprising to encounter specific verbal constructions that through repetition acquire an almost incantatory quality. Such is the case of expressions like 'On the day they were going to kill him', 'They've killed Santiago Nasar' and 'It was the last time they saw him alive', phrases that in their periodic appearance in the text would seem to mark the beat of the ceremonial proceedings. To this, one would have to add the clearly antiphonal structure that is so predominant in the novel. An intervention by the narrator will be followed by a 'response' offered by one of the witnesses, as in the following case:

No one would have even suspected . . . that Bayardo San Román had been in her [Angela's] life constantly from the moment he had brought her back home. It was a *coup de grâce*. 'Suddenly, when Mother began to hit me, I began to remember him', she told me. The blows hurt less because she knew they were because of him. She went on thinking about him with a certain surprise at herself as she lay sobbing on the dining-room sofa. 'I wasn't crying because of the blows or for anything that had happened', she told me. 'I was crying because of him.' (p. 120)

From this ritual perspective the entire narrative assumes a preparatory and propitiatory function for the sacrificial murder of Santiago Nasar with which the novel ends. The performative drive alluded to earlier would become a manifestation of this ritual dimension of the text. Its incongruity with the epistemic project of the investigative model is represented by the fact that the avowed inquest into the murder should end paradoxically with the repetition of the original crime. That the *telos* of the narrative is this re-enactment of the assassination is confirmed with enigmatic precision by García Márquez himself in the course of a recent interview: 'The story really ends almost twenty-five years after the murder, when the husband returns to the scorned wife, but to me it was always evident that the end of the book had to be the painstaking description of the crime.'[13]

In addition, the homologous relationship between the murder and the narrative is underscored by a series of similarities between the two registers. There is, for instance, a most telling scene in which the morning of the murder and the beginning of the investigation are explicitly equated: 'She [Santiago Nasar's mother] had watched him

from the same hammock and in the same position in which I found her
prostrated by the last lights of old age when I returned to this forgotten
town, trying to put back together the broken mirror of memory from
so many scattered shards . . . She was on her side, clutching the cords at
the head of the hammock in an attempt to get up, and there in the
shadows was the baptistery smell that had startled me on the morning
of the crime' (p. 13). By the same token, Santiago Nasar's obsession
with determining the cost of the wedding festivities parallels the many
references made by the narrator to the 'cost' of his investigation. By
gleaning relevant fragments from the novel, a rigorous account of the
chronological investment and of the effort spent on the construction of
the narrative can be obtained. Take, for instance, the following:

> There was no classification of files whatever, and more than a century of cases
> were piled up on the floor of the decrepit colonial building . . . The ground
> floor would often be flooded by high tides and the unbound volumes floated
> about the deserted offices. I myself searched many times with water up to my
> ankles in that reservoir of lost causes, and after five years of rummaging
> around, only chance let me rescue some 322 random pages from the more
> than 500 that the brief must have contained.   (p. 129)

And closely related to this parallel tallying is the all-too-precise
scansion of the temporal framework of the investigation, which
usually assumes the formulaic expressions 'x years later . . .' or 'x years
afterwards'.[14] One could plausibly argue that its presence in the
narrative is strongly reminiscent of the relentless chronological
indexing of Santiago Nasar's murder, and of which the very first
sentence of the novel may be the most appropriate example: 'On the
day they were going to kill him, Santiago Nasar got up at five-thirty in
the morning to wait for the boat the bishop was coming on' (p. 9).

All of these similarities attest to the performative intention that
rules the novel, that is, the desire to constitute the narrative as a ritual
repetition of the murder of Santiago Nasar.[15] There are a number of
fashions in which such a re-enactment could itself be understood as a
function of the events depicted in the novel. As Freud suggested in
Beyond the Pleasure Principle, the restaging of an unpleasant event allows
for the possibility of achieving mastery over – or at the very least some
degree of accommodation to – its disturbing consequences.[16] This
possibility would reside in the passage from passive experiencing to the
active re-enactment of the unsettling circumstance. In *Chronicle of a
Death Foretold* the need to internalize the murder of Santiago Nasar
goes from the individual (the narrator) to the collective (the entire

town), and can be identified in at least two of its manifestations: as the compulsion to understand the events that transpired and as a desire for absolution and catharsis. The following passage incorporates the two succinctly:

> For years we could not talk about anything else. Our daily conduct, dominated until then by so many linear habits, had suddenly begun to spin around a single common anxiety. The cocks of dawn would catch us trying to give order to the chain of many chance events that had made absurdity possible, and it was obvious that we were not doing it from a desire to clear up mysteries but because none of us could go on living with an exact knowledge of the place and the mission assigned to us by fate.   (p. 126)

In the projection of the narrative as a ritual re-enactment of the murder there is an attempt to endow the crime with the prescribed order of ceremony, thereby overcoming the centrifugal and fortuitous character of the original events. The narrative repetition of the murder would subsume the multiplicity of discrete and heterogeneous facts surrounding the tragedy under the homogenizing mantle of ritual discourse and performance. In this context, the novel would seem to give an almost literal rendition of the following phrase by Victor Turner: 'The unity of a given ritual is a dramatic unity. It is in this sense a work of art.'[17] The passage quoted earlier, in which the narrator describes his intention as that of 'trying to put back together the broken mirror of memory from so many scattered shards', becomes particularly significant here. Thus, understanding in this instance would not reside in a privileged moment of epiphany, but rather in the solace attained through the recognition of an efficacious teleology. Acting as a sort of officiant, the narrator would reassemble the collectivity once again through his narrative, seeking to achieve in the end the equilibrium and resolution of tension that, according to Lévi-Strauss, is the paramount concern of ritual ceremony:

> Ritual . . . conjoins, for it brings about a union (one might say communion in this context) or in any case an organic relation between two initially separate groups, one ideally merging with the person of the officiant and the other with the collectivity of the faithful . . . There is an asymmetry which is postulated in advance between profane and sacred, faithful and officiating, dead and living, initiated and uninitiated, etc., and the 'game' consists in making all the participants pass to the winning side.[18]

This project, based on a conception of writing as an efficient instrument for ritual closure and redemption, would seem to underwrite the entire novel. And yet, if *Chronicle of a Death Foretold* appears to exhibit the attributes of a cathartic ritual, its status from this standpoint becomes entirely problematic: there is no unpolluted agent in the text, no person who can legitimately conduct the ceremonial proceedings and certify the effective cleansing of the collectivity. This fact is a repostulation in a different sphere of the difficulty identified earlier when considering the novel as an investigative treatise. More importantly, the attempt to achieve cathartic release through the repetition of the original murder would carry with it the possibility of an endless cycle of contamination and atonement: the ritual to cleanse the crime would become itself a source of collective anxiety in need of purgation. We are therefore led to an impasse that can be resolved only by re-examining the homology identified earlier that conjoins the murder and the narrative.

In its desire to fashion itself as a re-enactment of the murder of Santiago Nasar, the text simultaneously establishes a relationship between the processes that yielded the two, that is, between victimage and writing. From this perspective, rather than functioning simply as the vehicle for purgation envisaged above, writing is revealed as sharing essentially in the attributes of the violent act it is supposed to master and transcend. This contamination is signalled pointedly in the text by the fact that there is structurally someone for whom the death of Santiago Nasar always occurs for the first time: the reader. For us, forced symbolically to witness the murder in an analogous position to that of the townspeople in the original crime, writing cannot provide any solace or redemption. Indeed, rather than engaging in a ritual cleansing, what *Chronicle of a Death Foretold* accomplishes is a process of ritual pollution, one that is repeated time and again with each successive reading of the text. It should not be surprising, then, to find that the novel itself has provided all along a metaphoric structure that established unambiguously the relationship between writing and violence that has been proposed. It is an association that is not preserved by the English translation, but which becomes readily apparent when the appropriate fragments from the original Spanish text are confronted. Santiago Nasar's autopsy, which is significantly referred to as a murder beyond murder,[19] includes the following passage: 'El cascarón vacío, embutido de trapos y cal viva, y *cosido* a la machota con bramante basto y agujas de enfardelar, estaba a punto de desbaratarse cuando lo pusimos en el ataúd nuevo de seda capitonada' (p. 101). The English version of Gregory Rabassa reads: 'The empty shell, stuffed with rags and quicklime and *sewn up* crudely with coarse twine and baling needles, was on the point of falling apart when we put it into the new coffin with its silk quilt lining.'[20] If we follow the thread of this metaphoric yarn, we find that it weaves its way through a number of specific allusions to writing and textuality in the novel. Thus, when Bayardo returns to the wife he had originally spurned, 'he was carrying a suitcase with clothing in order to stay and another just like it with almost two thousand letters that she had written him. They were arranged by date in bundles *tied* [i.e. sewn] with coloured ribbons, and they were all unopened' (p. 95). The English rendition blurs the perfect concordance that the Spanish original posits between this fragment and the previous quotation: 'Llevaba la maleta de la ropa para quedarse, y otra maleta igual con casi dos mil cartas que ella había escrito. Estaban ordenadas por sus fechas, en paquetes *cosidos* con cintas de colores, y todas sin abrir' (p. 125). The same relationship surfaces during the narrator's account of his research in the archives of the Palace of Justice in Riohacha. The first floor, we are told, 'se inundaba con el mar de leva, y los volúmenes *descosidos* flotaban en las oficinas desiertas' (p. 129). Once again, the English version obscures the metaphoric link. It reads: 'The ground floor would be flooded by high tides and the *unbound* [i.e. unsewn] volumes floated about the deserted offices' (pp. 98–9). Finally, while describing Bayardo San Román's almost mysterious disappearance after the events, the narrator reports that 'there is a declaration by him in the brief, but it is so short and conventional that it seems to have been *put together* [i.e. patched up] at the last minute to comply with an unavoidable requirement' (p. 87). The Spanish text, however, is relentless in its metaphoric consistency: 'Hay una declaración suya en el sumario, pero es tan breve y convencional, que parece *remendada* a última hora para cumplir con una fórmula ineludible' (p. 114). Also, one could note in this regard that the forlorn Angela Vicario divides her days between the nocturnal and surreptitious correspondence with Bayardo and an equally accomplished dedication to embroidery by daylight.[21]

Thus, the relationship between victimage and writing that is implicitly posited by the novel is distinctly underscored by the metaphoric structure identified above. Both the crumbling body of Santiago Nasar and the text show their seams, as it were, the crude remainders of their shared violent history.[22] For through the establishing of this association the text reveals its own necessarily concealed foundation in violence and suppression. I am alluding, in the terms offered by J. Derrida, to the imposition of a closed order of signification in the text, and the violent, expulsive 'logic of the supplement' that it inevitably sets in place.[23] This awareness of the supplement is expressed in the novel at both levels of the metaphoric association that confounds body and text. At the conclusion of Santiago Nasar's autopsy we read: 'Furthermore, the priest had pulled out the sliced-up intestines by their roots, but in the end he didn't know what to do with them, and he gave them an angry blessing and threw them into the garbage pail' (p. 100). Just as Nasar's entrails become a surplus, a supplement that must be discarded, the text repeats the same violent gesture by turning each reading, as was seen earlier, into an ever-renewed act of pollution. Writing, the suggestion appears to be, cannot serve as the instrument for redemption and cleansing that the novel envisions, since it is itself constituted and sustained through a violence that traverses it to the very core.

This knowledge, I would argue, also appears to be incorporated in the novel as a persistent attempt to eradicate the structure of differences on which the text is constructed. Seen in this light, *Chronicle of a Death Foretold* seems to be forever on the verge of reverting to a state of undifferentiation that would jeopardize the system of differences that rules the text. Instances of this desire to abolish difference are myriad. For example, the narrator is twice confused with Santiago Nasar, and he comes to the town manifestly from the outside, just as Bayardo San Román had many years earlier. Bayardo's supposed antagonist, Santiago Nasar, is alluded to in the narrative as a *boyardo* (master, lord), a transformation that could also yield *Bedoya*, the last name of the narrator's closest friend as one of its permutations. The onomastic similarities – whether literal or semantic – seem almost to dominate the text: the twins *Pedro* and *Pablo* Vicario; *Divino* Rostro, *Divina* Flor, *Angela* Vicario; Divina *Flor*, *Flora* Miguel, don Rogelio de la *Flor*, *Hortensia* Baute; Luisa *Santiaga*, *Santiago* Nasar; Father *Carmen* Amador, Purísima del *Carmen*. In addition, there is a dimension in the novel that appears to indicate the possibility of an interpretation of the events that would hinge specifically on the differentiation between the two meanings of the term *altanería*: haughtiness vs. falconry. This reading would centre on the epigraph to the text, borrowed from a poem of Gil Vicente, and which reads: 'The pursuit of love / is like falconry (haughtiness)' ('La caza de amor / es de altanería.') A fragment of the same poem is quoted later in the novel by the narrator:

'A falcon that chases / a warring crane / should expect no gain' ('Halcón que se atreve / con garza guerrera, / peligros espera') (p. 87), thereby proposing the existence of interpretative possibilities based on an explicit relationship with a previous text. But an examination of Vicente's poem reveals that it is itself sustained by the wilful ambiguity and oscillation between the two meanings that the novel seems intent on maintaining.[24] Moreover, Santiago Nasar, the person in relation to whom all the events and characters in the text delineate themselves, is depicted as a disassembler of identities, a veritable disseminator of non-difference:

Santiago Nasar had an almost magical talent for disguises, and his favourite entertainment was to confuse the identities of the mulatto girls. He would plunder the wardrobe of some to disguise the others, so that they all ended up feeling different from themselves and like the ones they were not. On a certain occasion, one of them found herself repeated in another with such exactness that she had an attack of tears. 'I felt like I'd stepped out of a mirror', she said.   (pp. 87–8)

This quality in turn assimilates him even more to Bayardo San Román, of whom it is said that he 'not only was capable of doing everything, and doing it extremely well, but also had access to inexhaustible resources' (p. 38). Examples like the foregoing could be multiplied almost endlessly. What must be emphasized is that in the drive to abolish the differences that constitute it, the text motions towards its own violent essence, demonstrating that it must speak the contradictory knowledge that it embodies even at the expense of its very being.

In sum, then, the novel's attempted passage from violence to the ritual containment of that violence is compromised by the text's awareness of its own primordial inscription through another kind of violent act. One could propose that in attempting such a passage the novel becomes a perfect analogue of writing, since it traces the unfolding of the inevitable self-mystification in which every instance of writing indulges. Finally, in the text's unmasking of a violence that precedes and underpins all subsequent violence, one can perhaps find the most literal, yet possibly the most significant interpretation of the title *Chronicle of a Death Foretold*.

Notes

1 Gabriel García Márquez, *Crónica de una muerte anunciada* (Bogotá: La Oveja Negra, 1981), p. 107. All subsequent page references will be to this edition, and will be noted parenthetically in the text. I have refrained for the most part from using Gregory Rabassa's English edition and have furnished my own translation since, as Randolph Pope has thoroughly demonstrated (in 'Transparency and Illusion in *Chronicle of a Death Foretold*', a lecture given at Wesleyan University, 9 April 1983), Rabassa's English rendition is uncharacteristically marred by mistranslations and mistakes.

The description of the murder includes the following significant passage as well: 'Then they kept on knifing him against the door with alternate and easy stabs, floating in the dazzling backwater they had found on the other side of fear. They did not hear the shouts of the whole town, *frightened by its own crime*' (my italics, p. 153).

2 'Santiago Nasar had been named for her [the narrator's mother] and furthermore, she was his godmother when he was christened, but she was also a blood relative of Pura Vicario, the mother of the returned bride' (p. 33). Later, the narrator's father protests: 'We've got the same ties with [Plácido Linero] that we have with the Vicarios' (p. 34).

3 ' "They [the Vicarios] were hard-looking, but of a good sort", the report said. I who had known them since grammar school would have written the same thing' (p. 24).

4 In a very provocative piece, Angel Rama pursues this line of questioning to the end, suggesting somewhat hastily that perhaps the narrator is the one to blame for Angela's dishonour: 'Is he [the narrator] the only one not to have been the victim of fate? Or had fate used him before, making him responsible for the loss of virginity of his cousin Angela Vicario? Could this be his place and this his mission in the working of the tragedy?' From 'García Márquez entre la tragedia y la policial o Crónica y pesquisa de la crónica de una muerte anunciada', *Sin Nombre*, 13: 1 (Oct.–Dec. 1982), p. 20. Other articles on the novel include the following: '*Crónica de una muerte anunciada*, la escritura de un texto irreverente', by Myrna Solotorevsky, *Revista Iberoamericana*, 128–9 (July–Dec. 1984), pp. 1077–91; Isabel Álvarez Borland, 'From Mystery to Parody: (Re)Readings of García Márquez's *Crónica de una muerte anunciada*', *Symposium*, 38:4 (Winter 1984), pp. 278–86; Dona M. Kercher's 'García Márquez's *Chronicle of a Death Foretold*: Notes on Parody and the Artist,' *Latin American Literary Review*, 13:25 (1985), pp. 90–103; and 'Ends and Endings in García Márquez's *Chronicle of a Death Foretold*', by Lois Parkinson Zamora, *Latin American Literary Review*, 13:25 (1985), pp. 104–16.

5 'In the chapters subsequent to the consummation of Santiago Nasar's crime . . . we learn, as we might in a soap-opera, that Angela finally fell in love with Bayardo after his rejection of her and spent most of her remaining days in a hallucinating correspondence which led her to write more than two thousand letters without really expecting a single reply. Yet, one day, Bayardo would calmly appear with a bundle of letters, in order and unopened: "Well", he would say, "here I am." ' The reader's perplexity at such simplicity could only permit him the following conjecture: ' "If this was the ending, opaque and pedestrian, then why such a high-sounding and moving opening?" ' From '*Crónica de una muerte anunciada*, de G. García Márquez: reportaje, profecía y recuento', by Germán D. Carrillo, in *Literature in Transition: the Many Voices of the Caribbean Area: a Symposium*, ed. Rose S. Minc (Gaithersburg, Md: Hispamérica and Montclair State College, 1982),

pp. 82–3. It could be argued that the disillusionment expressed by these critics is an expression of interpretative frustration, since this final reconciliation has been proposed by García Márquez himself as the scene that purportedly allowed him to discern the true meaning of the events as a secret and unfortunate story of love. From an article published in *El País* on 26 August and 2 September 1981, and reported by Richard Predmore in his 'El mundo moral de *Crónica de una muerte anunciada*', *Cuadernos Hispanoamericanos*, 390 (Dec. 1982), 703–12.

6 See, for instance, Gregory Rabassa's 'García Márquez's New Book: Literature or Journalism?' *World Literature Today*, 56:1 (1982), 48–51, and Raymond Williams, *Gabriel García Márquez* (Boston, 1984), specifically chapter 7, '*Chronicle of a Death Foretold* (1981) and Journalism', pp. 134–57. Needless to say, this relationship has been postulated by García Márquez himself on a number of occasions.

7 I am invoking to some degree the definition of the category 'performative' that is postulated by speech-act theory. More precisely, one could consider *Chronicle of a Death Foretold* as an extended illocutionary act, since I will argue that the production of the text constitutes in itself a significant act (See J. L. Austin's *How to do Things with Words*, New York, 1962; and J. R. Searle's *Speech Acts: An Essay in the Philosophy of Language*, Cambridge, 1969). Nevertheless, I would like to retain, for reasons that will become apparent presently, the theatrical/ritual connotations of the term as well.

8 In his exhaustive study of citation (*La seconde main, ou le travail de la citation*, Paris, 1979), Antoine Compagnon offers insights useful for a consideration of García Márquez's novel from this perspective. I have in mind in particular his examination of quotation as a kind of work that has an internal performative economy of its own.

9 Williams, *Gabriel García Márquez*, p. 137.

10 Proposing the category of *anunciación*, Josefa Salmón has enumerated the many ways in which the death of Santiago Nasar had been announced before the crime had been actually committed: 'El poder de la anunciación en *Cien años de soledad* y *Crónica de una muerte anunciada*', *Discurso Literario*, 1:1 (1983), 67–77. Mario Vargas Llosa had previously identified the use of this technique in *One Hundred Years of Solitude* in his *García Márquez: historia de un deicidio* (Barcelona, 1971), pp. 545–65.

11 I have had recourse to the following definition of ritual, proposed by S. J. Tambiah: 'Ritual is a culturally constructed system of symbolic communication. It is constituted of patterned and ordered sequences of words and acts . . . whose content and arrangement are characterized in varying degree by formality (conventionality), stereotypy (rigidity), condensation (fusion), and redundancy (repetition).' From 'A Performative Approach to Ritual,' in *Proceedings of the British Academy*, 65 (Oxford, 1981), pp. 113–69. I have also found useful the following: Victor Turner's *The Forest of Symbols* (Ithaca, 1967), *The Drums of Affliction* (Oxford, 1968), *The Ritual Process: Structure and Anti-Structure* (Ithaca, 1977), and 'Dramatic Ritual/Ritual Drama: Performative and Reflexive Anthropology', in *A Crack in the Mirror*, ed. Jay Ruby (Philadelphia, 1982), pp. 83–97; and James J. Fox, 'Roman Jakobson and the Comparative Study of Parallelism', in *Roman Jakobson: Echoes of his Scholarship*, ed. D. Armstrong and C. H. Van Schooneveld (Lisse, 1977), pp. 59–90.

12 'Many people coincided in recalling that it was a radiant morning with a sea breeze that came in through the banana groves, as it should have been on a fine February morning of that period. But most agreed that the weather was funereal, with a murky, low sky and the thick smell of still waters, and that at the moment of the tragedy a thin drizzle was falling' (p. 11).

13 In Plinio Apuleyo Mendoza, *El olor de la guayaba* (Barcelona, 1982), p. 38.

14 I am using these formulae as translations of 'x años después . . .' and 'x años más tarde . . .' respectively.

15 Given the general thrust of my argument, I believe the following marginal comment is called for. It is almost inevitable to read *Chronicle of a Death Foretold* and think of René Girard's ideas on mimetic rivalry and its attendant sacrificial crises. I contend, however, that to read the novel as a straightforward confirmation of Girard's theories would be unwarranted. How is one to deal, for instance, with the quasi-apocalyptical dissolution of the community as a result of the crime, or with Santiago Nasar's transformation into an 'enemy' after his sacrifice? If there is any unanimity achieved through the murder it is only in the universal reeking of the smell of Santiago Nasar that afflicts the entire town for days after the events. One *could* invoke Girard at this point and claim that what *Chronicle of a Death Foretold* details is the breakdown of the sacrificial mechanism, in other words, the impossibility of activating effectively the sacrificial process that would normally lead to a resolution of the mimetic crisis through the collective unanimity achieved in the act of victimage and the subsequent re-establishment of difference. (This development, and the consequences of this failure are addressed specifically in his book *Des choses cachées depuis la fondation du monde*, a series of interviews with J. M. Oughourlian and Guy Lefort, Paris, 1978.) However, if Girard can use the breakdown of the mechanism as a confirmation of his ideas, then he has placed his scheme in a position of theoretical unaccountability that is not consonant with the empirical pretensions of his work. For a penetrating critique of Girard's theories from an anthropological perspective, see Elizabeth Traube's 'Incest and Mythology: Anthropological and Girardian Perspectives', *Berkshire Review*, 14 (1979), 37–53.

16 *Beyond the Pleasure Principle*, ed. James Strachey (New York, 1961), pp. 9–11 *et passim*.

17 *The Drums of Affliction* (Oxford, 1968), p. 269. Here and elsewhere, Turner proposes the use of dramatic categories for the analysis of ritual performance, which makes him especially interesting from the perspective of the present study.

18 Claude Lévi-Strauss, *The Savage Mind* (Chicago, 1966), p. 32.

19 'The damage from the knives was only a beginning for the unforgiving autopsy that Father Carmen Amador had to undertake in Dr Dionisio Iguarán's absence. "It was as if we killed him all over again after he was dead" ' (p. 95).

20 *Chronicle of a Death Foretold*, trans. Gregory Rabassa (New York: Knopf, 1983), pp. 76–7. All subsequent references to the English translation will be to this edition and will be noted parenthetically in the text.

21 'Everyone who saw her [Angela] during that time agreed that she was absorbed and skilled at her embroidery machine, and that by her industry she had managed to forget' (p. 115).

22 With characteristic brilliance, William Gass has remarked: '*Chronicle of a Death Foretold* does not tell, but literally pieces together, the torn-apart body of a story.' In 'More Deaths than One', a review of *Chronicle of a Death Foretold, New York*, 11 April 1983, 83–4.

23 One could refer to a number of works by J. Derrida in this regard. See, for instance, *Of Grammatology*, trans. Gayatry Chakravorty Spivak (Baltimore and London, 1976) and 'Plato's Pharmacy', in *Dissemination*, trans. Barbara Johnson (Chicago, 1981).

24 The poem, in Spanish, is included in one of Vicente's Portuguese dramas, the *Comedia de Rubena*. It reads as follows:

Halcón que se atreve
con garza guerrera,
peligros espera.

Halcón que se vuela
con garza a porfía,
cazarla quería
y no la recela.
Más quien no se vela
de garza guerrera,
peligros espera.

La caza de amor
es de altanería:
trabajos de día,
de noche dolor.
Halcón cazador
con garza tan fiera,
peligros espera.

From *Poesías de Gil Vicente*, ed. Dámaso Alonso (México: Editorial Séneca, 1940), p. 33.

Free-play of fore-play: the fiction of non-consummation: speculations on *Chronicle of a Death Foretold*

BERNARD McGUIRK

'Speculations – On Freud'

> In his text something must answer for the speculation of which he speaks
> ... I also maintain that speculation is not only a mode of research named
> by Freud, not only the object of his discourse, but also the operation of
> his writing, what he is doing in writing what he is writing here, that
> which makes him do it and that which he causes to be done, that which
> makes him write and that which he causes to be written.   (Jacques
> Derrida)[1]

García Márquez's text, *Chronicle of a Death Foretold*, also opens with an
epigraph,[2] from the sixteenth-century Portuguese playwright Gil
Vicente: 'La caza de amor/es de altanería' (translated by Gregory
Rabassa as 'the hunt for love is haughty falconry'). A first speculation
concerns the multiple pun(ning) which opens the novel, for 'altanería'
means height, high flight, falconry, haughtiness and pride; 'de amor'
might also mean 'of love' and the second 'de', too, might mean 'of' or
'for'. To the Colombian ear, 'la caza (casa) de amor(es)', too, might
prefigure the brothel of María Alejandrina Cervantes. 'Opens the
novel', then, in all senses, invites open reading rather than interpretative closure. This study of *Chronicle* draws upon several of the
speculations applied by Derrida to Freud's *Beyond the Pleasure Principle*
and, in its turn, extends the mirroring process of 'speculary reflection'[3]
by adducing others. The guiding principle of the interaction between
this study and the host-text is Derrida's wish to mark the intersections
of the various speculations: 'If we wish to interlace, in another style,
with other questions, the networks of a so-called internal reading ...
the networks of autobiography, of auto-graphy, of auto-
thanatography, and those of the "analytical movement" inasmuch as
they are inseparable from it, we must at least, we must at least begin by

marking, in the reading hastily called "internal", the places that are *structurally* open to the crossing of the networks.'[4] Thus, this text will take the form of a series of overlapping speculations.

Speculation – speculary reflection

Q. How did the writing of *Chronicle of a Death Foretold* come about?

A. The novel is set 30 years ago and it's based on a real event, an assassination that took place in a town in Colombia. I was staying very near the participants in this 'drama' at a time when I'd written several short stories but still hadn't got my first novel published. I realized straight away that I'd got hold of some extremely important material, but my mother knew about this and asked me not to write this book while some of those involved were still alive, and then she told me their names. So I just kept putting it off. There were times I thought the 'drama' had ended, but it continued to develop and things kept on happening. If I'd written it then, I'd have left out a great amount of material which is essential to the understanding of the story.[5]

The mirroring of a 'real event' by a first-person narrator involved in, though recounting retrospectively, the 'drama' which shook Sucre, a small Colombian town, some thirty years previously, invites corroboration, not least beause of the *chronicling* promised by the title and by the presentation of testimony collected from eye-witnesses, participants and even the protagonists themselves. When the *chronicle* is published by the country's, the continent's, most famous author, the topical interest increases. Thus, the invasion of Sucre by journalists, shortly after the publication of García Márquez's book in 1981, resulted in a typically Latin American pseudo-literary event, a flood of interviews, opinions and memoirs drawn from those involved. The journalistic impact of the novel, however, is not merely *post hoc*; for García Márquez, the professional newspaperman, exploits the generic ambiguity of his text: 'For the first time I have managed a perfect integration of journalism and literature ... journalism helps maintain contact with reality, which is essential to literature. And vice-versa: literature teaches you how to write ... I learned how to be a journalist by reading good literature.'[6]

'Maintaining contact with reality', then, poses the perennial problem of realism. Yet, in another interview, the author admits the complication already implied, above, in this word 'drama':

... It's interesting to see now that the novel which finally emerged has nothing to do with the reality of the situation.

Q. Are any journalistic techniques used in the novel?

A. I've used a reporting technique but nothing of the actual drama or those taking part remains except the point of departure and the structure. The characters don't appear under their real names nor does the description tally with the real place. It's all been poetically transmuted. The only ones who retain their real names are members of my family because they've allowed me to do this. Of course, some of the characters are going to be recognized, but what really interests me, and I believe this must also interest the critics, is the comparison between reality and the literary work.

Q. Aren't you laying the novel open to a guessing game of who's who?

A. That's already happened. When the novel appeared a Bogotá magazine published an article written from where the events took place with photographs of who was supposed to have taken part. They've done a job which in journalistic terms, is, I think, excellent, but there's one snag: the story that the witnesses are now telling the journalists is totally different from what happens in the novel. Perhaps the word 'totally' is wrong here. The starting point is the same but the development is different. I'm pretentious enough to believe that the 'drama' in my book is better, that it's more controlled, more structured.[7]

When he uses the words 'drama', 'controlled, more structured', 'poetically transmuted', García Márquez betrays not only an author's awareness of the existence of what Derrida called 'the places that are *structurally* open to the crossing of the networks', but, at the same time, a reader's propensity to interpret, even to offer value judgements ('my book is better'). He does not go farther than a 'reading hastily called [by me] "internal"', a reading which merely acknowledges the impossibility of mimesis. Thus, 'we [as reader] must . . . begin by marking . . . the places that are *structurally* open to the crossing'. In the process, 'we do not aim for either priority or originality. We merely formulate speculative hypotheses to explain and describe the facts that we observe . . .'[8]

Fact	*Fiction*
Miguel Reyes Palencia marries and discovers his wife is not a virgin. He returns the bride, Margarita, to her parents after striking her and abusing her verbally. His friends give him a knife to kill her with. He refuses but offers her the knife to kill herself.	Bayardo San Román marries and discovers his wife is not a virgin. He returns the bride, Angela Vicario, to her parents' home where her mother, Pura, strikes her repeatedly.

However, the girl is forced to name her love, Cayetano Gentile Chimento, who is pursued and killed by her brother.

The girl is forced to name her lover. She names Santiago Nasar, who is pursued and eventually killed by her twin brothers, Pedro and Pablo.

García Márquez knows the protagonists. He does not himself witness the events. He promises his mother not to publish while protagonists are alive. She releases him from his promise. He writes *Chronicle* but says he will not publish until the Pinochet regime in Chile falls. He publishes *Chronicle* in 1981.

The narrator knows the protagonists and attends the wedding celebrations. He misses the actual crime because he is in the brothel of María Alejandrina Cervantes. The narrator 'pieces together' various eyewitnesses' versions of the death of Santiago Nasar and interviews the principal surviving protagonists. The narrator constantly refers to his text as a 'chronicle'.

The first two references to self on the part of the narrator in *Chronicle* are of different temporal orders. 'I was recovering from the wedding revels in the apostolic lap of María Alejandrina Cervantes' (p. 11) refers to the narrator at the time of Santiago Nasar's death: 'when I returned to this forgotten village, trying to put back together the mirror of memory from so many scattered fragments' points to the *construction* of the present narration, nearly thirty years later. The mirror is broken. But as scattered as the fragments are the instances of 'I'. The intervening instances are also chronicled in the text: 'I had a very confused memory of the festivities before I decided to rescue them piece by piece from the memory of others . . . In the course of the investigations for this chronicle, I recovered numerous marginal experiences . . . Many know that in the unconsciousness of the binge I proposed marriage to Mercedes Barcha . . . as she herself reminded me when we were wed fourteen years later' (pp. 71–2). Thus, apart from the collective nature of the fragmented memory, we are confronted with the literary convention which Philippe Lejeune has called the 'autobiographical contract':[9] that is, 'the affirmation in the text of the "identity" between the names of the author, narrator, and protagonist, referring in the last resort to the *name* of the author on the cover . . . manifesting an intention to "honour the signature" '. García Márquez's signature is honoured, in the first instance, by the presence in the text of Mercedes, his own wife, and later, by that of Margot his sister, Luis Enrique, his brother, Luisa Santiaga his mother, and Gerineldo, his illustrious forebear. Yet, here, analysis is further complicated by the mother's refusal to greet Bayardo San Román's father, General Petronio San Román, 'hero of the civil wars of the past century, and one of the most glorious of the Conservative regime because he had put to flight Colonel Aureliano Buendía in the disaster of Tucurinca . . . and a man who gave orders for Gerineldo Márquez to be shot in the back' (p. 55). For when we decide on the nature of the autobiographical contract, in this instance, it is not enough to follow Lejeune's view 'that all questions of *faithfulness* (this is the problem of "resemblance") depend in the last analysis on the question of *authenticity* (this is the problem of identity), which in itself is formulated in terms of the name of the author'.[10] Here, as elsewhere in *Chronicle*, the narrator refers not only to García Márquez's family as his own but also to García Márquez's *fictional* creations from other, earlier novels, in this case, *One Hundred Years of Solitude*. The crossing of networks, then, problematizes genre distinctions: autobiography, fiction and journalism. It also, concomitantly, highlights intertextuality: that is, the suggestion (beloved of García Márquez) that all his writing is but one text – *signature*. The extended signature loses the presence(s) of self(selves) – Being – 'in the differential character of the language-system and the arbitrariness of signs' in order *not* to succumb ultimately, as do Saussure and Husserl, 'to the metaphysics of presence'.[11]

Derrida's neologism *différance* is articulated by Vincent Leitch as: '(1) "to differ" – to be unlike or dissimilar in nature, quality, or form; (2) "differre" (Latin) – to scatter, disperse; and (3) "to defer" – delay, postpone'.[12] *Chronicle* splits the narrating presence into dissimilar natures, qualities and forms of 'I'. *Chronicle* scatters and disperses 'the fragmented mirror of memory'. *Chronicle* defers, delays, postpones the *writing* of 'a death foretold'. 'This is obviously what makes it threatening and necessarily dreaded by everything in us that desires a realm, the past or future presence of a realm.'[13]

Here, the realm of speculary reflection. And the writing achieves such a loss: 'Years later when I came back to search out the last pieces of testimony for this chronicle . . . things had been disappearing little by little despite Colonel Lázaro Aponte's stubborn vigilance, including the full-length wardrobe with six mirrors which the master craftsmen . . . had had to assemble inside the house since it would not fit through the door' (p. 139). The possibility of speculary reflection cannot exist outside the locus of the single, original *event*: here, the house of the widower Xius, where Angela's non-virginity is discovered on the wedding night.

And what of the 'I'? ' "It was a strange insistence", Cristo Bedoya told me. "So much so that sometimes I've thought that Margot already knew that they were going to kill him (Santiago Nasar) and wanted to hide him in your house" ' (p. 34). Not so strange while the certainty of authorship, of a future narrator to 'tell the tale', exists. But Margot's faith in concealing Santiago with the narrator conflicts with the narrator's own uneasiness regarding the self as a purveyor of writing: 'Much later, during an uncertain period when I was trying to understand something of myself by selling encyclopedias and medical books in the towns of Guajira . . . on seeing her like that, in the idyllic frame of the window, I refused to believe that that woman was the one I thought she was, because I didn't want to admit that life would end up so closely resembling bad literature. But it was she: Angela Vicario, twenty-three years after the drama' (p. 142).

The strange insistence is the notion of mimesis, the idyllic frame of bad literature which a *deferred* voice, a writing, will not admit.

Speculation – whodunnit?

. . . dans la langue il n'y a que des différences, sans termes positifs
(Saussure)[14]

'Someone who was never identified had pushed under the door an envelope containing a piece of paper warning Santiago Nasar that they were waiting for him to kill him and telling him, as well, the place, motives and other precise details of the plot. The message was on the floor when Santiago Nasar left the house but he didn't see it, nor did Divina Flor, nor anyone else, until long after the crime had been consummated' (p. 26).

'Place', 'motives', 'details of plot', 'crime': the *language* of detective-fiction. Since *Chronicle* manifests many traits of the detective genre, it is critically enticing to answer the question 'whodunnit' by speculation on the sign(s) provided by the text; in short, and in Saussurean terms, by regarding the genre as *langue* and the individual utterance, *Chronicle*, as *parole*. Given the traditional elements of victim, motive, weapon, criminal(s), and the refinements of legal trappings, police-man, autopsy, prosecution and judge, the sign, read as crime-novel, is virtually transparent. But the element 'missing' from the whodunnit model is mystery. The fact that the text reveals victim, criminals and motive so early has a concomitant effect on narrative sequence.

Instead of the *syntagmatic* progression associated with the detective genre which its subject matter evokes, namely Todorov's classic typology of enigma–pursuit–solution[15], *Chronicle* depends, rather, on an *associative* structure, again in Saussurean terms, in its generation of meaning. Thus, drawing for a moment on Roland Barthes, the hermeneutic (enigma) and the proaretic (action) codes, since they involve the apparatus of resolving a given sequence of actions, may be construed, here, as *misleading* the reader into identifying the utterance of *Chronicle* with the language of detective-fiction.

To what 'language', therefore, does *Chronicle* belong? Bearing in mind Barthes's fifth code, the referential, which points to the cultural setting of the text, it is perfectly possible, in the Spanish American perspective, to highlight and explain an associative structure of narrative. In the process, the semic code, relating to the development and understanding of character, and the symbolic code which controls symbolic and thematic interpretations, might be used to situate *Chronicle* in the system of *pundonor*, or 'honour code' literature. In this system, there is no deciphering of mystery or solution of crime; it is rather a matter of observing 'poetic' justice at work. Angela Vicario's lost honour, revealed only on her wedding night, must be recuperated, along with that of her family. Thus, the virtual complicity of the deceived husband and Angela's mother when he returns the bride: 'Bayardo San Román did not enter but pushed his wife gently into the house without saying a word. Then he kissed Pura Vicario on the cheek and spoke to her in a very deep and dejected voice but with great tenderness. "Thank you for everything, mother, you are a saint" ' (pp. 76–7). His subsequent withdrawal from the action and Pura Vicario's physical and mental punishment of her daughter are as little of a surprise to the reader, in *pundonor* tradition, as the subsequent assumption of the duty to kill Santiago Nasar, the named lover, by Angela's brothers. Once the 'tragedy' of dishonour occurs, the *action* of the narrative is irreversible. Society – and reader – awaits a known outcome whence the 'foretold' nature of death.

There do remain, however, in *Chronicle*, elements not of mystery but of the unexplained. The most obvious, and one central to any reading of the cultural code, is that of the possibility of Santiago Nasar's innocence. Very early, the text offers an 'open' or unread sign of such a possibility, namely, the anonymously delivered 'note under the door'. Unread by Santiago Nasar, the note, it will be remembered, told him 'the place, motives and other precise details of the plot'.

It is clear that it cannot be *exposed*. We can only expose what, at a certain moment, can become *present*, manifest; what can be shown, presented as present, a being – present in its truth, the truth of a present or the presence of a present.

The above refers not to Santiago Nasar's unread letter; it is Derrida's own formulation of *différance*, that *différance* 'which is neither a *word* nor a *concept*' but that which refers to 'the *play* of differences'.[16] My argument is that Santiago Nasar's letter is an instance of *différance* at work, unread, unexposed. Thus, 'the precise details of the plot', though pointed towards by the *unread* text of the note under the door, will not be revealed by the *read* text of *Chronicle*. *Chronicle* refutes the cause and effect and teleological structure of the detective-story (it begins *and* ends with the death); equally, it denies the placing of the *punto* (point, full stop) to *honour* . . . that is, it 'opens' a closed system, the *pundonor*. For the *pundonor* is a language, too: and 'in language there are only differences, without positive terms' (terminologies and terminations). That *Chronicle* itself constitutes a *trace*, a note slipped under the door of a closed system of writing, will be my fifth speculation, the free-play of a reading, a re-reading of 'thanatography'.

Speculation – money-making

The millionaire launching of Gabriel García Márquez
José Vicente Kataraín, director of 'La oveja negra' publishing house in Bogotá, explained how they obtained the García Márquez contract, negociating in Barcelona with Carmen Balcells, holder of the Colombian's publishing rights. '. . . we managed to produce, publish and sell one million copies of the complete works in two years, an unprecedented figure in so short a time. Because of this success, the company competed with a number of foreign publishers to launch *Chronicle of a Death Foretold*. Spain and Argentina are publishing another million, besides ours, that is, two million copies are on the Spanish-speaking market. By the end of the year, with world-wide sales, in thirty two languages, it will be the most successful publication in history.' The director says that they needed forty five aeroplanes to export the novel . . . bearing in mind that a 727 normally carries eight tons of cargo. By the author's request, the format of the book is light and easy for the reader; the large lettering is similar to that of a children's story. He also wanted it to be economically priced in order to reach the maximum readership.
      (Ana María Hernández de López, *Hispania*, 64, December 1981)

'Autobiography, auto-graphy, auto-thanatography'; writing about the self, writing the self, writing of the death of the self. The 'crossing of networks' has been confined, so far, in this 'reading hastily called "internal", [to] the places *structurally* open to the crossing'. Thus, in Derridan terms, the *presence, being* and *voice* of García Márquez are deconstructed by the *difference, trace* and *writing* of *Chronicle*.[17] While, as argued above, the signature need not succumb ultimately to the *metaphysics* of presence, it is the aim of the present speculation to situate *Chronicle* in an *economics* of signature. In this respect, the argument will draw upon Pierre Macherey's 'view of the author as someone who works upon a world of signs and codes from the inside, so that he or she is "written" by the language in the act of writing it'. That world entails 'a theory of reading which sees texts as necessarily *incomplete* and contradictory and which is crucially concerned with *ideology*'.[18]

However much García Márquez might complain of the traumatic impact of the sudden fame and responsibility thrust upon him by the success of *One Hundred Years of Solitude*,[19] the public demand for the authenticity of his signature, for 'recognizability', impinges on 'the world of signs and codes' from which *Chronicle* is produced: not only in the occasional cross-reference to Colonel Aureliano Buendía or to a Petra Cotes, but also in the replicated Buendía dynasty of the Vicario family – Poncio, the father, 'seated alone on a stool in the centre of the patio' (p. 73), Pablo 'who learned to work with precious metals in his father's workshop and became an elegant goldsmith' (p. 134), Pedro 'who reenlisted . . . went into guerilla territory singing whoring songs and was never heard of again' (p. 134) and Pura, the mother, Ursula reincarnate. The list of possible parallels is long, from the comic, Pedro Crespi impact of the newcomer, Bayardo San Román, to the elaborated inclusion of a certain Gabriel, this time the name on the cover rather than the Paris-bound friend of the last of the Buendías, Aureliano Babilonia.

The temptation to counterfeit the successful currency of a previous best-seller, then, constitutes another speculation, a speculation, as Derrida has it, 'in the sense of the production of a surplus value and in the sense of calculation or gambling on the stock-market or issuing more or less fictitious bills'.[20] To José Vicente Kataraín and to Carmen Balcells, no doubt, praise-worthy – but, no less, prize-worthy. Nobel prize-worthy. (And were I Derrida, or even writing in French, I should not resist the temptation either. *Prix Nobel*, Nobel prize . . . and Nobel *price*.)

Yet this is no condemnation. For, it must be recalled, it is nothing other than a theory of reading – in this case, my own reading of 'someone who works upon a world of signs and codes *from the inside*' (my italics). How the signature *García Márquez* 'is "written" by the language in the act of writing it' yet remains 'necessarily *incomplete* and contradictory' will be the substance of my next, ideological, speculation.

Speculation – free play

> The self, like the world, is a text . . . readers who are astonishingly eager to see shattered or social selves in novels and poems are a good deal more reluctant to acknowledge the consequences of such a deconstruction for their own relations to texts . . . neutrality itself is a fiction . . . and the literary critic, whose avowed subject is fiction, need not find this embarrassing.   (Walter Benn Michaels)[21]

The fantastic enterprise of the last Buendía, in *One Hundred Years of Solitude*, of reading his own destiny in the very act of fulfilling it, may be taken as one metaphor of the erroneous reading-practice of the assumption of realism. Aureliano Babilonia's fate is sealed by his attachment to a supposed link between the text he is reading and his own act of reading it. For him, that link is one of a transparent, mimetic relationship, a 'realist' characterization *par excellence*. For this reason, his reading is *closed*; he has no second chance in the closed cycle of one hundred years, the final chapter of which he himself constitutes. Since this might be construed as García Márquez's attack not merely against the notion of realism but specifically against the reading-practice which renders it possible, it becomes necessary for the reader – now liberated from the notion of 'text as speaking mirror' (*One Hundred Years of Solitude*, Editorial Sudamericana ed., 1975, p. 350) – to redefine the link, the relationship. Apparently audaciously, then, by returning to a *supposed* documented event, *Chronicle* cuts the umbilicus, renders non-fiction fiction, but not simply, dismissively, as in the throw-away (Borgesian?) notion that 'all writing is fiction' but rather in terms of *reading*, that reading-practice which insists on perpetuating the confusion of transparent realism. In short, *Chronicle's* reference is plurivalent, despite having paid the fares to Sucre of all those journalists.

Concomitantly, there can be many answers to the question(s) 'whodunnit?'.

'Come on, girl', he said, trembling with rage, 'tell us who it was'. She hesitated no more than the time it took to say the name. She sought it from within the darkness, found it at first sight amongst the many, many confusable names of this world and the other one, and she pinned it to the wall with her well-aimed dart, like a butterfly with no will of its own, whose sentence had been written forever. 'Santiago Nasar', she said.   (p. 78)

Fulfilling the promise that my fifth speculation would constitute a pursuit of the trace left by the note slipped under the door of a closed system of writing, I come to the necessary free-play of any, of all reading. Of my reading. Of a reading prompted both by the title of 'a death foretold' and of Derrida's notion of 'auto-thanatography', but one of the many networks of reading. I begin with 'confusable names'.

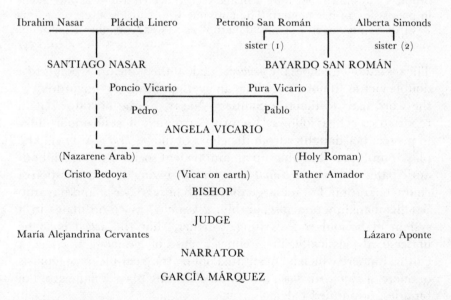

The above lay-out, while less than arbitrary, is nonetheless an unembarrassing non-neutrality. It may serve to focus attention on the free-play of names which follows.

'From within the darkness' of 'the many, many confusable names of this world and the other one' comes the *name* Santiago Nasar. Born of the Arab intruder Ibrahim, master of falconry (p. 16), deflowerer (p. 19), and of the Christian mother, inaccurate decipherer of dreams, Santiago Nasar is the outsider, 'just like all Turks' (p. 162), 'the stranger in the house'[22] of a Holy Roman dominance. Part Nazarene, victim 'with no will of its own, whose sentence had been written forever', whose fate it is to die against the tree, the wooden door of his own house, in the helpless proximity of his placid mother. Part saint (if martyr), but SANT/IAGO . . . thus, part perpetrator, 'distiller' of doubt – the doubt which destroys the *Moor*. Notorious womanizer, would-be deflowerer both of Divina Flor (pp. 18–19) and of the church for his own funeral (p. 69), he is sacrificed by raisers of hogs who cannot bring themselves to kill *named* pigs, except when these are called after flowers (p. 86). Yet there is a complication:

For the immense majority there was only one victim: Bayardo San Román. They assumed that the other protagonists of the tragedy had fulfilled with dignity, and even with a certain grandeur, the part which, as a favour, life had assigned them. Santiago Nasar had expiated the insult, the Vicario brothers had shown they were men and their ridiculed sister was once again in possesssion of her honour. The only one who had lost everything was Bayardo San Román. 'El pobre Bayardo', as he was remembered for many years.   (p. 134)

The text at once echoes the *pundonor* and, at the same time, points to a double victim. If not a doubling, an overlap. Bayardo/'boyardo'? . . . the word used to describe Santiago Nasar, by the narrator but in reported speech, as follows: 'Victoria Guzmán . . . lost no opportunity to protect her daughter from the claws of the *seigneur*' (p. 110). The play is multiple, throwing up an ambivalent social code which both anticipates and accepts a *droit de seigneur*, throwing *open* the question of characterization. For it is arguable that Santiago Nasar and Bayardo San Román function inseparably, *actantially*, as co-ordinates in a system of honour-code writing. Further, that the *actant* is to be understood classically, in Greimas's sense of *the sphere of action*, a cultural sphere which is constituted not by the 'real-life' protagonists of Sucre, a *characterization*, but by an elaborate play of names and of binaries, of punned pairs.

Speculation – word play

The 'anagram' should not be defined as a regulated dislocation lacking completeness, but as an indeterminable multiplicity, a radical undecidability, which undoes all codes.[23]

In the juxtaposition of Santiago Nasar/Bayardo San Román, an anagrammatical free-play breeds saints and martyrs ('y ardo'/'and I burn'), Christians versus Moor, incomplete Nazarene, Holy Roman obedience to a severe marriage-code. And the play remains incomplete, always leaves a *trace*:

two men carried Bayardo San Román down on a hammock . . . Magdalena Oliver thought he was dead.
'Collons de déu!' she exclaimed. 'What a waste.'
. . . his right arm was dragging on the ground . . . so that he left a trail from the edge of the precipice to the deck of the boat. That was all that we had left of him: the memory of a victim.   (pp. 137–8)

The silent mark traced on the memory by the limp victim's hand finds an accompanying, coded (Catalan) voice: 'God's balls!' – the coming together of religion and sexuality. What a waste.

One sphere of action chronicled, then, is that of sexual politics. And the complicity of church and state. 'What is important in the work', Macherey writes, 'is what it does not say.'[24] It does not say much of the bishop, Christ's *vicar(io)* on earth. His role is one of neglect. An absence . . . who 'hates this town' (p. 17), makes 'the sign of the cross because he has to' (p. 17) and (almost) visits to pick up the tribute of *machismo*, 'coxcomb soup, his favourite dish' (p. 30). This neglect of spirituality, of justice, cannot be made up for by the incapable saviour *Cristo* Bedoya, in his frantic, failed attempt to live up to Clotilde Armenta's confidence that 'in that town of poofters [*maricas*/faggots] only a man like him could prevent the tragedy' (p. 174).

Justice? Nominally, Colonel Lázaro Aponte, like Lazarus, given a *second* chance to preserve life:

'I saw them two minutes ago and each one had a pig-killing knife', Cristo Bedoya said.
'Oh, fuck', the mayor said, 'they must have come back with two others.' He promised to take care of it at once, but went into the Social Club to confirm a date for dominoes that night, and when he came out the crime was already consummated.   (p. 175)

And what of our Peter and Paul? Since Poncio (Pontius) Vicario, Angela's father, is too senile to act, having 'lost his sight doing so much delicate work with gold-jewellery in order to maintain the honour of the house' (p. 50), his hands are washed of active responsibility. Thus, the binary, clichéd duo of instrumentality, Pedro and Pablo, vicarious defenders of an un-thought-out faith and a social code sanctioned by a community unwilling or unable to combat the 'foretold' nature of their act.

There had never been a death more foretold. After their sister revealed the name to them, the Vicario twins went to the shed in the pig-sty where they

kept their sacrificial tools and chose the two best knives: one for quartering, ten by two and a half, and the other one for trimming, seven by one and a half. They wrapped them in a rag and went to sharpen them at the meat-market ... There were only a few customers at such an early hour but twenty-two people declared that they had heard everything and all were agreed that the only reason they said it was to be overheard ...
'We're going to kill Santiago Nasar.'   (pp. 83–5)

This Nasar-ene, then, is to be killed by his own friends and drinking companions; his own 'apostles' collude (Pedro plus eleven, Pablo plus eleven), in a Gethsemane of sleepy inactivity, despite the twins' manifold statement of murderous intent. And the second requirement for mortal sin, 'responsibility', they admit, too:

'We killed him in full awareness of what we were doing', said Pedro Vicario, 'but we're innocent.'
'Perhaps before God', said Father Amador.
'Before God and before men', said Pablo Vicario. 'It was a matter of honour.'   (p. 80)

The *instrumentality* of the twins' actant-status is underscored by several elements. First, the shift from 'Fact' (Margarita's one brother) to 'Fiction' (Angela's twin brothers); second, the play of 'apostolic' naming, duty and innocence; and third, the anti-realist characterization of Pedro and Pablo, expressed either through their reduction to mere wielders of the knife so often a fetish-object of the narrative or, more uproariously, through their hilarious inseparability:

'He (Pedro) spent about half an hour changing the gauze he had his prick wrapped in', Pablo Vicario told me. Actually he hadn't spent more than ten minutes doing that, but it was something so difficult and so enigmatic for Pablo Vicario, that he interpreted it as some new trick on the part of his brother to waste time until dawn. So he put the knife in his hand and dragged him off almost by force in pursuit of their sister's lost honour.
'There's no other way', he told him. 'It's as if it had already happened.'
(pp. 99–100)

Culmination of the brothers' only 'disagreement' (p. 99), namely, as to whose responsibility had been the final, fatal decision, this passage at once constructs, reconstructs and deconstructs the *pundonor* sphere of action. Irreversible, vengeful action at the *hands* of blood-relatives; delay, *agonizing* (though hardly expressed as a matter of conscience) before the act; and, finally, the grasping of the *instrument*, the instrument of honour-code responsibility. 'Knife' . . . or 'prick'?

Speculation – *cherchez la femme!*

Sexual politics centre on Angela Vicario, already broached in mention of Poncio, Pura, Pedro and Pablo. The axial, unresolved question is not whether Santiago Nasar was her seducer; that comes subsequently. Virgin or non-Virgin (technically)? Despite her unscheming refusal to cover up her own, *undisclosed* knowledge of why her hymen is not intact, the wedding night frankness that triggers the honour-code action, it is *society* that asks not *how*? but *who*? The *how*?, possibly more interesting, would surely have made for a shorter narrative; as it is, in Derridan terms, it is an *espacement*, a hidden spacing, opened wide and dwelled upon. But this instance of *aperture* gives rise to the wrong question – *who*? For Angela's society (a kind of traditional 'readership'?) is ill-equipped to reason, only to react. Thus, when forced (verbally; that is all we know) to name a perpetrator, she plucks from the darkness not only a 'son of man', whom she names *thrice*, but the name of *man*: 'a butterfly with no will of its own, whose sentence had been written forever'.

Once, the Angel of the Annunciation had visited upon a Pure, Vicarious, virgin-instrument (Mary) the weight of bearing the Nazarene. Now, the roles of angel and vicar are subsumed into but a single *actant*, the one 'sphere of action' where, vicariously, Angela both announces and condemns. Her hand bears (bares) the responsibility of authorship – 'he was my author' ('fue mi autor'). She names Santiago Nasar responsible for what her own finger has traced, has written, in blood. After his death, in ink, her hand is able to write in full (almost two thousand letters). Her hand weaves the fabric of writing, the seemingly endless act of *écriture* which serves to cover up her act of (carnal) self-knowledge and self-penetrating analysis. It is a more original cover-up than the traditional method of linen sheets with the stain of honour ('la mancha del honor') recommended by her girl-friend confidantes – a more writerly (*scriptible*) display of stained sheets.

Thereafter, all is but a play of names, the ploy of plural, interchangeable victims; the aperture of a *social* membrane, pointed at and pierced by her penetrative, accusing finger, and a fabric falsely woven to cover up the long-standing 'gap' of honour, of honour-code, of honour-code writing. A fabric now undone by the readerly (*lisible*). A reading which refutes *whodunnit*? A feminist reading of the 'macho' code?

Speculation – reading

> The writing changes the very surface of what it is written on. This non-
> belonging unleashes speculation.   (Jacques Derrida)[25]

The instability of the writing surface, of the *scene* of writing, unleashes,
as we have now seen, myriad unstable readings, incomplete,
uncompletable speculations, investigations, guess-work(s), narra-
tions. Internally, the text contains many readers, many readings.
Father Amador, vicarious and obscene pathologist, haruspex, picking
over (and out) the entrails of the dead Santiago Nasar in a Rabelaisian
fusion of name and functions; gruesome priest, *amateur* physician. The
instructing judge, incapable of clinical, dispassionate reading:

> The judge's name didn't appear on any of the pages of the brief, but it was
> evident that he was a man burning with the fever for literature . . . The
> marginal notes, and not just because of the colour of the ink, seemed to be
> written in blood. He was so perplexed . . . that often he fell into lyrical
> distractions contrary to professional rigour. Above all, it never seemed
> legitimate to him that life should make use of so many coincidences forbidden
> to literature merely to achieve without obstacle a death so clearly foretold . . .
> On folio 416, in his own handwriting and in red ink . . . he wrote a marginal
> note: *Give me a prejudice and I will move the world.* Under that disillusioned
> paraphrase, with a felicitous sketch in the same blood ink, he drew a heart
> pierced by an arrow. For him, as for Santiago Nasar's closest friends, the
> latter's own behaviour in his last hours was a final proof of his innocence.
>   (pp. 158–61)

At play, here, is *slippage*; away from one text as verifiable presence and
towards a margin where another *trace*, a parallel *écriture* not confined to
ink but extended to blood, is generated by the 'unprofessional'
doodling of the arbiter of justice. It constitutes the arbitration of a
judgement: a judgement not as to Santiago Nasar's implied innocence
(the function of social justice which the unnamed judge supposedly
represents) but on the political power derivable from prejudice. A
case, perhaps, of Louis Althusser's 'symptomatic reading':

> . . . when we write, we do not just record what we see and fail to record what
> lies outside our field of vision; rather, we see all the elements of reality about
> which we write, but our written text cannot always make the right
> connections between them. A text thus tends to present reality partially or
> incoherently, leaving gaps. Through these gaps, however, an informed
> reader can see what the text was hiding from itself.[26]

Not only does the judge's marginal note offer an Althusserian 'symptomatic reading', it performs (without signature) the function of *supplementing* the narrator's version of events. Politically manipulated, 'life' can 'make use of' the 'coincidences forbidden to literature'. A theory of *production*, then, derives from such 'making use'. But this judge, exceptionally, appears to stand aside, helpless and 'perplexed', from society's manipulated 'world' (his *Give me* . . . is, after all, an unfulfilled imperative). He is, rather, 'a man burning with the fever for literature' and, as such, a duplication of that other, most important of readers within *Chronicle*, its own narrator.

María Alejandrina Cervantes had left the door of the house unbolted. I took leave of my brother, crossed the passage-way where the mulatto-girls' cats were curled up, asleep, amongst the tulips, and pushed open the bedroom door without knocking. The lights were out, but as soon as I entered I caught the smell of warm woman and saw her insomniac leopard's eye in the dark and then I knew nothing more of myself until the bell began to ring.

(pp. 110–11)

The narrator withdraws from the scene of action at the actual time of Santiago Nasar's death, into the brothel, the 'house of mercies' (p. 74), which sucks the equally 'fevered' male protagonists, sporadically, away from a social reality of 'prejudice' into a temporary oblivion:

It was she who did away with my generation's virginity . . . Santiago Nasar lost his senses the first time he saw her. I warned him: *A falcon which takes on a warrior crane, merely risks a life of pain.* But he didn't listen, bewildered by the chimerical whistling of María Alejandrina Cervantes. She was his unbridled passion, his mistress of tears at fifteen, until Ibrahim Nasar whipped him out of her bed and shut him up for over a year on *The Divine Face*.   (pp. 105–6)

Withdrawal from the scene of action to a scene of *writing*. For this is no ordinary brothel, but the brothel of chimerae, of enchantment, of withdrawal into the *literature* of its Madame Cervantes, mother (Mary), classical (Alexandrine) lap of adolescent consolation, spontaneous sensuality and anathema to conscience or guilt – or contemplation of the Divine Face (nominally, the Nasars' ranch). Therein, discourse is literary, proverbial, picking up yet never closing the falconry-theme of Gil Vicente's epigraph. Therein, activity is but play, the loss and confusion of *presence*, of identity:

Santiago Nasar had an almost magical knack for disguises, and his favourite pastime was to confuse the identities of the mulatto-girls. He would rifle the wardrobes of some to disguise others, so they all ended up feeling different from themselves and the same as the ones they weren't. Once, one of them saw herself repeated in another so accurately that she burst into tears. 'I felt as if I'd been taken out of the mirror', she said. But that night, María Alejandrina Cervantes wouldn't let Santiago Nasar indulge himself for the last time in his transformer's trickery, and with such frivolous excuses that the bad taste of that memory changed her life.   (pp. 106–7)

The scene of writing as brothel, as evasion, as oblivion, as loss of identity (or a 'metaphysics of presence') is denied, fatally, not only to Santiago Nasar, 'changing his life' (to death) by depriving him of his indulgence in 'transformer's trickery'. It is denied, too, subsequently, to the narrator. Yet differently, obversely, in another mirror-image. For Santiago Nasar passes from scene of writing to scene of action; the narrator is expelled from his scene of action ('suddenly she stopped, coughed from far off, and slipped out of my life. "I can't", she said. "You smell of him" ', pp. 125–6) to a deferred (thirty years) scene of writing – and the 'transformer's trickery' which is *Chronicle*.

Notwithstanding this expulsion, all literariness is not lost to the narrator. His absence from the scene of action, of the death, permits him a decentring of point of view, away from omniscience, towards the 'piecing together' of a narrative which is always but another reading. 'The investigating judge looked for even one person who had seen him, and he did so with as much persistence as I, but it was impossible to find anyone. On folio 382 of the brief, he wrote another marginal pronouncement in red ink: *Fatality makes us invisible*' (p. 180). For the anonymous judge (reader), entry into investigation (speculation), for the narrator (reader), entry into María Alejandrina's (house of speculation), for Santiago Nasar, entry into the antipode of brothel – the house of Flora Miguel and arranged marriage (speculation) – all are forms of non-omniscience. It is the 'fatality' of their status in the text – in literature – which makes them invisible. Invisible readers. Readers without *signature*, who have not *written*.

Speculation – writing

It engages a new speculation. 'The details of the process by which repression turns a possibility of pleasure into a source of unpleasure are not yet clearly understood or cannot be clearly represented (described, expounded, pictured); but there is no doubt that all neurotic unpleasure is of that kind – pleasure that cannot be felt as such'. (Jacques Derrida)[27]

He who has written, who speculates (money makes) with *signature*, is

Gabriel García Márquez. But does the deconstruction of this series of speculations reduce his writing, his discourse, to that signature alone? '... the widespread opinion that deconstruction denies the existence of anything but discourse, or affirms a realm of pure difference in which all meaning and identity dissolves, is a travesty of Derrida's own work and of the most productive work that has followed from it.'[28] García Márquez's signature begins with death;[29] this novel is the chronicling of a death. At play, perhaps, is the 'neurotic unpleasure' of death which, dwelt upon, returned to again and again, becomes, is, the 'pleasure that cannot be felt as such'. Thus, through *writing*, the *difference* operates; in the overlay of apparent opposites –pleasure, unpleasure – there is a residue, a remainder. And that remainder, here, for me, writing on García Márquez, as for Derrida writing on Freud, takes the form of a question: 'How does death wait at the end, at all the ends ... of this structure, at all the moves of this speculation?'[30] *Chronicle of a Death Foretold* rehearses from prediction to event the narration of the death, *The Passion*, of a banal Nasar-ene. In the dramatic set-piece of pinning against wood, the end announced throughout – which everyone knows, which no one prevents, which, retrospectively and by piecing together conflicting versions, everyone would *mythologize*, reliving, exaggerating and exulting in their own part – *Chronicle* rewrites another chronicle: the dominant chronicle of Spanish American consciousness. Yet it would be a travesty of García Márquez to affirm but the 'neurotic unpleasure' of a death (recalled) turning to 'a possibility of pleasure' – the pleasure of the text, the *jouissance* of the 'literariness' of death, and no more than that. For meaning does not dissolve; it multiplies and concentrates. In the process, it deconstructs all possible mythification of a Santiago Nasar; he of absent father (Ibrahim) and of present (dominant, irrelevant, pure) mother responsible, thinking him 'upstairs' already, for the closed door to salvation; he who transmutes an 'Eloi, Eloi, lama sabachthani?' to an '¡Ay, mi madre!', repeating not an augury of despair against the Father (Psalm 22), but despairing of his *mother's* futile augury, of her failure to decipher his own repeated dreams of trees (p. 10).

Santiago, Hispanic patron-saint, 'Matamoros' ('Moor-killer' but, here, only of the self); false, *ersatz* Nazarene, victim of a Holy Roman (San Román)-descended code, a religion, a society (Catholicism) and its culture, its customs, its politics, its history. A history of 'stained' honour, of hypocritical sexual ethics; a history, an *écriture* written (unofficially, in the margin) in *blood*. *Chronicle of a Death Foretold* deconstructs a version of the New Testament; it cannot but do the same for the original.

Pure speculation is still waiting
(Jacques Derrida)[31]

Notes

1 *The Oxford Literary Review*, 3:2 (1978), 78–97, trans. Ian McLeod. Further references to Derrida's text will follow the pattern 'Speculations', p. 92.
2 All references to *Chronicle of a Death Foretold* are to the Bruguera edition (Barcelona, 1981).
3 'Speculations', p. 92.
4 'Speculations', p. 86.
5 'An Interview with Gabriel García Márquez', *Cencrastus*, 7, 6–7 (a translation by David Cole of an original *El País* interview).
6 Edith Grossman, 'Truth is Stranger than Fact', *Review*, 30 (New York), pp. 71–2.
7 *Cencrastus*, 7.
8 'Speculations', p. 88.
9 Philippe Lejeune, 'The Autobiographical Contract', in *French Literary Theory Today* (Cambridge, 1982), pp. 192–207. Lejeune uses Gérard Genette's categories of point of view; by these, *Chronicle* (almost) assumes the homodiegetic form of the 'eye-witness' account.
10 *Ibid.*, p. 203.
11 Vincent B. Leitch, *Deconstructive Criticism* (Colombia, 1983), p. 44.
12 *Ibid.*, p. 41.
13 Jacques Derrida, *Speech and Phenomena: and Other Essays on Husserl's Theory of Signs*, trans. David B. Allison (Evanston, Ill., 1973). This volume contains a translation of Derrida's 'La Différance', 1968; further references to this essay will follow the pattern of 'Différance', p. 153.
14 See the discussion of 'Saussure's Key Ideas', in Rex Gibson, *Structuralism and Education* (London, 1984), pp. 15–29, especially note 3, p. 29, where Gibson outlines his disagreement with Jonathan Culler over the primacy of the arbitrariness of the sign in Saussure's thought.
15 Tzvetan Todorov, 'The Typology of Detective Fiction', *The Poetics of Prose* (Ithaca, 1977), p. 46.
16 'Différance', pp. 130–4.
17 See Leitch, *Deconstructive Criticism*, p. 40.
18 David Forgacs, 'Marxist Literary Theories', in *Modern Literary Theory. A Comparative Introduction*, ed. Ann Jefferson & David Robey (London, 1982), p. 146.
19 Plinio Apuleyo Mendoza, *El olor de la guayaba* (Barcelona: Bruguera, 1982), p. 89.
20 'Speculations', p. 92.
21 'The Interpreter's Self', in *Reader-Response Criticism: from Formalism to Post-Structuralism*, ed. Jane P. Tompkins (Baltimore and London, 1980), pp. 199–200.

22 I echo the 'Stranger in the House' section of Tony Tanner's 'Introduction' to *Adultery in the Novel* (Baltimore, 1979). It begins resoundingly: 'Western literature as we know it starts with an act of transgression, a violation of boundaries that leads to instability, asymmetry, disorder, and an interfamilial, intertribal clash that threatens the very existence of civilization . . .' (p. 24).

23 Leitch, *Deconstructive Criticism*, p. 10.

24 Forgacs, 'Marxist Literary Theories', p. 149.

25 'Speculations', p. 92.

26 Forgacs, 'Marxist Literary Theories', p. 149.

27 'Speculations', p. 96. The internal quotation is from Freud's *Beyond the Pleasure Principle*.

28 Terry Eagleton, *Literary Theory: an Introduction* (Oxford, 1983), p. 148.

29 'La tercera resignación' (3 September 1947); 'Eva está dentro de su gato' (25 October 1947); 'Tubalcaín forja una estrella' (18 January 1948); all in *El Espectador* of Bogotá.

30 'Speculations', p. 93.

31 'Speculations', p. 97.

A prospective post-script: apropos of *Love in the Times of Cholera*

ROBIN FIDDIAN

Love in the Times of Cholera is the first novel by García Márquez to be published since the award of the Nobel Prize for Literature in October 1982. As abundant publicity surrounding the book's appearance in December 1985 revealed, the author was already working on a sequel to *Chronicle of a Death Foretold* (1981) when the Nobel committee's decision was announced; with the award there came numerous public commitments which obliged García Márquez to interrupt the progress of his project until January 1984, when he resumed work on the existing material. *Love in the Times of Cholera* was eventually completed in August 1985 and published three months ahead of schedule in a first edition of 1,200,000 copies for distribution in Spanish America and a further 250,000 reserved for the Spanish market.[1]

Initial critical response has taken the form of summary notices and reviews, the most enthusiastic of which asserts that *Love in the Times of Cholera* is 'one of the great living classics of the Spanish language'.[2] It is not my intention to debate that claim here. In the absence of any properly established critical guidelines, my role will be restricted to providing a brief description of the essential features of *Love in the Times of Cholera* and to indicating possible avenues of approach which readers may decide to explore at greater length in the future.

Love in the Times of Cholera is an accomplished work which exhibits many aspects of interest, including a dynamic discursive form. Its six chapters, ranging from 71 to 98 pages in length, progress smoothly along a linear axis punctuated by frequent parentheses and reprises. The story is told by a single narrative voice which recounts certain events in duplicate in order to represent the overlapping experiences of its multiple protagonists. In terms of narrative design, the novel incorporates three temporal perspectives, the most immediate of which focuses on a period of slightly less than two years during which a seventy-six-year-old romantic, Florentino Ariza, courts and finally consummates a lifetime's love for Fermina Daza who had broken their engagement 'fifty-one years, nine months and four days previously' (p. 418)[3] and married a handsome young doctor whose accidental death, narrated in chapter 1, eventually leaves her a widow at the age of seventy-two. The events set in motion by Doctor Juvenal Urbino's fatal fall are overlain by a second level of the narrative which extends some sixty years back into the past in order to account for Florentino, Fermina and Juvenal's family backgrounds; at the same time, it registers the principal social developments which shape the life of their community during the period concerned, and surveys the political history of Colombia since that country achieved independence in 1819. A still more remote perspective encompassing the period of Spanish colonial rule completes the range of temporal references in the book.

The spatial setting of *Love in the Times of Cholera* concentrates on the social and racial microcosm of a formerly prosperous community situated at the mouth of the Magdalenas River in northern Colombia. The city, which had been 'the habitual residence of the viceroys of the New Kingdom of Granada' (p. 35), is in fact a composite image of Cartagena de Indias, Santa Marta, Barranquilla and other locations on the Caribbean coast.[4] The story line also takes in several points along the Magdalenas River, as well as some countries in Western Europe which Fermina Daza and her husband visit on their honeymoon (chapter 3) and again some years later (chapter 4); other journeys along the river, related in chapters 2 (Fermina in the company of her father, Lorenzo Daza), 3 (Florentino, alone), 5 (Fermina, alone), and 6 (Fermina and Florentino, together), reinforce the novel's expansive spatial projection, thereby setting it strikingly apart from previous works by García Márquez, including *Leaf Storm*, *No One Writes to the Colonel* and *Chronicle of a Death Foretold*.

The generic status of the novel is of particular interest here. In effect, *Love in the Times of Cholera* masquerades as a nineteenth-century work; on García Márquez's own admission, he had set out 'to write a nineteenth-century novel as examples of the type were written in the nineteenth century, as if it were actually written at that time'.[5] His text displays many conventional features of realist or naturalist fiction, 'as exemplified by the schools of Emile Zola or Gustave Flaubert';[6] in its documentation of social custom and historical fact, it partakes of the qualities of a chronicle; above all, it draws conspicuously on a type of nineteenth-century writing to which other Spanish American novelists, including Manuel Puig and Mario Vargas Llosa, have also turned for creative inspiration, that is, the 'folletines de amor' (p. 220) and 'folletines de lágrimas' (pp. 101 and 117) (sentimental and lachrymose love stories, or *feuilletons*) which enjoyed wide popularity with nineteenth-century readers in Europe and America, appearing in serialized form in the newspapers on a weekly or monthly basis (see pp. 207 and 426). It is not the first time that the *folletín* is cited in García Márquez's work: the *juez-instructor* (or official investigator) in *Chronicle of a Death Foretold* had been unable to cast off the influence of the *folletín* when reporting on the circumstances of Santiago Nasar's death. Imitation of the *folletín*, arguably an embryonic and incidental feature of that text, becomes the basis of *Love in the Times of Cholera*, where Florentino Ariza models himself, from the earliest years of his adult life, on the romantic stereotypes associated with the genre.

During the 'medicinal journey' (p. 205) which Florentino takes up the Magdalenas River in search of a cure for the sickness of love,

At night, when the boat was tied up and most of the passengers walked disconsolately up and down the deck, he would reread the illustrated stories that he knew almost off by heart, by the light of the carbide lamp in the dining room, the only one which stayed alight throughout the night. The stories charged with drama which he had read so often would recover their original magic when he substituted people whom he knew in real life for the imaginary protagonists, and reserved the roles of lovers thwarted by circumstances for himself and Fermina Daza. (p. 211)

The very first love letters he writes to Fermina incorporate 'entire paragraphs from the Spanish Romantics, undigested'; as the narrator explains, 'By then he had moved one step closer to the tear-jerking serial stories and other even more profane prose writings of his times' (a reference to a well-known volume of poetry published in 1896 by the Nicaraguan *modernista*, Rubén Darío) (p. 117).[7]

Fermina Daza is not immune to the infectious appeal of the *folletín*. The picture which she forms of the young Florentino and his mother bespeaks a naivety fostered by the commonplaces of a facile culture:

He was the son of a hard-working and serious woman who had not married but who displayed the irremediable mark of a fiery stigma which had its origins in a single false step she had taken in her youth. [Fermina] had discovered that he was not the telegraphist's messenger boy, as she had assumed, but a well-qualified assistant with a promising future... (p. 104)

Although soon displaced by the down-to-earth pragmatism typical of so many of García Márquez's women characters (for example, Ursula Buendía and the colonel's anonymous, asthmatic wife), Fermina's attraction to the stylized and improbable world of the *folletín* is revived in the early days of widowhood when she would 'fill her empty hours with tear-jerking serial stories transmitted on the radio from Santiago de Cuba' (p. 460).

García Márquez draws as systematically as his characters on the conventions of the *folletín*. He fashions a novel which, besides featuring the stock figure of the solitary, love-sick poet who, like many a Romantic hero, finds refuge, as though he were the victim of a fateful shipwreck (p. 258), in the remote seclusion of a light-house (p. 144), also reproduces the stereotype of a three-cornered love relationship. In this the more passionate male plays a serenade beneath the window of the woman he adores, writes her interminable love letters, and, when she cuts short their engagement, distraughtly returns a lock of her hair which he had displayed 'like a holy relic' in a glass case hanging on his bedroom wall (p. 157). A no less familiar chord is struck by the scene in which Florentino 'planted a clump of roses on [his dear mother's] grave' (p. 318) and transplanted a cutting to that of a lover, Olimpia Zuleta, who died violently at the hands of her jealous, cuckolded husband (p. 318).

The author introduces into the story-line of *Love in the Times of Cholera* a number of 'unlikely coincidences' (p. 200) of the sort which 'were common currency in the novels of the time, but which nobody believed actually happened in real life' (p. 387). See, for example, the 'exceptional' occurrence, on the day of Pentecost, of 'two extraordinary events: the death of one of Doctor Juvenal Urbino's friends and the silver-wedding celebrations of an eminent pupil of his' (p. 25); and, the unlikely arrival of a telegram informing Florentino of the death of América Vicuña – an adolescent school-girl put in his charge – as he cruises along the Magdalenas River with Fermina, oblivious to the banalities of life (p. 485). The arbitrary intrusion here of an adverse element of fate is at once reminiscent of the world of the *folletín* and of the classic nineteenth-century novel, *María*, written by García Márquez's fellow Colombian, Jorge Isaacs.[8]

In *Love in the Times of Cholera*, some of Florentino's statements are culled directly from the pages of the *folletín*, as when he exclaims that 'There is no greater glory than to die for love' (p. 127), or when he confides to Fermina that 'I kept my virginity for you' (p. 490). The narrator imitates this hackneyed language, describing Florentino on one occasion as 'prostrate with grief' (p. 217), using variants of the word 'desgarrado' ('heart-rending') to the point of excess, and frequently employing stilted metaphors: at a delicate stage of Fermina and Juvenal Urbino's love-making on their honeymoon voyage, the doctor 'realized that they had rounded the Cape of Good Hope' (p. 233); Lorenzo Daza's progress in fulfilling his ambition to 'make Fermina into a fine lady' had been pictured earlier as a journey along 'a long and uncertain road' to social acceptance (p. 125).

The verbal clichés, character types and narrative situations illustrated here are evidence of a clear intent on García Márquez's part to write a pastiche of the *folletín*. His description of *Love in the Times of Cholera* as 'practically a "telenovela" [television soap opera]'[9] encourages the view that the book is a recreation of the sentimental episodic melodramas of a previous age, as perceived through the prism of late-twentieth-century generic equivalents such as 'Dallas' and 'The Colbys'. Arguably, the resulting form of a literary *telenovela* provides an ideal mould for the hyperbolic style characteristic of much of García Márquez's writing. The story of Florentino Ariza's uncle, León XII, who out of necessity 'kept spare sets of dentures everywhere, in different places throughout the house, in the drawer of his desk and one set in each of the three ships belonging to his business' (p. 385), rests comfortably within the bounds of the narrative, as does the extravagant account of the Olivella silver-wedding celebrations which are attended by 122 guests, and the description of the huge breakfast which the Gargantuan Diego Samaritano devours on the last morning of the period covered in the story.

García Márquez's personal brand of humour, including elements of bathos and ridicule and an acute sense of irony, also acquires appropriate expression through the vehicle of an up-dated *folletín*. *Love in the Times of Cholera* contains many comic ingredients which make it at times hilarious (see the episode of the scalding of Juvenal Urbino's parrot in chapter 1), at times black and tragi-comic in the manner of *Belarmino y Apolonio* by Ramón Pérez de Ayala. In keeping with this design, García Márquez presents Florentino Ariza both as a pathetic character whom adult female citizens regard compassionately as 'a solitary person in need of love and affection' (p. 226), and as 'a squalid, timid and insignificant [wretch]' (p. 93) whose 'vigil' in the park attracts Fermina's attention more than it does her sympathy. The 'cagada', or bird-shit, that soils a love letter he sends her (p. 97) is

a typical instance of the author's deflationary procedures which serve
to ridicule Florentino's idealistic pretensions. To the same end, García
Márquez endows his protagonist with defective eyesight, makes him
prone to 'chronic constipation' (p. 86), and imposes on him the
affliction of premature baldness, a characteristic not generally
associated with his type.

In this way, the topoi and values of a lachrymose and implausible
romanticism are subjected to sustained debasement, their excesses
kept in check by an author who maintains a humorous detachment
from a world of melodrama rooted in literary convention. García
Márquez's strategy in this regard carries resounding echoes of that of
Gustave Flaubert in *Madame Bovary*, a text with which *Love in the Times
of Cholera* bears numerous resemblances, as it does with *L'Éducation
sentimentale* by the same author, and *Don Quixote* by Cervantes. Many
of the representative themes of traditional and nineteenth-century
fiction are superimposed on the *folletín*-esque framework of *Love in the
Times of Cholera*. They include the problematic relationship between
essence and appearance, the conflict between an individual's private
aspirations and the established norms of public life, the view of
reading as an 'insatiable vice' (p. 116) which distorts our perception of
ourselves and the world and, lastly, the theme of disillusionment,
illustrated most strikingly in the experience of Doctor Juvenal Urbino
who, on the very last day of his life, discovers distressing truths about
his friend, Jeremiah de Saint-Amour. According to García Márquez,
'Juvenal Urbino discovers the fraudulent foundation of his love for
Jeremiah. And he is deeply disillusioned. He comes to realize on the
very last day of his life only hours before he dies, that he had given his
affection to someone who was not quite the person he thought he
was.'[10] Florentino Ariza's acknowledgement of 'the fallacy of his own
life' (p. 292) two years later is a similarly chastening admission of
error. As happened regularly in the classical novel, the experience of
desengaño (i.e. of being disabused of one's illusions) heightens a
character's 'sense of reality' (p. 35) and forces a retreat from naive
idealism of the sort indulged in by the *folletín*. On this evidence we
observe how García Márquez employs the themes and conventions of
one literary genre to undermine assumptions implicit in another,
thereby providing an interesting illustration of the principle, enunci-
ated in one of Jorge Luis Borges's fictions, that 'A text which does not
incorporate its counter-text is considered to be incomplete.'[11]

Desengaño and the consequences of an unstable view of reality are concerns which are articulated throughout García Márquez's work. Other themes characteristic of his writing also reappear in *Love in the Times of Cholera*. Foremost among them are: dreams, memory and nostalgia, personal identity, sex and solitude, death, fate and destiny (with associated imagery of chess and card games), the historical experience of Colombia and Spanish America, social and sexual emancipation, patriarchy and the family, and the nature of – and relations between – the sexes. Such a broad range of interests promises to stimulate a variety of critical responses. In the remainder of this essay a number of themes and issues are considered which may prove likely to figure prominently in criticism of *Love in the Times of Cholera*. Three complementary readings of the novel are advanced from standpoints which may loosely be defined as 'humanist', 'feminist' and 'Americanist'. Needless to say, in choosing these categories there is no pretence that the interpretative possibilities of a many-sided text have been exhausted.

Love in the Times of Cholera is susceptible to a humanist reading of the sort illustrated in Giovanni Pontiero's study of *No One Writes to the Colonel*.[12] The narrative highlights the themes of love, marriage and old age, and promotes the value of human dignity, happiness, compassion, and (sensual) pleasure in defiance of cultural constraints, the strongest and most insidious of which is a sense of shame and remorse. In his mature writings Florentino Ariza develops his own ideas about 'life, love, old age and death' (p. 433) which challenge 'the conventional beliefs of his times' (p. 378) and are a source of 'prodigious consolation' to Fermina in her hours of grief (p. 459). Florentino insists on the propriety and dignity of love in old age, a belief shared by Fermina's daughter-in-law who counters the puritanical intolerance of Ophelia Urbino Daza with 'a serene justification of love at any age'. Ophelia, Fermina's daughter, 'was unable to conceive of an innocent relationship between two people of the opposite sex at the age of five, let alone at the age of eighty' and, in a heated family exchange, exclaims indignantly to her older brother, Urbino: 'Love is ridiculous at our age, but at [Florentino and Fermina's] it is disgusting' (p. 467). Her attitude offends Fermina to such an extent that she bans Ophelia from the family house, in an episode which secures our sympathy and admiration for her and elicits our firm disapproval of all forms of mean-minded moralism.

Heterosexual love, irrespective of age and in an almost infinite variety of forms, is García Márquez's single most important concern in *Love in the Times of Cholera*. He remarked to a journalist that 'What interests me most in the novel is the analysis it conducts of love at all ages.'[13] Arguably, some of Florentino Ariza's experiences as, alternately, a shy and vulnerable idealist and a selfish, calculating 'night-time prowler', who in his relations with several women 'gave nothing and wanted everything in return' (pp. 316–17), are less than exemplary and result in the most trite of revelations: see, for example, his discovery that 'one can be friendly with a woman without going to bed with her' (p. 276). But, his unfaltering devotion to Fermina and 'his infinite capacity for sustaining hope' (p. 336) are eventually rewarded by an author who is convinced that 'If we persevere, our bodies persevere. I think that we persevere if there is love. Always.'[14] Without underestimating the claims of the body, the novel proposes an idealistic conception of love as 'a state of grace which [is] not a means to anything but, rather, a beginning and an end in itself' (p. 425), and celebrates its realization in Fermina and Florentino's relationship:

They carried on in silence like an old couple whom life has taught to act warily, beyond the range of the pitfalls of passion, beyond the range of the unkind tricks played on us by our hopes and by our failure to learn from our disappointments: beyond the range of love. For they had shared enough experiences to know by now that love is love in any period and in any place, but that it increases in intensity the closer we are to death.   (p. 499)

The fulfilment of the couple's desires provides *Love in the Times of Cholera* with a narrative conclusion which several reviewers have interpreted as an affirmation of hope, life and love. Fermina and Florentino's dogged achievement may indeed be seen as a victory over the rigours of old age, the obstacles of fate and the prejudices of an unsympathetic society. Yet, the ending of the novel is deliberately left open and cannot be said unequivocally to be a happy one. The couple's position on the *New Fidelity* ('*Nueva Fidelidad*') which is destined to sail up and down the Magdalenas River (i.e. the river of life) as long as they remain alive, strikes us as being not only an acute form of social isolation – or quarantine, as it is termed in the symbolic idiom of the book – but also a wilfully artificial situation. García Márquez implicitly acknowledges this in an interview with Françesc Arroyo, in which he carefully evades the issue of whether his novel ends on an affirmative or negative note and confesses, instead, to 'a great curiosity': 'How do they end up? I mean, how do they really end up? What eventually happened to them?' In effect, García Márquez admits to providing a rhetorical denouement for his novel, which, he declares, '[is] a problem for the critics to solve'.[15] A brief examination of the scenes which immediately precede the conclusion may help to reveal the full implications of the final chapter.

In the period which leads up to the consummation of their love, Fermina and Florentino have to contend with a series of set-backs and obstacles to their happiness. First, Florentino breaks his ankle in a fall on a flight of stairs and is prevented from seeing Fermina for four months. When he recovers and invites her to take a cruise on the *New Fidelity*, she brushes aside her children's open opposition to her romance with Florentino and embarks with him, but the sound of the ship's horn as the *New Fidelity* sets sail damages her left ear, leaving her hearing permanently impaired. Finally, just as the couple begin to experience a fragile happiness, a telegram arrives bringing the disturbing news of América Vicuña's suicide. Now, it is possible to explain Florentino's accident merely as a comic narrative device and to attribute the onset of Fermina's deafness, which nicely matches Florentino's physical deficiencies, to a perverse symmetry. But, América Vicuña's suicide resists a reductive interpretation of this kind and requires to be accounted for at a deeper level of analysis which involves renewed consideration of the themes of love, happiness, moral responsibility, and death.

Leona Cassiani's telegraphic message attributes the suicide to mysterious causes: 'América Vicuña died yesterday cause unknown' (p. 485). The reader, however, is left in no doubt that the girl kills herself because she cannot bear the pain and humiliation caused by Florentino's abandoning her for Fermina Daza. Some three years previously, Florentino had wasted no time in seducing América when, as a teenager, she had been placed in his care by distant relations; now, still standing *in loco parentis*, he treats her with peremptory indifference and is to be held largely responsible for her death. In the book's final chapter the sudden announcement of América's suicide thereby signifies the intrusion, into Fermina and Florentino's idyll, of disturbing realities of selfishness, cruelty and death. The central importance of these ideas is enhanced by a newspaper report about an elderly couple who are battered to death by a boatman as he ferries them to the location where they had enjoyed their honey-moon forty years before (pp. 460–1). Fermina is haunted by this story which provides an approximate but telling reflection of her position with Florentino on the *New Fidelity*; it is also a compelling intimation of mortality. The old folk's murder, coupled with América Vicuña's suicide, thus modifies the mood of the narrative at a climactic point and persuades us that García Márquez's vision of humanity is best understood in nuanced terms, not simply as generous and humane, but, fundamentally, as 'a fatalistic brand of humanism' (p. 23) which rests on a mature recognition of 'the certainty of death' (p. 35).

The relationship between feminist ideology and the values of liberal humanism is at once intricate and controversial; as Toril Moi observes in a recent critical survey,[16] some feminist positions in fact reproduce the aesthetic and philosophical assumptions of patriarchal humanism, while others engage in a radical critique of them. By virtue of its ideological complexity, *Love in the Times of Cholera* is sure to attract the attention of egalitarian and radical feminists alike.

The questions of marriage and the curtailment of personal freedom preoccupy García Márquez in this novel. *Pace* José Font Castro, who sees *Love in the Times of Cholera* as a *roman à clef* designed to pay homage to García Márquez's own parents and their marriage,[17] I discern in the book substantial evidence of an indictment of that particular institution. For, if on one occasion Fermina and Juvenal's marriage is credited with certain positive achievements (see p. 328), on countless others it is presented as a form of 'sterile captivity' (p. 296) and 'servitude' (p. 405) endured by Fermina. Her experience of married life testifies emphatically to the dehumanizing effect of an institution which traps women 'in [a] web of conventions and prejudices' (p. 305), forcing them to compromise their individuality and, ultimately, to sacrifice their personal identity to their husband's will. In a singular passage, the narrative records the disappointment which Fermina feels as a mature housewife:

about never having become what she had dreamt of becoming when she was young, in the Park of the Evangelists, but instead, something which she did not dare to admit even to herself: a high-class serving maid . . . She always felt as if she were living a life that was being leased to her by her husband: with absolute control over a vast empire of happiness established by him and for him alone. She knew that he loved her above all else, more than anyone else in the world, but only for himself: she was at his beck and call.   (p. 323)

A later reference to Juvenal Urbino's 'patriarchal demands' (p. 434) adds a conclusive touch to the picture of her entrapment by the insidious mechanisms of 'benevolent' patriarchy.

It is no surprise that Fermina finds in widowhood a source of liberation and an opportunity to recover 'all that she had had to give up in the course of half a century's servitude which unquestionably had made her happy but which, in the wake of her husband's death, left her without the slightest trace of an identity' (p. 405). We note that her experience is representative of that of a wider community of women who, in striving to adjust to their new circumstances, 'would discover that the only honest way to live was as their bodies dictated, eating only when they felt hungry, making love without the need to tell lies, sleeping without having to pretend to be asleep in order to avoid the indecency of a conjugal routine' (p. 297). In the guise of a general statement about widowhood, this quotation reiterates condemnation of the constraints placed on women in marriage, and conveys a message of protest which has relevance beyond the boundaries of Colombian society in the late nineteenth century.

García Márquez's attitude to the position which women occupy within the broader framework of society is expressed indirectly through recurrent images of 'maternal manatees' (p. 488). These sea-cows 'with huge breasts for suckling their young, and plaintive voices like those of disconsolate women' (see pp. 211 and 497) are symbols of motherhood; according to legend, they are also 'the only creatures without a male in the animal kingdom' (p. 479), and thereby embody an ideal of sexual self-sufficiency which institutionalized patriarchy is bound to regard as an unnatural form of independence. Whenever he sees a manatee, Diego Samaritano, the ship's captain, is reminded of 'women whom society has condemned for having taken a false step in love' (p. 479); he thus conveys his society's hostility towards behaviour which does not conform to established norms. Manatee imagery also acts as a vehicle for García Márquez's denunciation of the predatory spirit of the male. His story of 'a huntsman from North Carolina who had disobeyed regulations and shot a mother manatee in the head with a bullet from his Springfield rifle' (p. 480) indicates the extremes of cruelty and abuse to which the female of the species is exposed within a supposedly civilized world.

Seen in this light, *Love in the Times of Cholera* stands out as a novel which passes strong censure on the order of patriarchy. However, García Márquez's reliance on the image of woman as a vulnerable mother-figure betrays a conservative sexual ideology which, in its perpetuation of given assumptions about the function of gender in social relations, may actually further that system's interests. If we assume that the narrative voice in the novel embodies overall the attitudes of an implied author, then it is possible to identify certain moments in *Love in the Times of Cholera* which reveal a suspect essentialism in García Márquez's account of the nature of the sexes. An early description of Juvenal and Fermina's house as a place which displays throughout 'the good judgement and careful attention of a woman who had her feet firmly on the ground' (p. 37) raises the spectre of a sexist mystique which attributes *a priori* one set of characteristics (for example, pragmatism and reliability) to women, represented here by Leona Cassiani as well as by Fermina Daza, and another quite distinct set to men, who are depicted as helplessly idealistic and impractical. A subsequent portrayal of Fermina disembarking at Riohacha, 'looking radiant, every inch a woman' (p. 191), increases our sense of unease, as does a statement to the effect that 'Women think more about the meanings behind the questions than about the questions themselves' (p. 417). The same narrator goes on to attribute Juvenal's dependence on his wife, not so much to personal psychological peculiarities, as to the fact that 'He is a man and weaker [than she is]' (p. 328). Such statements may possibly ring true to certain readers, but we cannot help but dispute the essentialist foundations on which they appear to rest; future commentators will almost certainly wish to undertake a systematic deconstruction of García Márquez's position on this issue which is of profound concern to several types of feminist inquiry.

This reading of *Love in the Times of Cholera* concludes with some reflections on the theme of America. This important area of García Márquez's writing embraces considerations of history, politics, class, race and culture, expressed here in literal, symbolic and allegorical terms. From a detailed historical vantage point, the narrative evokes the era of Spanish colonial rule as a time of prosperity for the local *criollo* merchant class and, on a wider scale, as a period of slavery and abuse by the Inquisition in 'the sinister palace where the Holy Office's prison was located' (p. 197). Hazardous open sewers 'inherited from the Spanish' (p. 27) are a pungent image of the colonial heritage of a city which 'had now existed on the margins of history . . . for four hundred years'; during that time 'nothing had happened except that it had grown old slowly midst its withered laurel trees and putrid cess pools' (p. 33). This vision of secular inertia holds true for the post-colonial era, as the experience of Juvenal Urbino's family illustrates: 'Independence from Spanish rule, followed by the abolition of slavery, precipitated the circumstances of honourable decline in which [Juvenal] was born and grew up' (p. 34). According to García

Márquez, at this juncture in their history those 'families that had been influential in days gone by' (p. 34) cultivated a fatalistic acceptance of 'the sad and oppressive world which God had provided for them' (p. 163) and sought refuge in an artificial order of social snobbery, racial prejudice and political mystification.

In this respect, Juvenal Urbino exemplifies the contradictions of his class. His conciliatory liberal views, which he holds 'more out of habit than conviction' (p. 74), are at variance with the inflexible moral stance of an 'old-style Christian' (p. 68). On an innocent reading, the name 'Juvenal Urbino' connotes qualities of youthful dynamism and commitment to a civilizing mission which are echoed in the narrator's remark about Juvenal's 'spirit of renovation and his maniacal civic sense' (p. 164); yet, we learn that in private the doctor displayed 'a narrow-mindedness which did not conform to his public image' (p. 56). On his death, the Urbino dynasty is shown to be a spent force which leaves no significant political legacy: the narrative describes Juvenal's children by Fermina as 'two mediocre tail-ends of a race' and attests to his status as 'the last bearer of a surname doomed to extinction' (p. 75).

García Márquez deliberately contrasts *criollo* decadence with the instinctual vitality of 'the impoverished mulattoes' (p. 33). In an image of visionary proportions, the masses of mixed racial origins 'infused the dead city with a frenzy of human jubilation smelling of fried fish: [they infused it] with new life' (p. 34). This affirmation is redolent of the author's Nobel speech which celebrates the vital potential of the people of Latin America. However, in neither context is that belief translated into any clearly outlined philosophy of political action which might lead to an improvement in the people's lives. In fact, at a level of significance to which we now turn, *Love in the Times of Cholera* recounts not the revival but the death of America in the allegorical figure of América Vicuña, whose name identifies her as an emblem of the natural and political life of the sub-continent (recalling that the vicuña is a mammal peculiar to some parts of South America).

As already stated, responsibility for América Vicuña's death may be imputed to Florentino Ariza, who is pictured in symbolic terms 'leading her by the hand with the gentle cunning of an apparently well-meaning grandfather towards a hidden place of slaughter' (p. 396). This image, which evokes a famous story, *The Slaughterhouse*, by the nineteenth-century Argentinian writer, Esteban Echeverría, provides graphic confirmation of Florentino's involvement in the death of América, and opens up the possibility of an allegorical reading of their relationship as a re-enactment of the treacherous destruction of young America by the Florentine (i.e. the Columbus Renaissance) spirit of Europe. The killing, by a huntsman from North Carolina, of a second species of mammal indigenous to the Caribbean (the manatee) further enhances the novel's figurative dimension and contributes to the projection of a poetic image of Latin America as a living body which European and American interests have courted and stalked as prey since the colonization of the New World began in the sixteenth century. Western readers may feel that they have a particular obligation to examine the view of Latin American history which, on this interpretation, is implied in the narrative of *Love in the Times of Cholera*.

These observations on García Márquez's representation of Latin America bring this study of his most recent novel to a close. In this essay I have attempted to convey a sense of the generic and ideological complexity of *Love in the Times of Cholera*, by demonstrating its capacity to accommodate various readings. My reluctance to impose a reductive or unitary interpretation on the book reflects a belief in the principle, expressed by Mario Vargas Llosa, that 'The richness of a work of art derives from the diversity of elements which it comprises and from the number of readings which it admits.'[18] In my view, *Love in the Times of Cholera* affords generous opportunities to future commentators who may wish to extend appreciation of a richly allusive and open work beyond the confines of this introductory study.

Notes and references

1 Information on the circumstances of the novel's composition and publication is provided by Antonio Caballero, 'La increíble y divertida historia de la novela de García Márquez', *Cambio 16*, 736 (Madrid, 6 January 1986), 102–3, and in a special report entitled 'El amor en los tiempos del Nobel', published in *Semana*, 187 (Bogotá, 3–9 December 1985), 28–35.

2 See Carlos Monsiváis, 'García Márquez, al margen del Nobel', in *Culturas* (Suplemento semanal de *Diario 16*), 38 (Madrid, 29 December 1985), i–ii.

3 Gabriel García Márquez, *El amor en los tiempos del cólera* (Barcelona, Bruguera, 1985). All page references cited in the text of this study are to this edition. All translations of material into English are mine.

4 As confirmed by García Márquez and reported in 'El amor en los tiempos del Nobel', p. 29.

5 See García Márquez's declarations to Françesc Arroyo, reproduced in 'El amor, la vejez, la muerte: un paseo con Gabriel García Márquez por la trama y la

historia de su última novela', *El País* (*Libros*), Year 7, 321 (Madrid, 12 December 1985), 1–3 (p. 1).

6 Ex-President Dr Alfonso López Michelsen referred to this and other properties of *Love in the Times of Cholera* in a public address celebrating the book's publication in Bogotá, in December 1985. The text of Dr López Michelsen's address, entitled 'El amor en los tiempos del cólera', was supplied by Sr Mario Ramírez of the Colombian Embassy in London. I wish to take this opportunity of thanking Sr Ramírez and his staff for providing a wide range of bibliographical information connected with this project.

7 Other echoes of Darío are to be found in this novel as well as in the pages of *The Autumn of the Patriarch*.

8 In 'El amor en los tiempos de cólera', Dr López Michelsen reminded his Colombian audience that *María* 'was obligatory reading' in the age of Romanticism.

9 See Antonio Caballero, 'La increíble y divertida historia de la novela de García Márquez', p. 103.

10 See García Márquez's declarations to Françesc Arroyo, mentioned in note 5 above, p. 2.

11 Jorge Luis Borges, 'Tlön, Uqbar, Orbis Tertius', in *Ficciones*, 11th ed. (Madrid, 1982), p. 28.

12 Gabriel García Márquez, *El coronel no tiene quien le escriba*, edited with an introductory study by Giovanni Pontiero (Manchester, 1981).

13 See García Márquez's declarations to Françesc Arroyo, p. 2.

14 *Ibid.*, p. 3.

15 *Ibid.*, p. 2.

16 Toril Moi, *Sexual/Textual Politics: Feminist Literary Theory* (London and New York, 1985).

17 Font Castro documents numerous similarities in the experience of the characters in *Love in the Times of Cholera* with the courtship and marriage of García Márquez's parents, in 'Las claves reales de *El amor en los tiempos del cólera*', *El País* (*Domingo*) (Madrid, 19 January 1986), 14–15.

18 See Vargas Llosa's remarks on the film 'Furtivos', by the Spanish director, José Luis Borau, in *Vuelta*, 9 (Mexico City, August 1977), 44–8 (46).

The solitude of Latin America:
Nobel address 1982

GABRIEL GARCÍA MÁRQUEZ

Antonio Pigafetta, the Florentine navigator who accompanied Magellan on the first circumnavigation of the world, kept a meticulous log on his journey through our Southern American continent which, nevertheless, also seems to be an adventure into the imagination. He related that he had seen pigs with their umbilicus on their backs and birds without feet, the females of the species of which would brood their eggs on the backs of the males, as well as others like gannets without tongues whose beaks looked like a spoon. He wrote that he had seen a monstrosity of an animal with the head and ears of a mule, the body of a camel, the hooves of a deer and the neigh of a horse. He related that they put a mirror in front of the first native they met in Patagonia and how that overexcited giant lost the use of his reason out of fear of his own image.

This short and fascinating book, in which we can perceive the germs of our contemporary novels, is not, by any means, the most surprising testimony of our reality at that time. The Chroniclers of the Indies have left us innumerable others. Eldorado, our illusory land which was much sought after, figured on many maps over a long period, changing in situation and extent according to the whim of the cartographers. The mythical Alvar Núñez Cabeza de Vaca, in search of the fount of Eternal Youth, spent eight years exploring the north of Mexico in a crazy expedition whose members ate one another; only five of the six hundred who set out returned home. One of the many mysteries which was never unravelled is that of the eleven thousand mules, each loaded with one hundred pounds weight of gold, which left Cuzco one day to pay the ransom of Atahualpa and which never arrived at their destination. Later on, during the colonial period, they used to sell in Cartagena de India chickens raised on alluvial soils in whose gizzards were found gold nuggets. This delirium for gold among our founding fathers has been a bane upon us until very recent times. Why, only in the last century the German mission appointed to study the construction of a railway line between the oceans across the Panamanian isthmus concluded that the project was a viable one on the condition that the rails should be not of iron, a scarce metal in the region, but of gold.

The independence from Spanish domination did not save us from this madness. General Antonio López de Santana, thrice dictator of Mexico, had the right leg he lost in the so-called War of the Cakes buried with all funereal pomp. General García Moreno governed Ecuador for sixteen years as an absolute monarch and his dead body, dressed in full-dress uniform and his cuirass with its medals, sat in state upon the presidential throne. General Maximilian Hernández Martínez, the theosophical despot of El Salvador who had thirty thousand peasants exterminated in a savage orgy of killing, invented a pendulum to discover whether food was poisoned and had the street lamps covered with red paper to combat an epidemic of scarlet fever. The monument to General Francisco Morazán, raised up in the main square of Tegucigalpa is, in reality, a statue of Marshall Ney which was bought in a repository of second-hand statues in Paris.

Eleven years ago, one of the outstanding poets of our time, Pablo Neruda from Chile, brought light to this very chamber with his words. In the European mind, in those of good – and often those of bad – consciences, we witness, on a forceful scale never seen before, the eruption of an awareness of the phantoms of Latin America, that great homeland of deluded men and historic women, whose infinite stubbornness is confused with legend. We have never had a moment of serenity. A Promethean president embattled in a palace in flames died fighting single-handed against an army, and two air disasters which occurred under suspicious circumstances, circumstances which were never clarified, cut off the life of another of generous nature and that of a democratic soldier who had restored the dignity of his nation. There have been five wars and seventeen *coups d'état* and the rise of a devilish dictator who, in the name of God, accomplished the first genocide in Latin America in our time. Meanwhile, twenty million Latin American children have died before their second birthday, which is more than all those born in Europe since 1970. Nearly one hundred and twenty thousand have disappeared as a consequence of repression, which is as if, today, no one knew where all the inhabitants of

Uppsala were. Many women arrested during pregnancy gave birth in Argentinian prisons but, still, where and who their children are is not known; either they were passed on into secret adoption or interned in orphanages by the military authorities. So that things should not continue thus, two thousand men and woman have given up their lives over the continent and more than one hundred thousand in three tiny, wilful countries in Central America: Nicaragua, El Salvador and Guatemala. Were this to happen in the United States the proportional ratio would be one million six hundred violent deaths in four years. A million people have fled from Chile, a country noted for its tradition of hospitality: that is, ten per cent of the population. Uruguay, a tiny nation of two and a half million inhabitants, a nation which considered itself one of the most civilized countries of the continent, has lost one in five of its citizens into exile. The civil war in El Salvador has created, since 1979, virtually one refugee every twenty minutes. A country created from all these Latin Americans either in exile or in enforced emigration would have a larger population than Norway.

I dare to believe that it is this highly unusual state of affairs, and not only its literary expression, which, this year, has merited the attention of the Swedish Literary Academy: a reality which is not one on paper but which lives in us and determines each moment of our countless daily deaths, one which constantly replenishes an insatiable fount of creation, full of unhappiness and beauty, of which this wandering and nostalgic Colombian is merely another number singled out by fate. Poets and beggars, musicians and prophets, soldiers and scoundrels, all we creatures of that disorderly reality have needed to ask little of the imagination, for the major challenge before us has been the want of conventional resources to make our life credible. This, my friends, is the nub of our solitude.

For, if these setbacks benumb us, we who are of its essence, it is not difficult to understand that the mental talents of this side of the world, in an ecstasy of contemplation of their own cultures, have found themselves without a proper means to interpret us. One realizes this when they insist on measuring us with the same yardstick with which they measure themselves, without recalling that the ravages of life are not the same for all, and that the search for one's own identity is as arduous and as bloody for us as it was for them. To interpret our reality through schemas which are alien to us only has the effect of making us even more unknown, even less free, even more solitary.

Perhaps venerable old Europe would be more sympathetic if it tried to see us in its own past; if it remembered that London needed three hundred years to build her first defensive wall and another three hundred before her first bishop; that Rome debated in the darkness of uncertainty for twenty centuries before an Etruscan king rooted her in history, and that even in the sixteenth century the pacifist Swiss of today, who so delight us with their mild cheeses and their cheeky clocks, made Europe bloody as soldiers of fortune. Even in the culminating phase of the Renaissance, twelve thousand mercenary lansquenets of the Imperial armies sacked and razed Rome, cutting down eight thousand of its inhabitants.

I have no desire to give shape to the ideals of Tonio Kröger, whose dream of a union between the chaste North and a passionate South excited Thomas Mann in this place fifty three years ago. But I believe that those clear-sighted Europeans who also struggle here for a wider homeland, more humane and just, could help us more if they were to revise fundamentally their way of seeing us. Their solidarity with our aspirations does not make us feel any less alone so long as it is not made real by acts of genuine support to people who desire to have their own life while sharing the good things in the world.

Latin America has no desire to be, nor should it be, a pawn without will, neither is it a mere shadow of a dream that its designs for independence and originality should become an aspiration of the western hemisphere. Nevertheless, advances in methods of travel which have reduced the huge distances between our Americas and Europe seem to have increased our cultural distance. Why are we granted unreservedly a recognition of our originality in literature when our attempts, in the face of enormous difficulties, to bring about social change are denied us with all sorts of mistrust? Why must they think that the system of social justice imposed by advanced European nations upon their peoples cannot also be an objective for us Latin Americans but with different methods in different conditions? No: the violence and disproportionate misery of our history are the result of secular injustice and infinite bitterness and not a plot hatched three thousand leagues distance from our home. But many European leaders and thinkers have thought so, with all the childlike regression of grandfathers who have forgotten the life-giving madness of youth, as if it were not possible to live a destiny other than one at the mercy of the two great leaders and masters of the world.

Nevertheless, in the face of oppression, pillage and abandonment, our reply is life. Neither floods nor plagues, nor famine nor cataclysms, nor even eternal war century after century have managed to reduce the tenacious advantage that life has over death. It is an advantage which is on the increase and quickens apace: every year there are seventy-four million more births than deaths, a sufficient number of new living souls to populate New York every year seven times over. The majority of them are born in countries with few resources, and among these, naturally, the countries of Latin America. On the other hand, the more prosperous nations have succeeded in accumulating sufficient destructive power to annihilate one hundred times over not only every human being who has ever existed but every living creature ever to have graced this planet of misfortune.

On a day like today, my master William Faulkner said in this very place, 'I refuse to admit the end of mankind.' I should not feel myself worthy of standing where he once stood were I not fully conscious that, for the first time in the history of humanity, the colossal disaster which he refused to recognize thirty-two years ago is now simply a scientific possibility. Face to face with a reality that overwhelms us, one which over man's perceptions of time must have seemed a utopia, tellers of tales who, like me, are capable of believing anything, feel entitled to believe that it is not yet too late to undertake the creation of a minor utopia: a new and limitless utopia for life wherein no one can decide for others how they are to die, where love really can be true and happiness possible, where the lineal generations of one hundred years of solitude will have at last and for ever a second chance on earth.

TRANSLATED BY RICHARD CARDWELL

Select bibliography

COMPILED BY

JOHN WAINWRIGHT

EDITIONS OF THE WORKS OF GARCÍA MÁRQUEZ

Fiction (in order of first publication)

La hojarasca. Bogotá: Sipa, 1955, 137pp.
    Buenos Aires: Sudamericana, 1969 [etc.], 133pp.
    Barcelona: Bruguera, 1981, 160pp.
El coronel no tiene quien le escriba. Medellín: Aguirre, 1958, 90pp.
    México: Era, 1963 [etc.], 105pp.
    Buenos Aires: Sudamericana, 1968 [etc.], 91pp.
    Barcelona: Bruguera, 1981, 160pp.
La mala hora. Madrid: Talleres de Gráficas Luis Pérez, 1962, 224pp. [Edition
    repudiated by García Márquez.]
    México: Era, 1966, 198pp. [Regarded by García Márquez as the 1st
    edition.]
    Barcelona: Bruguera, 1981, 224pp.
Los funerales de la Mamá Grande. Xalapa: Univ. Veracruzana, 1962, 151pp.
    Buenos Aires: Sudamericana, 1967 [etc.], 147pp.
    Madrid: Alfaguara, 1981, 192pp.
Cien años de soledad. Buenos Aires: Sudamericana, 1967 [etc.], 351pp.
    Madrid: Alfaguara, 1982, 353pp.
    Edición de J. Joset. Madrid: Cátedra, 1984, 493pp.
Isabel viendo llover en Macondo. Buenos Aires: Estuario, 1967, 45pp. [Subsequently
    included in *Ojos de perro* (see below). This edition also contains 'Los
    cuentos de Gabriel García Márquez o el trópico desembrujado', by E.
    Völkening.]
Relato de un náufrago . . . Barcelona: Tusquets, 1970, 88pp.
La increíble y triste historia de la cándida Eréndira y de su abuela desalmada. Barcelona: Barral,
    1972, 163pp.
    Buenos Aires: Sudamericana, 1972 [etc.], 163pp.
    Barcelona: Bruguera, 1981, 160pp.
Ojos de perro azul. Rosario: Equiseditorial, 1972, 95pp.
    Buenos Aires: Sudamericana, 1974 [etc.], 133pp. [This edition does not
    include 'Monólogo de Isabel viendo llover en Macondo'].
    Barcelona: Bruguera, 1982, 160pp.
El negro que hizo esperar a los ángeles. Rosario: Alfil, 1972, 119pp. [Contains the same
    stories as *Ojos de perro azul* in a different sequence but excluding 'La

noche de los alcaravanes' and 'Monólogo de Isabel viendo llover en
   Macondo'.]
El otoño del patriarca. Barcelona: Plaza & Janés, 1975, 271pp.
   Buenos Aires: Sudamericana, 1975 [etc.], 271pp.
   Barcelona: Bruguera, 1982, 352pp.
Crónica de una muerte anunciada. Bogotá: La Oveja Negra, 1981, 156pp.
   México: Diana, 1981, 156pp.
   Buenos Aires: Sudamericana, 1981, 193pp.
   Barcelona: Bruguera, 1981, 193pp.
El rastro de tu sangre en la nieve; El verano feliz de la Señora Forbes. Bogotá: William
   Dampier, 1982, 74pp.
El secuestro: relato cinematográfico. Salamanca: Lóguez, 1983, 143pp.
El amor en los tiempos del cólera. Bogotá: La Oveja Negra, 1985, 473pp.
   México: Diana, 1985, 473pp.
   Buenos Aires: Sudamericana, 1985, 451pp.
   Barcelona: Bruguera, 1985, 503pp.

Selections:

*El coronel no tiene quien le escriba; La increíble y triste historia de la cándida Eréndira y de su
   abuela desalmada.* Selección y estudio preliminar por N. Jitrik. Buenos
   Aires: Librería del Colegio, 1975, 175pp.
Todos los cuentos de Gabriel García Márquez (1947–1972). Barcelona: Plaza & Janés, 1975
   [etc.], 320pp. [Contains the stories from *Los funerales de la Mamá Grande,
   La increíble y triste historia de la cándida Eréndira* . . . and *Ojos de perro azul.*]

English editions:
'La prodigiosa tarde de Baltazar', in *Seven Stories from Spanish America,* selected and
   introduced by G. Brotherston and M. Vargas Llosa. Oxford: Pergamon
   Press, 1968, pp. 1–9.
El coronel no tiene quien le escriba. Ed. with introd., notes and vocabulary by G. Pontiero.
   Manchester: UP, 1981, 90pp.

Non-fictional writings

Cuando era feliz e indocumentado. Caracas: El Ojo del Camello, 1973, 151pp.
   Barcelona: Plaza & Janés, 1976 [etc.], 157pp.
Chile, el golpe y los gringos. Bogotá: Editorial Latina, 1974, 91pp.
Crónicas y reportajes. Bogotá: Instituto Colombiano de Cultura, 1976, 518pp. [Articles
   published in *El Espectador.*]
Operación Carlota. Lima: Mosca Azul, 1977, 31pp.
Periodismo militante. Bogotá: Son de Máquina 1978, 250pp.
De viaje por los países socialistas: 90 días en la 'Cortina de Hierro'. 5th ed. Bogotá: La Oveja
   Negra, 1980, 208pp.
Obra periodística. Recopilación y prólogo: J. Gilard. 4 vols. (1. Textos costeños. 891pp.
   2.,3. Entre cachacos. 986pp. 4. De Europa y América (1955–1960).
   861pp.). Barcelona: Bruguera, 1981–4.

English translations of the works of García Márquez

No One Writes to the Colonel and other stories, trans. J. S. Bernstein.
   New York: Harper & Row, 1968, 170pp. [Contains *No One Writes to the
   Colonel* and the stories of *Big Mama's Funeral.*]

Retitled *No One Writes to the Colonel* but still containing the stories of *Big Mama's Funeral*.
    London: Jonathan Cape, 1971, 170pp.
    Harmondsworth: Penguin, 1974, 157pp.
    London: Pan Books/Picador, 1979 [etc.], 170pp.
One Hundred Years of Solitude, trans. G. Rabassa.
    New York: Harper & Row, 1970, 422pp.
    London: Jonathan Cape, 1970, 422pp.
    Harmondsworth: Penguin, 1972, 383pp.
    London: Pan Books/Picador, 1978 [etc.], 336pp.
Leaf Storm and other stories, trans. G. Rabassa.
    New York: Harper & Row, 1972, 146pp.
    London: Jonathan Cape, 1972, 146pp.
    London: Pan Books/Picador, 1979 [etc.], 146pp.
The Autumn of the Patriarch, trans. G. Rabassa.
    New York: Harper & Row, 1976, 229pp.
    London: Jonathan Cape, 1977, 229pp.
    London: Pan Books/Picador, 1978 [etc.], 206pp.
Innocent Eréndira and other stories, trans. G. Rabassa.
    New York: Harper & Row, 1978, 183pp.
    London: Jonathan Cape, 1979, 183pp.
    London: Pan Books/Picador, 1981, 126pp.
In Evil Hour, trans. G. Rabassa.
    New York: Harper & Row, 1979, 183pp.
    London: Jonathan Cape, 1980, 183pp.
    London: Pan Books/Picador, 1982, 183pp.
Chronicle of a Death Foretold, trans. G. Rabassa.
    New York: Harper & Row, 1982, 122pp.
    London: Jonathan Cape, 1982, 122pp.
    London: Pan Books/Picador, 1983, 122pp.
    New York: Knopf, 1983, 122pp.
Collected Stories, trans. G. Rabassa & S. J. Bernstein.
    New York: Harper & Row, 1984, 311pp.

'The Day after Saturday', trans. J. Franco, in *Latin American Writing Today*, ed. J. Cohen. Harmondsworth: Penguin, 1967, pp. 182–202.
'Someone Has Been Disarranging these Roses', trans. G. Rabassa, *New Yorker*, 54 (27 March 1978), 34–5.
'Night of the Curlews', trans. G. Rabassa, *New Yorker*, 54 (1 April 1978), 30–1.

CONVERSATIONS AND INTERVIEWS WITH GARCÍA MÁRQUEZ
(IN CHRONOLOGICAL ORDER)

La novela en América Latina (*diálogo*) with M. Vargas Llosa.
    Lima: Carlos Milla Batres, 1968, 58pp.
Durán (Armando). 'Conversations with Gabriel García Márquez', *70 Review* [New York], 3 (1971), 109–18.
González Bermejo (Ernesto). 'Con Gabriel García Márquez: ahora doscientos años de soledad', in his *Cosas de escritores*. Montevideo: Biblioteca de Marcha, 1971, pp. 11–51.
Guibert (Rita), 'Gabriel García Márquez', in *Seven Voices: Seven Latin American Writers Talk to Rita Guibert*, trans. F. Partridge. New York: Alfred A. Knopf, 1973, pp. 303–37.

Rodman (Selden). 'Gabriel García Márquez', in his *Tongues of Fallen Angels: Conversations*. New York: New Directions, 1974, pp. 113–33.
Mendoza (Plinio Apuleyo). *El olor de la guayaba*. Barcelona: Bruguera, 1982, 189pp. Trans. as *The Fragrance of the Guava: Plinio Apuleyo Mendoza in Conversation with Gabriel García Márquez*, trans. T. Nairn. London: Verso, 1983, 160pp.
'A Talk with Gabriel García Márquez', *New York Times Book Review*, 5 Dec. 1982, 7, 60.

IMPORTANT CRITICISM IN SPANISH

Arnau (Carmen). *El mundo mítico de Gabriel García Márquez*. Barcelona: Península, 1971, 136pp.
Carrillo (Germán Darío). *La narrativa de Gabriel García Márquez*. Madrid: Castalia, 1975, 165pp.
Collazos (Óscar). *García Márquez: la soledad y la gloria: su vida y su obra*. Barcelona: Plaza & Janés, 1983, 248pp.
Dorfman (Ariel). 'La muerte como acto imaginativo en *Cien años de soledad*', in *La novela hispanoamericana actual*, ed. A. Flores & R. Silva Cáceres. New York: Las Américas, 1971, pp. 177–220.
Earle (Peter), ed. *Gabriel García Márquez* (El escritor y la crítica). Madrid: Taurus, 1981, 294pp.
Fernández-Braso (Miguel). *Gabriel García Márquez* (*una conversación infinita*). Barcelona: Planeta, 1972, 139pp.
Giacoman (Helmy F.), ed. *Homenaje a Gabriel García Márquez: variaciones interpretativas en torno a su obra*. New York: Las Américas, 1972, 311pp.
González del Valle (Luis) & Cabrera (Vicente). *La nueva ficción hispanoamericana a través de Miguel Ángel Asturias y Gabriel García Márquez*. New York: Eliseo Torres, 1972, 164pp.
Gullón (Ricardo). *García Márquez o el olvidado arte de contar*. Madrid: Taurus, 1970, 73pp.
Jara Cuadra (René) & Mejía Duque (Jaime). *Las claves del mito en García Márquez*. Valparaíso: Ediciones Universitarias, 1972, 96pp.
Levine (Suzanne Jill). *El espejo hablado: un estudio de 'Cien años de soledad'*. Caracas: Monte Ávila, 1975, 163pp.
Ludmer (Josefina). *'Cien años de soledad': una interpretación*. Buenos Aires: Tiempo Contemporáneo, 1972, 222pp.
Martínez (Pedro Simón), ed. *Sobre García Márquez*. Montevideo: Biblioteca de Marcha, 1971, 248pp.
Maturo (Gabriela). *Claves simbólicas de García Márquez*. 2nd ed. Buenos Aires: García Cambeiro, 1977, 253pp.
Nueve asedios a García Márquez. Santiago de Chile: Editorial Universitaria, 1969, 190pp.
Palencia-Roth (Michael). *Gabriel García Márquez: la línea, el círculo y las metamorfosis del mito*. Madrid: Gredos, 1983, 318pp.
Shaw (Donald L.). 'Gabriel García Márquez', in his *Nueva narrativa hispanoamericana*. Madrid: Cátedra, 1981, pp. 108–18.
Vargas Llosa (Mario). *García Márquez: historia de un deicidio*. Barcelona: Barral, 1971, 667pp. Caracas ed.: Monte Avila Editores, 1971.
Völkening (Ernst). 'Anotado al margen de *Cien años de soledad*', in *Nueva novela latinoamericana*, ed. J. Lafforgue, vol. 1. Buenos Aires: Paidós, 1969, pp. 142–79.

A SELECTION OF CRITICISM IN ENGLISH

Aaron (M. Audrey). 'Remedios la Bella or the Myth of Convention', *Proceedings of the Pacific Northwest Conference on Foreign Languages*, 28:1 (1977), 130–3.

Aaron (M. Audrey). 'Remedios la Bella and "The Man in the Green Velvet Suit" ', *Chasqui*, 9:2–3 (1980), 39–48. [Re. *Cien años de soledad*.]

Aaron (Audrey M.). 'García Márquez' *mecedor* as Link between Passage of Time and Presence of Mind', in *The Analysis of Literary Texts: Current Trends in Methodology: Third and Fourth York College Colloquia*, ed. R. D. Pope. Ypsilanti, Mich.: Bilingual Press, 1980, pp. 21–30.

Acker (Bertie). 'Religion in Colombia as Seen in the Works of García Márquez', in *Religion in Latin American Life and Literature*, ed. L. C. Brown & W. F. Cooper. Waco, Texas: Baylor U.P., 1980, pp. 339–50.

Alegría (Fernando). 'García Márquez: the Reality of Latin America', in *Essays on Gabriel García Márquez*, ed. K. Oyarzún & W. W. Megenney. Riverside: Univ. of California, 1984, pp. 4–13.

Álvarez Borland (Isabel). 'From Mystery to Parody: (Re)Readings of García Márquez's *Crónica de una muerte anunciada*', *Symposium*, 38:4 (1984), 278–86.

Arenas (Reinaldo). 'In the Town of Mirages', *70 Review* [New York], 3 (1971), 101–8. [Re. *Cien años de soledad*.]

Barros-Lémez (Álvaro). 'Beyond the Prismatic Mirror: *One Hundred Years of Solitude* and serial fiction', *Studies in Latin American Popular Culture*, 3 (1984), 105–14.

Bell-Villada (Gene H.). 'Names and Narrative Pattern in *One Hundred Years of Solitude*', *Latin American Literary Review*, 9:18 (1981), 37–46.

Bell-Villada (Gene H.). 'García Márquez and the Novel', *Latin American Literary Review*, 13:25 (1985), 15–23.

Berg (Mary G.). 'Repetitions and Reflections in *Chronicle of a Death Foretold*', in *Critical Perspectives on Gabriel García Márquez*, ed. B. A. Shaw & N. Vera-Godwin. Lincoln: Univ. of Nebraska, 1986, pp. 139–56.

Berger (John). 'Márquez's Tolerance', *New Society*, 40:757 (28 April 1977), 180–1. [Re. *El otoño del patriarca*.]

Bjornson (Richard). 'Cognitive Mapping and the Understanding of Literature', *Substance*, 30 (1981), 51–62. [Re. *Cien años de soledad*.]

Borinski (Alicia). 'What do we Do When we Read?' [review of Vargas Llosa's *García Márquez: historia de un deicidio*], *Diacritics*, 4:2 (summer 1974), 20–3.

Boschetto (Sandra Maria). 'The Demythification of Matriarchy and Image of Women in *Chronicle of a Death Foretold*', in *Critical Perspectives on Gabriel García Márquez*, ed. B.A. Shaw & N. Vera-Godwin. Lincoln: Univ. of Nebraska, 1986, pp. 125–37.

Box (J.B.H.). *Gabriel García Márquez: El coronel no tiene quien le escriba*. London: Grant & Cutler, 1984, 109pp. (Critical Guides to Spanish Texts, 38).

Brotherston (Gordon). 'An End to Secular Solitude: Gabriel García Márquez', in his *The Emergence of the Latin American Novel*. Cambridge: UP, 1977, pp. 122–35.

Brotherston (Gordon). 'García Márquez and the Secrets of Saturno Santos', *Forum for Modern Language Studies*, 15:2 (1979), 144–9. [Re. *El otoño del patriarca*.]

Brushwood (John S.). 'The Year of *Cien años de soledad* (1967)', in his *The Spanish American novel: a twentieth-century survey*. Austin: Univ. of Texas Press, 1975, pp. 267–304.

Brushwood (John S.). 'Reality and Imagination in the Novels of García Márquez',

Latin American Literary Review, 13:25 (1985), 9–14.

Bryan (Avril). 'Myth and Superstition in *Cien años de soledad*', in *Myth and Superstition in Spanish-Caribbean Literature*, Conference papers, 5th Conference of Hispanists, Univ. of the West Indies, Mona Campus, Jamaica, 6–9 July 1982. Mona: Univ. of West Indies, 1982, pp. 68–84.

Bryan (Avril). 'Virginity: Contrasting Views in the Works of Miguel de Unamuno and Gabriel García Márquez', in *La mujer en la literatura caribeña*, Sexta Conferencia de Hispanistas, Univ. of the West Indies, St Augustine, Trinidad, 6–8 April 1983. St Augustine: Univ. of the West Indies [?1985], pp. 168–84.

Buford (Bill). 'Haughty Falconry and Collective Guilt' [review of *Chronicle of a Death Foretold*], *Times Literary Supplement*, 4145 (10 Sept. 1982), 965.

Castro Klarén (Sara). *The Space of Solitude in 'Cien años de soledad'*. Washington, DC: The Wilson Center, 1978, 76pp.

Ciplijauskaité (Biruté). 'Foreshadowing as Technique and Theme in *One Hundred Years of Solitude*', *Books Abroad*, 47:3 (1973), 479–84.

Clark (Stella T.). '*Cien años de soledad*: a *texte de plaisir*, a *texte de jouissance*', *The American Hispanist*, 4:30–1 (Nov.–Dec. 1978), 17–19.

Coleman (Alexander). 'The Transformation of the Chivalric Novel', *World Literature Today*, 52:1 (1978), 24–9. [Re. *Cien años de soledad*.]

Coover (Robert). 'The Master's Voice', *American Review*, 26 (1977), 361–88.

Dauster (Frank). 'The Short Stories of García Márquez', *Books Abroad*, 47:3 (1973), 466–70.

Dauster (Frank). 'Ambiguity and Indeterminacy in *La hojarasca*', *Latin American Literary Review*, 13:25 (1985), 24–8.

Davis (Mary Eunice). 'The Voyage beyond the Map: "El ahogado más hermoso del mundo" ', *Kentucky Romance Quarterly*, 26:1 (1979), 25–33.

Deas (Malcolm). 'Unnecessary Town: *Leaf Storm and other stories*' [review], *The Listener*, 89 (1 Feb. 1973), 157.

Deas (Malcolm). 'No-Cage-Birds Sing: *The Autumn of the Patriarch*' [review], *The Listener*, 97 (21 April 1977), 526.

Dixon (Paul B.). '*Cien años de soledad*'s Unending End', in his *Reversible Readings: Ambiguity in Four Modern Latin American Novels*. Univ. of Alabama Press, 1985, pp. 89–124.

Dreifus (Claudia). 'Playboy Interview: Gabriel García Márquez', *Playboy*, 30:2 (Feb. 1983), 65–77, 172–8.

Ekstrom (Margaret V.). 'Los Márquez en Macondo: Surnames for a Family of Characters', *Literary Onomastic Studies* [Brockport, NY], 7 (1979), 235–55.

Faris (Wendy). 'Magic and Violence in Macondo and San Lorenzo', *Latin American Literary Review*, 13:25 (1985), 44–54.

Fiddian (Robin W.). 'Two Aspects of Technique in *El coronel no tiene quien le escriba*', *Neophilologus*, 69:3 (1985), 386–93.

Foster (David William). 'García Márquez and Solitude', *Americas*, [Washington DC], 21 (Nov.–Dec. 1969), 36–41. [Re. *Cien años de soledad*.]

Foster (David William). 'García Márquez and the *écriture* of Complicity: "La prodigiosa tarde de Baltazar" ', in his *Studies in the Contemporary Spanish-American Short Story*. Columbia & London: Univ. of Missouri Press, 1979, pp. 39–50.

Foster (David William). 'The Double Inscription of the *narrataire* in *Los funerales de la Mamá Grande*', in his *Studies in the Contemporary Spanish-American Short Story*. Columbia & London: Univ. of Missouri Press, 1979, pp. 51–62.

Foster (David William). 'Latin America Documentary Narrative', *Publications of the Modern Language Association of America*, 99:1 (1984), 49–51. [Re. *Relato de un náufrago . . .*]

Foster (David William) & Foster (Virginia Ramos). 'Gabriel García Márquez', in their *Modern Latin American Literature*, vol. 1. New York: Frederick Ungar, 1979, pp. 374–91. (A Library of Literary Criticism).

Franco (Jean). 'Stranger in Paradise: *Cien años de soledad*' [review], *Times Literary Supplement*, 3428 (9 Nov. 1967), 1054.

Franco (Jean). 'Gabriel García Márquez', in her *An Introduction to Spanish American Literature*. Cambridge: UP, 1969, pp. 343–7.

Franco (Jean). '*El otoño del patriarca*' [review], *Times Literary Supplement*, 3839 (10 Oct. 1975), 1172.

Franco (Jean). 'The Limits of the Liberal Imagination: *One Hundred Years of Solitude* and *Nostromo*', *Punto de Contacto* [New York]; 1:1 (1975), 4–16.

Fuentes (Carlos). 'Macondo, Seat of Time', *70 Review* [New York], 3 (1971), 112–14.

Gallagher (David). 'Cycles and Cyclones' [review of *One Hundred Years of Solitude*], *The Observer*, 28 June 1970, 6.

Gallagher (David). 'Gabriel García Márquez', in his *Modern Latin American Literature*. London: Oxford UP, 1973, pp. 144–63.

Gerlach (John). 'The Logic of Wings: García Márquez, Todorov and the Endless Resources of Fantasy', in *Bridges to Fantasy*, ed. G. E. Slusser, E. S. Rabkin & R.E. Scholes. Carbondale: S. Illinois UP, 1982, pp. 121–9. [Re. 'Un hombre muy viejo con unas alas enormes'.]

Goetzinger (Judith A.). 'The Emergence of a Folk Myth in *Los funerales de la Mamá Grande*', *Revista de Estudios Hispánicos*, 6:2 (1972), 237–48.

González (Eduardo). 'Beware of Gift-Bearing Tales: Reading García Márquez According to Mauss', *Modern Language Notes*, 97:2 (1982), 347–64.

González Echevarría (Roberto). 'Polemic: with Borges in Macondo', *Diacritics*, 2:1 (spring 1972), 57–60.

González Echevarría (Roberto). 'The Dictatorship of Rhetoric/the Rhetoric of Dictatorship: Carpentier, García Márquez and Roa Bastos', *Latin American Research Review*, 15:3 (1980), 205–28.

González Echevarría (Roberto). '*Cien años de soledad*: the Novel as Myth and Archive', *Modern Language Notes*, 99:2 (1984), 358–80.

Gordon (Ambrose). 'The Seaport beyond Macondo', *Latin American Literary Review*, 13:25 (1985), 79–89.

Graham-Yool (Andrew). 'Back in the Bullring: García Márquez in Bogotá', *London Magazine*, 21 (1984), 87–91.

Grossman (Edith). 'Truth is Stranger than Fact', *Review* [New York], 30 (Sept.–Dec. 1981), 71–3. [Re. *Crónica de una muerte anunciada*.]

Gullón (Ricardo). 'Gabriel García Márquez and the Lost Art of Storytelling', *Diacritics*, 1:1 (autumn 1971), 27–32.

Halka (Chester S.). *Melquíades, Alchemy and Narrative Theory: the Quest for Gold in 'Cien años de soledad'*. Lathrup Village, Mich.: International Book Publishers, 1981, 197pp.

Hancock (Joel). 'Gabriel García Márquez's "Eréndira" and the Brothers Grimm', *Studies in Twentieth Century Literature*, 3:1 (1978), 43–52.

Harss (Luis) & Dohmann (Barbara). 'Gabriel García Márquez or the Lost Chord', in their *Into the Mainstream*. New York: Harper & Row, 1967, pp. 310–41.

Hedeen (Paul M.). 'Gabriel García Márquez's Dialectic of Solitude', *Southwest Review* [Dallas], 68:4 (1983), 350–64. [Re. *Cien años de soledad*.]

Higgins (James). 'The Political Symbolism of the Letter and the Cock in *El coronel no tiene quien le escriba*', *Vida Hispánica* [Sutton-on-Derwent], 31:3 (1982), 19–24.

Incledon (John). 'Writing and Incest in *One Hundred Years of Solitude*', in *Critical Perspectives on Gabriel García Márquez*, ed. B. A. Shaw & N. Vera-Godwin. Lincoln: Univ. of Nebraska, 1986, pp. 51–64.

Janes (Regina). 'The End of Time in *Cien años de soledad*, and *El otoño del patriarca*', *Chasqui*, 7:2 (1978), 36–45.

Janes (Regina). *Gabriel García Márquez: Revolutions in Wonderland.* Columbia & London: Univ. of Missouri Press, 1981, 115pp.

Janes (Regina). 'Liberals, Conservatives and Bananas: Colombian Politics in the Fictions of Gabriel García Márquez', *Hispanófila*, 82 (1984), 79–102.

Jelinski (Jack B.). 'Memory and the Remembered Structure of *Cien años de soledad*', *Revista de Estudios Hispánicos*, 18:3 (1984), 323–33.

Kadir (Djelal). 'The Architectonic Principle of *Cien años de soledad* and the Vichian Theory of History', *Kentucky Romance Quarterly*, 24:3 (1977), 251–61.

Kappeler (Susanne). 'Voices of Patriarchy: Gabriel García Márquez' *One Hundred Years of Solitude*', in *Teaching the Text*, ed. S. Kappeler & N. Bryson. London: Routledge, 1983, pp. 148–63.

Kercher (Dona M.). 'García Márquez's *Crónica de una muerte anunciada* [*Chronicle of a Death Foretold*]: Notes on Parody and the Artist', *Latin American Literary Review*, 13:25 (1985), 90–103.

Kirsner (Robert). 'Four Colombian Novels of Violence', *Hispania* [Appleton, Wis.], 49:1 (1966), 70–4. [Re. *La hojarasca*.]

Koldewyn (Phillip). 'Anthropological Approaches to Novels of Carpentier and García Márquez', in *Essays on Gabriel García Márquez*, ed. K. Oyarzún & W. W. Megenney. Riverside: Univ. of California, 1984, pp. 88–102.

Kulin (Katalin). 'Reasons and Characteristics of Faulkner's Influence on Juan Carlos Onetti, Juan Rulfo and Gabriel García Márquez', in *Proceedings of the 7th Congress of the International Comparative Literature Association*, vol. 1. Stuttgart: Bieber, 1979, pp. 277–80.

Kutzinski (Vera M.). 'The Logic of Wings: Gabriel García Márquez and Afro-American Literature', *Latin American Literary Review*, 13:25 (1985), 133–46.

Lawrence (Gregory). 'Marx in Macondo', *Latin American Literary Review*, 2:4 (1974), 49–57.

Levine (Suzanne Jill). '*One Hundred Years of Solitude* and *Pedro Páramo*: a Parallel', *Books Abroad*, 47:3 (1973), 490–5.

Levitt (Morton P.). 'From Realism to Magic Realism: the Meticulous Modernist Fictions of García Márquez', in *Critical Perspectives on Gabriel García Márquez*, ed. B.A. Shaw & N. Vera-Godwin. Lincoln: Univ. of Nebraska, 1986, pp. 73–89.

Levy (Kurt L.). 'Planes of Reality in *El otoño del patriarca*', in *Studies in Honor of Gerald E. Wade*, ed. S. Bowman &c. Madrid: Porrúa Turanzas, 1979, pp. 133–41.

Lichtblau (Myron I.). 'In Search of the Stylistic Key to *Cien años de soledad*', in *Essays on Gabriel García Márquez*, ed. K. Oyarzún & W.W. Megenney. Riverside: Univ. of California, 1984, pp. 103–12.

Lipski (John M.). 'Embedded Dialogue in *El otoño del patriarca*', *The American Hispanist*, 2:14 (Jan. 1977), 9–12.

Luchting (Wolfgang A.). 'Gabriel García Márquez: the Boom and the Whimper', *Books Abroad*, 44:1 (1970), 26–30.

Luchting (Wolfgang A.). 'Lampooning Literature: *La mala hora*', *Books Abroad*, 47:3
    (1973), 471–8.
Luna (Norman). 'The Barbaric Dictator and the Enlightened Tyrant in *El otoño del
    patriarca* and *El recurso del método*', *Latin American Literary Review*, 8:15
    (1979), 25–32.
MacAdam (Alfred J.). 'Gabriel García Márquez: a Commodius Vicus of Recircula-
    tion', in his *Modern Latin American Narratives: the Dreams of Reason*.
    Chicago: Univ. of Chicago Press, 1977, pp. 78–87. [Re. *Cien años de
    soledad*.]
MacAdam (Alfred J.). 'Realism Restored', *Review* [New York], 35 (July–Dec.1985),
    34–8. [Re. *El amor en los tiempos del cólera*.]
McGowan (John P.). '*À la recherche du temps perdu* in *One Hundred Years of Solitude*',
    Modern Fiction Studies, 28:4 (1982–3), 557–67.
McMurray (George R.). 'Reality and Myth in García Márquez's *Cien años de soledad*',
    Bulletin of the Rocky Mountain Language Association, 23 (1969), 175–82.
McMurray (George R.). *Gabriel García Márquez*. New York: Frederick Ungar, 1977,
    182pp.
McMurray (George R.). '«The Aleph» and *One Hundred Years of Solitude*: two
    Microscopic Worlds', *Latin American Literary Review*, 13:25 (1985),
    55–64.
Megenney (William W.). 'The Origin of Francisco el Hombre in *Cien años de soledad*',
    Romanische Forschungen, 92:1–2 (1980), 132–3.
Menton (Seymour). 'In the Beginning . . .', in *Essay on Gabriel García Márquez*, ed. K.
    Oyarzún & W.W. Megenney. Riverside: Univ. of California, 1984, pp.
    14–26. [Re. *Cien años de soledad*.]
Merrel (Floyd). 'José Arcadio Buendía's Scientific Paradigms: Man in Search of
    Himself', *Latin American Literary Review*, 2:4 (1974), 59–70.
Miller (John C.). 'Onomatology of Male Characters in the *Hundred Years of Solitude* of
    Gabriel García Márquez', *Literary Onomastic Studies* [New York], 1
    (1974), 66–73.
Millington (Mark). 'Actant and Character in García Márquez's *La increíble y triste
    historia de la cándida Eréndira y de su abuela desalmada*', in *Essays in honour of
    Robert Brian Tate from his Colleagues and Pupils*, ed. R.A. Cardwell.
    University of Nottingham Monographs in the Humanities, II, 1984,
    pp. 83–90.
Montes-Huidobro (Matías). 'From Hitchcock to García Márquez: the Methodology
    of Suspense', in *Critical Perspectives on Gabriel García Márquez*, ed. B.A.
    Shaw & N. Vera-Godwin. Lincoln: Univ. of Nebraska, 1986, pp. 105–
    23.
Morello-Frosch (Marta). 'The Common Wonders of García Márquez's Recent
    Fiction', *Books Abroad*, 47:3 (1973), 496–501.
Morello-Frosch (Marta). '*One Hundred Years of Solitude* by Gabriel García Márquez, or
    Genesis Rewritten', in *Essays on Gabriel García Márquez*, ed. K. Oyarzún
    & W.W. Megenney. Riverside: Univ. of California, 1984, pp. 27–35.
Morgan (Beverley). '*Crónica de una muerte anunciada*: Myth stood on its Head', in *Myth
    and Superstition in Spanish–Caribbean Literature*, Conference papers, 5th
    Conference of Hispanists, University of the West Indies, Mona
    Campus, Jamaica, 6–9 July 1982. Mona: Univ. of West Indies, 1982,
    pp. 85–100.
Morrison (Robert W.). 'Literature in an Age of Specialization', in *Brave New Universe:
    Testing the Values of Science in Society*, ed. T. Henighan. Ottawa:
    Tecumseh, 1980, pp. 112–24.

Mount (F.). 'The Autumn of the Patriarch' [review], Encounter 48 (Jan. 1977), 51–8.

Müller (Gerd F.). 'On the Mythical Structure of Cien años de soledad', in Studies in Language and Literature: Proceedings of the 23rd Mountain Interstate Foreign Language Conference, ed. C. Nelson. Richmond: Eastern Kentucky Univ., 1976, pp. 447–50.

Müller-Bergh (Klaus). 'Relato de un náufrago, García Márquez's Tale of Shipwreck and Survival at Sea', Books Abroad, 47:3 (1973), 460–6.

Oberhelman (Harley Dean). 'The Absurd in Three Representative Spanish American Novelists', in From Surrealism to the Absurd, ed. W.T. Zyla. Lubbock: Texas Technological Univ., 1970, pp. 95–110.

Oberhelman (Harley Dean). 'García Márquez and the American South', Chasqui, 5:1 (1975), 29–38.

Oberhelman (Harley Dean). 'Faulknerian Techniques in Gabriel García Márquez's Portrait of a Dictator', in Ibero-American Letters: a Comparative Perspective, ed. W.T. Zyla & W.M. Aycock. Lubbock: Texas Technological Univ., 1978, pp. 171–81. (Proceedings of the Comparative Literature Symposium, vol. 10.) [Re. El otoño del patriarca.]

Oberhelman (Harley Dean). The Presence of Faulkner in the Writings of García Márquez. Lubbock: Texas Technological Univ., 1980, 43pp.

Ollivier (Louis L.). 'One Hundred Years of Solitude: Existence is the Word', Latin American Literary Review, 4:7 (1975), 9–14.

Ondaatje (Michael). 'García Márquez and the Bus to Aracataca', in Figures in a Ground: Canadian Essays on Modern Literature Collected in Honor of Sheila Watson, ed. D. Bessai & D. Jackel. Saskatoon: Western Producer Prairie, 1978, pp. 19–31.

Ortega (Julio). 'One Hundred Years of Solitude', in his Poetics of Change: the New Spanish–American Narrative, trans. G.D. Greaser. Austin: Univ. of Texas, 1984, pp. 85–95.

Ortega (Julio). 'The Autumn of the Patriarch: Text and Culture', in his Poetics of Change: the New Spanish-American Narrative, trans. G.D. Greaser. Austin: Univ. of Texas, 1984, pp. 96–119.

Palencia-Roth (Michael). 'Prisms of Consciousness: the "New Worlds" of Columbus and García Márquez', in Critical Perspectives on Gabriel García Márquez, ed. B.A. Shaw & N. Vera-Godwin. Lincoln: Univ. of Nebraska, 1986, pp. 15–32.

Peel (Roger M.). 'The Short Stories of Gabriel García Márquez', Studies in Short Fiction, 8:1 (1971), 159–68.

Penuel (Arnold M.). 'Death and the Maiden: the Demythologization of Virginity in García Márquez's Cien años de soledad', Hispania [University, Miss.]. 66:4 (1983), 552–60.

Penuel (Arnold M.). 'The Sleep of Vital Reason in García Márquez's Crónica de una muerte anunciada', Hispania [University, Miss.], 68:4 (1985), 753–66.

Pinard (Mary C.). 'Time in and out of Solitude in One Hundred Years of Solitude', in Critical Perspectives on Gabriel García Márquez, ed. B.A. Shaw & N. Vera-Godwin. Lincoln: Univ. of Nebraska, 1986, pp. 65–72.

Pontiero (Giovanni). 'Art and Commitment in Gabriel García Márquez's El coronel no tiene quien le escriba', Kentucky Romance Quarterly, 22:4 (1975), 443–57.

Porter (Laurence M.) & Porter (Laurel). 'Relations with the Dead in Cien años de soledad', Mosaic [Winnipeg], 15:1 (1982), 119–27.

Prescott (Peter S.). 'Murder and Machismo', review of Chronicle of a Death Foretold, Newsweek, 1 Nov. 1982, 82.

Pritchett (V.S.). '*One Hundred Years of Solitude*' [review], *New Statesman*, 85 (9 February 1973), 200.

Pritchett (V.S.). '*The Autumn of the Patriarch*' [review], *New Statesman*, 93 (22 April 1977), 531.

Rabassa (Gregory). 'Beyond Magic Realism: Thoughts on the Art of Gabriel García Márquez', *Books Abroad*, 47:3 (1973), 444–50.

Rabassa (Gregory). 'Gabriel García Márquez's New Book: Literature or Journalism?', *World Literature Today*, 56:1 (1982), 48–51. [Re. *Crónica de una muerte anunciada*.]

Reid (A.). 'Basilisks' Eggs' [review of *The Autumn of the Patriarch*], *New Yorker*, 52 (8 Nov. 1976), 175–80.

Rodríguez Monegal (Emir). 'A Writer's Feat', *70 Review* [New York], 3 (1971), 122–8. [Re. *Cien años de soledad*].

Rodríguez Monegal (Emir). '*One Hundred Years of Solitude*: the Last Three Pages', *Books Abroad*, 47:3 (1973), 485–9.

Saine (Ute M.). 'Einstein and Musil in Macondo: *One Hundred Years of Solitude* and the Theory of Relativity', in *Essays on Gabriel García Márquez*, ed. K. Oyarzún and W.W. Megenney. Riverside: Univ. of California, 1984, pp. 36–50.

Saldívar (José David). 'Ideology and Deconstruction in Macondo', *Latin American Literary Review*, 13:25 (1985), 29–43.

Schwartz (Ronald). 'García Márquez: a New Colombian Cosmology', in his *Nomads, Exiles & Emigrés: the Rebirth of the Latin American Narrative, 1960–80*. Metuchen, NJ: Scarecrow Press, 1980, pp. 34–45.

Schweitzer (S. Alan). *The Three Levels of Reality in García Márquez's 'Cien años de soledad'*. New York: Plaza Mayor, 1972, 16pp.

Scott (Nina M.). 'Vital Space in the House of Buendía', *Studies in Twentieth Century Literature*, 8:2 (1984), 265–72. [Re. *Cien años de soledad*].

Shaw (Donald L.). 'Concerning the Interpretation of *Cien años de soledad*', *Ibero-Amerikanisches Archiv*, 3:4 (1977), 318–29.

Shaw (Donald L.). '*Chronicle of a Death Foretold*: Narrative Function and Interpretation', in *Critical Perspectives on Gabriel García Márquez*, ed. B.A. Shaw & N. Vera-Godwin. Lincoln: Univ. of Nebraska, 1986, pp. 91–104.

Sheppard (R.Z.). 'Where the Fiction is *fantástica*', *Time*, 7 March 1983, 79 [Re. *Crónica de una muerte anunciada*].

Siemens (William L.). 'Gabriel García Márquez and the Tainted Hero', *West Virginia University Philological Papers*, 21 (1974), 92–6.

Siemens (William L.). 'The Devouring Female in Four Latin American Novels', *Essays in Literature* [Western Illinois Univ.], 1:1 (1974), pp. 118–29. [Re. *Cien años de soledad* &c.]

Silva-Cáceres (Raúl). 'The Narrative Intensification in *One Hundred Years of Solitude*', *70 Review* [New York], 3 (1971), 143–8.

Sims (Robert L.). 'Claude Simon and Gabriel García Márquez: the Conflicts between *histoire-Histoire* and *historia-Historia*', in *Papers on Romance Literary Relations*, ed. C. De Coster. Evanston: Northwestern Univ., Ill., 1975, pp. 1–22.

Sims (Robert L.). 'García Márquez' *La hojarasca*: Paradigm of Time and Search for Myth', *Hispania* [Worcester, Mass.], 59:4 (1976), 810–19.

Sims (Robert L.). 'The Creation of Myth in García Márquez's *Los funerales de la Mamá Grande*', *Hispania* [Worcester, Mass.], 61:1 (1978), 14–23.

Sims (Robert L.). 'The Banana Massacre in *Cien años de soledad*', *Chasqui*, 8:3 (1979), 3–23.

Sims (Robert L.). 'Theme, Narrative *bricolage* and Myth in García Márquez', *Journal of Spanish Studies: Twentieth Century*, 8:1–2 (1980), 143–59.

Sims (Robert L.). *The Evolution of Myth in García Márquez from 'La hojarasca' to 'Cien años de soledad'*. Miami: Universal, 1981, 153pp.

Sims (Robert L.). 'Matriarchal and Patriarchal Patterns in Gabriel García Márquez's *Leaf Storm*, "Big Mama's Funeral" and *One Hundred Years of Solitude*: the Synergetic, Mythic and *bricolage* Synthesis', in *Critical Perspectives on Gabriel García Márquez*, ed. B.A. Shaw & N. Vera-Godwin. Lincoln: Univ. of Nebraska, 1986, pp. 33–49.

Stevens (L. Robert) & Vela (G. Roland). 'Jungle Gothic: Science, Myth and Reality in *One Hundred Years of Solitude*', *Modern Fiction Studies*, 26:2 (1980), 262–6.

Sturrock (John). 'The Unreality Principle' [review of *The Autumn of the Patriarch*], *Times Literary Supplement*, 3918 (15 April 1977), 451.

Tobin (Patricia). 'García Márquez and the Genealogical Imperative', *Diacritics*, 4:2 (summer 1974), 52–5. [Re. *Cien años de soledad*.] [See also pp. 55–7 ('Response, 2') for reply by R. González Echevarría.]

Tobin (Patricia). 'García Márquez and the Subversion of the Line', *Latin American Literary Review*, 2:4 (1974), 39–48. [Re. *Cien años de soledad*.]

Tobin (Patricia). 'Everything is Known: Gabriel García Márquez, *One Hundred Years of Solitude*', in her *Time and the Novel*. Princeton: UP, 1978, pp. 164–91.

Tobin (Patricia). 'The Autumn of the Signifier: the Deconstructionist Moment of García Márquez', *Latin American Literary Review*, 13:25 (1985), 65–78. [Re. *El otoño del patriarca*.]

Valdés (Mario J.). 'Myth and Reality in *Cien años de soledad* and *La muerte de Artemio Cruz*', *Reflexión* [Ottawa], 2nd series, 3–4 (1974–5), 245–55.

Vargas Llosa (Mario). 'García Márquez : from Aracataca to Macondo', *70 Review* [New York], 3 (1971), 129–42.

Vargas Llosa (Mario). 'A Morbid Prehistory (the Early Stories)', *Books Abroad*, 47:3 (1973), 451–60.

Vázquez Amaral (José). 'Gabriel García Márquez: *One Hundred Years of Solitude*', in his *The Contemporary Latin American Narrative*. New York: Las Américas, 1970, pp. 135–56.

Wilkie (James W.), Monzón de Wilkie (Edna) & Herrera-Sobek (María). 'Elitelore and Folklore: Theory and a Test Case in *One Hundred Years of Solitude*', *Journal of Latin American Lore*, 4:2 (1978), 183–223.

Williams (Linda I.). 'Edenic Nostalgia and the Play of Mirrors in *Hopscotch* and *One Hundred Years of Solitude*', *Latin American Literary Review*, 6 :11 (1977), 53–67.

Williams (Raymond Leslie). 'The Dynamic Structure of García Márquez's *El otoño del patriarca*', *Symposium*, 32:1 (1978), 56–75.

Williams (Raymond Leslie). *Gabriel García Márquez*. Boston: Twayne, 1984, 176pp.

Williams (Raymond Leslie). 'An Introduction to the Early Journalism of García Márquez: 1948–1958', *Latin American Literary Review*, 13:25 (1985), 117–32.

Woods (Richard D.). 'Time and Futility in the Novel *El coronel no tiene quien le escriba*', *Kentucky Romance Quarterly*, 17:4 (1970), 287–95.

Zamora (Lois Parkinson). 'The Myth of Apocalypse and Human Temporality in García Márquez's *Cien años de soledad*', *Symposium*, 32:4 (1978), 341–55.

Zamora (Lois Parkinson). 'The End of Innocence: Myth and Narrative Structure in Faulkner's *Absalom! Absalom!* and García Márquez' *Cien años de soledad*', *Hispanic Journal*, 4:1 (1982), 23–40.

Zamora (Lois Parkinson). 'Ends and Endings in García Márquez's *Crónica de una muerte anunciada* [*Chronicle of a Death Foretold*]', *Latin American Literary Review*, 13:25 (1985), 104–16.

BIBLIOGRAPHIES

Becco (Horacio Jorge) & Foster (David William). *La nueva narrativa hispano-americana.* Buenos Aires: Casa Pardo, 1976, pp. 119–37.

Coll (Edna). *Índice informativo de la novela hispanoamericana*, vol. 4 (Colombia). Río Piedras: Univ. de Puerto Rico, 1980, pp. 195–224.

Earle (Peter). 'Bibliografía de Gabriel García Márquez', in his *Gabriel García Márquez* (El escritor y la crítica), [see p. 216 above], pp. 287–94.

Fau (Margaret Eustella). *Gabriel García Márquez: an Annotated Bibliography, 1947–1979.* Westport, Conn.: Greenwood Press, 1980, 198pp.

Fau (Margaret Eustella) & González (Nelly Sfeirde). *Bibliographical Guide to Gabriel García Márquez, 1979–1985.* Westport, Conn.: Greenwood Press, 1986, 189pp.

Flores (Ángel). *Bibliografía de escritores hispanoamericanos 1609–1974.* New York: Gordian Press, 1975, pp. 112–15, 182–4.

Foster (David William). *The 20th Century Spanish-American Novel: a Bibliographical Guide.* Metuchen, NJ: Scarecrow Press, 1975, pp. 105–16.

Joset (Jacques). 'Bibliografía selecta', in his ed. of *Cien años de soledad*, [see p. 213 above], pp. 47–65.

Lozano (Stella). *Selected Bibliography of Contemporary Spanish-American Writers.* Los Angeles: California State Univ., 1979, pp. 61–72.

Martínez (Pedro Simón). 'Bibliografía', in *Sobre García Márquez* [see p. 216 above], pp. 236–44.

Mendoza (Roseanne B. de). 'Bibliografía de y sobre Gabriel García Márquez', *Revista Iberoamericana*, 41: 90 (1975), 107–43.

Ocampo (Aurora M.). *Novelistas iberoamericanos contemporáneos: obras y bibliografía crítica*, part 1, section 3. Mexico: UNAM, 1974, pp. 44–56.

Porras Collantes (Ernesto). *Bibliografía de la novela en Colombia.* Bogotá: Instituto Caro y Cuervo, 1976, pp. 251–89.

Vargas Llosa (Mario). 'Bibliografía', in his *García Márquez: historia de un deicidio*, [see p. 216 above], pp. 643–64.

Index